PRAISE FOR *MY JAMS*

Anthony Pinn's *My Jams* instinctively weaves theory, embodiment, and personal experience into a reflective exploration of hip-hop's sonic and lyrical landscapes. Pinn fuses musicology with deep theoretical insight, crafting an inventive narrative where rhythm, philosophy, and ethics collide. His unique voice moves between autobiographical reflection and intellectual critique, making hip-hop's beats pulse with new meaning. This work not only celebrates the music but offers a profound understanding of its cultural and epistemic power, making *My Jams* an essential read for anyone seeking a fresh, interdisciplinary look at hip-hop's transformative impact on identity and society.

—Robert Beckford, professor and broadcaster

The brilliant and often infamous Dr. Pinn once again shows us the deep intersections of rhetoric, race, religion, music, and popular culture. This book adds a much-needed conversation around manhood and what masculinity looks like in a post-truth world. Dr. Pinn, in his poignant voice, has given us a guide to better understanding the myriad of complexities embedded in the music we listen to. As always, his work is a must-read!

—Daniel White Hodge, professor of communication arts, North Park University; coeditor of *Marveling Religion: Critical Discourses, Religion, and the Marvel Cinematic Universe* and author of *Baptized in Dirty Water: Reimagining the Gospel according to Tupac Amaru Shakur*

If William James and Lauryn Hill had a love child, his name would be Anthony Pinn. *My Jams* brilliantly chronicles varieties of religious experience that intersect with artistic imagination and forms of resistance, recuperation, and restoration found in the bodies of belief, flesh, and music that bridge the human and the divine. This beautiful book is a monumental spiritual and cultural jam session.

—Michael Eric Dyson, author of *Entertaining Race: Performing Blackness in America*

MY JAMS

MY JAMS

Reflections on the Relationship between Music and Religion

ANTHONY B. PINN

Fortress Press
Minneapolis

MY JAMS
Reflections on the Relationship between Music and Religion

30 29 28 27 26 25 24 1 2 3 4 5 6 7 8 9

Library of Congress Cataloging-in-Publication Data

Names: Pinn, Anthony B., author.
Title: My jams : reflections on the relationship between music and religion / Anthony B. Pinn.
Description: Minneapolis, MN : Fortress Press, [2025] | Includes bibliographical references and index.
Identifiers: LCCN 2024032782 (print) | LCCN 2024032783 (ebook) | ISBN 9798889833734 (print) | ISBN 9798889833741 (ebook)
Subjects: LCSH: Popular music—Religious aspects. | Rap (Music)—Religious aspects. | African Americans—Religion. | Hip-hop—Religious aspects.
Classification: LCC ML3921.8.P67 P56 2025 (print) | LCC ML3921.8.P67 (ebook) | DDC 781.64/112—dc23/eng/20240726
LC record available at https://lccn.loc.gov/2024032782
LC ebook record available at https://lccn.loc.gov/2024032783

Cover image: Illustration using LP vinyl record album drawing from MAXSHOT/Getty Images
Cover design: Kristin Miller

Print ISBN: 979-8-8898-3373-4
eBook ISBN: 979-8-8898-3374-1

Dedicated

to

Those who modeled how to listen to and learn from *music*

CONTENTS

INTRODUCTION

Framing Decades of Listening

Hey this is my jam;
Y'all don't understand.

—Flo Rida, "In the Ayer"

When it comes to music, I am what most would call an "old head"—privileging songs from earlier decades, typically pre-twenty-first-century streaming platform tunes. "Old head," yes, but this status is a natural process of prioritized memory tied to a set of sound-based markers of meaning—particular rhythms, beats, and lyrics. Reflecting back over the years, it is difficult for me not to connect life with some type of music. And so, as the years passed, I came to mark off and commemorate major moments of my maturation through songs—my fears, desires, anxieties, and sorrows. My connection to music has involved both a personal appreciation for various genres—especially Hip Hop—and more recently a professional commitment to writing about the importance of music for understanding the nature and meaning of Black (religious) life. In this way, music nurtures my private life while also serving as either the subject matter or a source of hermeneutical insight that shapes how I view sociopolitical, economic, and cultural developments within my scholarship. Over the decades

I've made an effort to keep these two motivations intertwined. In a word, both my personal and professional growth have a soundtrack.

The sound, rhythm, melody, harmony, and beat that came together to constitute music were found throughout the geography defining my life arrangements and activity. It's almost as if, like in the movies, music marked out the ebb and flow of my experiences—amplifying their affective and epistemological significance. There was something musical about my effort to travel through the world with an increased sense of who I was and what I wanted to accomplish—while larger circumstances always made me remember how the world would push back against me. Music refocused language—ripping, opening, and reshaping it through shortening or elongation of vibration—so that it could reflect reality colored by a certain set of concerns and possibilities.

SOUND. RHYTHM. MELODY. HARMONY. BEAT.

My first independent music purchase (as far as a weekly allowance can signal independence) was an album of Scott Joplin's "ragtime." The songs by this artist, working in the late nineteenth and early twentieth centuries, aren't exactly the type of music one would expect a preteen to find appealing, let alone buy. But they appealed, and I did. I don't recall why Joplin caught my attention, but I can still hear "The Entertainer" (not the more famous "Maple Leaf Rag") whenever I think of him. Perhaps it was the 1977 movie *Scott Joplin*, starring Billy Dee Williams, that sparked my interest by amplifying his prestige, importance, and allure, and creating a curiosity about the musician important enough to make a movie about him.[1] Maybe it was his picture on the album cover—a Black

1. *Scott Joplin*, Universal Studies/Motown Productions, released February 11, 1977.

man dignified and stoic like a preacher but making music rather than writing sermons. It could have been the subtle irreverence, the provocative playfulness—almost the equivalent of a defiant smile in the face of social terror—of the music that captured me, although at the time I wasn't able to name it as such. My understanding of Joplin's impact beyond the tunes on that particular album would come far along in life. However, maybe I sensed back then what I would only come to appreciate years later as I grew to understand that, despite his preference for concert halls and social refinement as the proper orientation for his music, there's an earthy "something" within it that made it just as fitting for the more casual and less refined "honky-tonk" environment. And, that organic fluidity aided its transformation into musical genres like jazz. In a word, his genius informed many of the musical genres that moved and motivated me over the years.

Whatever the impetus, after that purchase of Joplin's ragtime, walking to the big music store—the long-gone Record Theatre[2]—about twenty to thirty minutes from my house to buy or browse was a marker of my shifting identity in relationship to the social world. During my treks to that store, I occupied time and space on my own terms (temporarily of course), and that framed some of my growing independence as the ability to go my own way. I anticipated what I would find and looked forward to the familiar faces I might see. Moving down the store's aisles bumping against the shelves and display cabinets crowded with albums organized by genre and in alphabetical order, I would hum along with the songs played through the sound system. And then, holding tight my purchase, I'd make my way back home continuing to hum the music I'd heard at the shop. The sound moved against, around, and through my changing body.

2. Record Theatre at 1800 Main Street opened in Buffalo in 1976, when I was twelve years old, and it closed in 2017.

Going alone to the record store was tied to another marking of maturation: the ability to use the stereo or record player without supervision. That "freedom of expression" said a lot in that it spoke to a "right" level of responsibility, a move away from pure childhood connoted by a firm enough appreciation for music (and expensive household items) to orchestrate it and to determine what song(s) marked a particular moment. It was an honor to use the stereo, a welcomed introduction to a new technology for encountering the world. It wasn't long before folks in the neighborhood heard word—the care you took with your records, and the taste that marked your music collection. Your LPs were sociopolitical (and at times religious or at least "soulful") commentary. Mindful of this, the record player wasn't just a piece of equipment. It was a prized possession, a type of "magical" device with the ability to transport you to different times and places—blurring past and present. And, with the right artist like Parliament and the Funkadelic (aka, P-Funk), or Sun Ra, the future also was expressed through a new and imaginative grammar and vocabulary of relationship (e.g., Parliament and the Funkadelic's "Supergroovalisticprosifunkstication," track 4 on the B-side of *Mothership Connection*[3]), punctuated by a cosmic sound often perceived as free from some of the typical music and social conventions.[4] P-Funk, during periods of trauma and misery within the social world expressed through heightened anti-Blackness on the heels of the civil rights movement, offered alternate worlds with patterns of interaction that signified US structures of difference as dilemma. I can't forget these words from "P-Funk Wants to Get Funked Up":

---

3. Parliament, "Supergroovalisticprosifunkstication" on *Mothership Connection*, Casablanca, 1975.

4. I have in mind, for example: Parliament's *Funkentelechy vs. Placebo Syndrome*, Casablanca, 1977, and Sun Ra's *The Futuristic Sounds of Sun Ra*, Savoy Records, 1962.

Do not attempt to adjust your radio, there is nothing wrong
We have taken control as to bring you this special show
We will return it to you as soon as you are grooving.[5]

As a reviewer noted concerning the futuristic sounds of Sun Ra on *The Futuristic Sounds of Sun Ra*, "What exactly are these new, otherworldly emotions? For me to try and pin it down for you would be go [*sic*] against the grain of what the music is trying to say. We all have to find out for ourselves. Personally, *The Futuristic Sounds of Sun Ra* sounds like the imagination at work."[6] P-Funk and Sun Ra explored a future growing out of a vibrant Blackness—in other words, Afrofuturism. While my thinking doesn't move in the direction of Afrofuturism as an intellectual and moral orientation, there was (and remains) something special about the music that inspired and that speaks an imaginative resistance to things as they were, whether or not new worlds actually emerge.[7] Music served as a powerful dynamic of expressive culture that shaped how many named and processed physical and psychosocial encounters in and with the world.

My brother-in-law, Terry Bryant, recently reminded me of this function of music by sharing a song—"Black Man in America," by October London—that describes the social world and captures our relationship to it. Surely, it doesn't describe all the workings of the social world, and it pronounces the sociopolitical and economic context in terms

5. Parliament, "P-Funk Wants to Get Funked Up" on *Mothership Connection*.

6. Matthew Wuethrich, "Sun Ra: The Futuristic Sounds of Sun Ra," AllAboutJazz, posted on January 19, 2003. Found at: https://www.allaboutjazz.com/the-futuristic-sounds-of-sun-ra-sun-ra-savoy-jazz-review-by-matthew-wuethrich. Accessed on February 18, 2024.

7. I find Afropessimism incomplete, but more compelling than Afrofuturism, or Afro-optimism. See, for example: *Deathlife: Hip Hop and Thanatological Narrations of Blackness* (Durham, NC: Duke University Press, 2024) for an example of my take on Afropessimism.

of a particular gender—both struggle and freedom named through a graphic masculinity. It is important to be mindful of such limitations while also acknowledging the truth of what it does describe in such a somber fashion. London's haunting 2016 proclamation moves back and forth through time, identifying a tragic past as well as ongoing dilemmas. Many might find something melancholic about London's imagery of degraded Black life, maybe akin to the misnamed "sorrow songs" that troubled W. E. B. Du Bois;[8] but for me the poetic depiction is simply a mode of existential "sho 'nuffness"—that is, *real*-ness:

> You won't let me live
> It's hard to be a Black man, a Black man in America.[9]

What my brother-in-law and I find in the song is an example of a larger commonality. Across time and space, there is something familiar about the existential concerns and the lament expressed so vividly. That so many outside October London's immediate orbit can find something compelling about the song suggests music has the ability to account for experience in such a way as to blur present and past—to syncopate encounters along a different register. Its poetic quality allows for reimagining and taming the harshness of paradox as the song both reduces and amplifies locality. Sitting and listening, I can't help but think that the world presented over against Black (male) well-being is all too familiar, feels too present, too impactful, and too close for comfort.

---

8. W. E. B. Du Bois, "Of the Sorrow Songs," in *The Souls of Black Folk* (New York: The Library of America, 1990). Zora Neale Hurston challenges Du Bois's depiction of the spirituals as simply sorrowful in, for example, Hurston, "Spirituals and Neo-spirituals," in *The New Negro*, ed. Henry Louis Gates Jr. and Gene Andrew Jarrett (Princeton, NJ: Princeton University Press, 2007).

9. October London, "Black Man in America," on *Color Blind: Love*, Cadillac Music, 2016.

Not just this song, but music in general did heavy lifting: sounds emanating (sometimes more like exploding) through an intentional manipulation of vibration amplified and explored experience, and elicited multidimensional response(s). Music was accessible but also distant as it spoke of worlds both familiar and beyond full grasp. At other times, this distance was constituted by the world of interactions lamented and the world of possibilities believed more desirable. In either case, in either way, music spoke a reality full of complexities, layered situations, and competing possibilities. October London reminds listeners that music isn't always a celebratory perspective regarding circumstances; but, that notwithstanding, it offers a way to process those conditions so as to avoid being consumed by them. Even musical laments serve to signify through a call to lucidity, of awareness, that enables continuation despite all. In a sense, music could be called the sound of persistence.[10] There is something about the almost-episodic quality of a "what" and "what if" expressed across a register of sound that makes music so very vital, as the orchestrated vibrations of sound waves captured by the ears and filtered through psychosocial concerns serve to amplify and interrogate the times.[11]

MUSIC'S ALMOST "SACRED" QUALITY AND PLACE

The technology for music making and listening has radically changed, but back in the day, as was the case for most in my neighborhood, the

10. I don't want to overromanticize music, its production, and the arrangements of it for our consumption. There, of course, could be competing claims—neighbors competing to be the loudest, etc. But, while such scenarios call to the differences in preference and the limitations encountered, music—despite such issues—maintained its appeal and importance.

11. This is not to suggest that musicians have some type of moral obligation to promote this push for existential clarity and ontological substance.

record player or stereo system was prized, and was a central component of the living room (or for some the more formal "front room"). In many of these homes, the record player's place was as central and assumed as that of the family Bible—and just as guarded from foolishness and disrespect. The Bible's pages were turned with intentionality, and a steady hand gently guided the needle forward in just the right way. The pages of the Bible had to be held with great care. Causing a rip would get you sent to your room (or worse) because they weren't just pages in a book; they were the physical containers of cosmic concerns made material. And, the records (later 8-track tapes, cassettes, then CDs would have their own maintenance practices) had to be treated with the same care—wiped off, kept away from direct sunlight, and the needle gently lowered onto the LP or 45. The "sacred book" in some cases provided a link to family and community, as the names of newborns often were added to the family tree outlined in the space for such reflections at the front or back of the Bible. On the other hand, the album collection served as a kind of "listening tree" representing a host of family and friends whose presence was tied to memories around moments of life connected to particular songs. In this way, both albums and the Bible spoke a world acknowledged through the senses. One might think of them as constituting linguistically arranged modes of meaning.

Music guided the structuring of time in two of the most significant locations of life for me. Church moved along in part through the music that communicated shifts in the order of service—in other words, the music of the procession indicated worship had started; a song of fellowship encouraged us to greet each other; a choir selection prepared us for the preacher to move to the pulpit; the song after the sermon marked a time for people to come to Christ; a somber song of reflection led folks to the altar; and, a final upbeat hymn led people out of their pews and to the back of the church as service ended. We went home holding our everyday Bible (as opposed to a family Bible that stayed in its place in the house), humming a favorite tune from the service, and signifying any member of the choir who happened to be off-key or whose movements during choir selections failed to impress. Or, maybe a particular choir selection "hit" just right and we couldn't stop thinking and talking about it. Whatever the motivating scenario, even the walk back home rehearsed the nature of music as a mode of orientation and sonic guide. At home, gospel music might give way to the familiar defiant sounds of R&B, blues, jazz, and Hip Hop—and as the music played the sound offered opportunity for reflection that informed movement through the world when the "sacred book" wasn't in hand. Even so-called secular music—like religious engagement—had a kind of "sacred" quality in that it exposed, signified, and transported by harnessing language and manipulating sound, thereby opening listeners to intensified affective registers of encounter both personal and tragically unfamiliar. Music could be the data and occasion for life lessons meant to hold us in "place," while also calling us to journey and find joy even when engulfed in a social world more inclined to offer misery and pain. The Bible could spark imagining that transported the reader into alternate historical occurrences, but there remained a type of gap in the form of an unawareness and cultural disconnect between the one reading and the worlds encountered. The biblical text is a code of sorts that offers moral and ethical insights gleaned through a range of scripted experiences; but even the most avid reader appreciates these cosmically framed narratives only from an epistemological-existential distance. The stereo was something different—a device for a type of engagement that closed distance and blurred distinction through shared affective responses to the world, a similarity of experience that *didn't always* require the same bracketing of cultural worlds required often by the Bible. That is to say, the stereo afforded not an identical experience but one that was plausible for the most part. Even wild dreams within certain genres were tethered to a familiar social world.

Music touched the world and is touched by the world, and we find engrossing the sound of this contact.

What the stereo produced offered an alternate type of "salvation"—introspection, encouragement, or discipline newly energized epistemological engagement with the world . . . and with a beat. This is not to say all my musical selections (or all biblical passages) were celebratory; many were warnings of pending judgment, like the spiritual reimagined by Nina Simone:

> Sinnerman where you gonna run to?
> Where you gonna run to on that day?[12]

The symbolism (expressed biblically in this case) in religion and the symbolism embedded in music are intertwined at times. When saying this I am mindful of Ralph Ellison's reflection on the jazz musicians he encountered as a young man in Oklahoma City. These musicians spent time and energy working to fine-tune their ability to produce an "eloquent expression of idea-emotion." He continues, and this is the important point of convergence of commitment that draws the devotee into their calling, some wore their instruments "as a priest wears the cross."[13] In this situation both the musical instrument and the cross serve as signs of sacrifice for the sake of something significant and transformative—a something that calls humans to imagine worlds different than the circumstances that hold them bound. Drawing on the religious-theological imagery provided by Ellison, both the "secular" and "sacred" spark imagination as they reframe and refine time and space.

My goal with the above comparison to the biblical text isn't to force a theological rendering of music constituting a spiritualized

12. Nina Simone, "Sinnerman" on *Pastel Blues*, Philips, 1965.

13. Ralph Ellison, "Living with Music," in *Shadow and Act* (New York: Vintage International, 1995), 189.

sameness, but rather to give some sense of how I perceive music's relationship to the human in the process of *becoming*—the manner in which music holds importance as a tool of interpretation that exposes and deciphers the questions and concerns that amplify existence. Such is to also acknowledge that in doing this work, music is multidirectional because it is concerned with both horizontally and vertically situated questions. Despite what I've argued, connection between the Bible and secular music may seem odd; but, experience for many is tied to these two as mechanisms of metaphysical expansion, or as communicative technologies that occasion the speaking of worlds. Both harness the energy of sound—words in one case, and sound/rhythm/melody/harmony in the other. Both "secular" (i.e., nontheologically motivated) albums and the Bible presented arrangements of wonder with moral and ethical codes and conditions lodged behind the signs and symbols.[14] Both the Bible and music involve fluidity of perspective to the extent they call for looking forward and backward simultaneously. Stevie Wonder framed well this multidirectionality through the soulful "Songs in the Key of Life." Music, as Wonder demonstrates, could urge listeners to look forward by reflecting back: "Thinking back on when I was little nappy headed boy . . ."[15] Or,

> I wish those days could come back once more
> Why did those days ever have to go?[16]

---

14. I use the term *secular* here as an identifier of different engagement. I believe there is little that is captured actually through the traditional "secular" and/or "sacred" divide in that both point to the amplification of human experience, the isolation of particular dimensions and interpretations of that experience. I use it here not to point out some sort of ontological distinction but rather to point in the direction of a difference in assumed epistemological locale.

15. Stevie Wonder, "I Wish," on *Songs in the Key of Life*, Talma Records, 1976.

16. Wonder, "I Wish."

But even without that brilliant album we would have known the role of music in illustrating the dynamics of our daily lives. And this connection would have been displayed through other artists and genres that filled the airways and punctuated activities in Black neighborhoods across the nation. Music mattered—in more than one sense. Again, music is important because it is a vital expression of who we (re)present and understand ourselves to be in relationship to a world that shows little love and fights us on every front. This introspectiveness enabled by music is substantive, an expression of our being that announces an alternate materiality lodged in a refreshed epistemological connection to experiences, concerns, and possibilities.

WHAT THE MUSIC DOES

Is it too much to say where there is music there is life? This isn't the same as saying music is life; but rather that music punctures, punctuates, and wrestles with experiences that structure life. In so doing, music may amplify particular dimensions of existential meaning, might encourage particular life orientation and movements, or might warn against particular uses of one's time or caution against heartbreak. But most importantly, music brings attention to patterns of thought that inform how we see and understand our movement through the world. In this way, it functions as an interpretive device equipped to capture the nuance, the tone, the texture, the rhythmic nature of life and present its dynamics through the power of the poetic. Music points toward multiple routes at the same time and codes this dynamic positionality through a grammar and vocabulary of human reflexivity. It cuts across time and connects to worlds of thought in a manner reminiscent of the trickster's ability to open relationships between realms of existence. In fact, for some, listening to music with focused intent might qualify as a type of mystical experience to the degree mysticism is concerned with the intersections of the seen and the unseen—the contemplation of what can't be fully named—an affective turn where logic fails but feeling is sublime, which is to name a more elastic sense of possibility's dimensions and reach.

I liked the aural vulnerability and the sonic jaggedness of the LP—the skips, popping, and crackling that came with the needle moving across the surface of the vinyl record caused by dust and static electricity[17]—in part because of the mystical element. Yet, for many, that popping sound wasn't music, but rather noise—a distraction from the real intent of the artist. That wasn't the case for me. There was a beauty in the full range of sounds—including sonic inconsistencies—coming from that LP, and this beauty wasn't tied to completeness or sonic creativity as a type of perfection. Rather, it was to be found in the ability of music to hold in creative tension both intentionality and flaw. Placement of the needle on the vinyl was key, marking the start of this intersection of intentional sound and "noise." The compelling presentation of song as message was accompanied by sound as imperfection, and there was a type of harmony in the disjunction.[18] (The Hip Hop DJ knew this and made those alternate sounds an artform!) For me, there was a splendor in the skipping and in the popping sound, which constituted the unplanned elements of the musical experience—a reminder of our fragility, incompleteness that nonetheless speaks a "firm" significance that is compelling and affirming. Something of our humanity is captured in that complexity of sound—a reminder of our anthropology as a messy configuration of contradictions and (im)possibilities. Too technologically enhanced and "cleaned" a presentation of that arrangement of sound would deny the incomplete nature of human creativity. In a way, such

17. All this could be fundamentally altered if that record came into prolonged and direct contact with too much heat, sunlight, or clumsy handling.

18. And there was an embodied connection to this disjunction no longer present with streaming service (which isn't a lament of our current technology).

refinement might serve to damper the humanity of the humans—the interaction between imperfect humans and their engagement with other "things"—involved in the making and the expression of music.

Experience of the song came with accountability, a mode of responsibility associated with engaging the LP and the record player or stereo that spoke a confluence of forces pointing out both the power and vulnerability of sonic play. Touch signaled a transformationalist impulsiveness with and between things (e.g., the body, the needle, the record, electricity) involved in a type of mutuality. The senses are engaged and the mind expresses the world as it is, while also seeing what it was and what one might want it to be. As I've noted before, this application of sound doesn't necessarily change physical conditions but it has the potential to increase awareness that allows for a different type of connection with self and others through a more defiant positioning: love in a world that denies *Love*; resistance within a world demanding compliance; friendships in a world promoting radical individualism attached to empty nationalism; and imagination in a world that seeks conformity.[19] Continuing this pattern of thought, novelist Richard Wright understood his writing to be the equivalent of the blues—raw, subversive, signifying an unconquered expression of life in a death-dealing social world—and he was the bluesman marginalized and defiant. That said, I'm not calling for a sense of music as being of necessity a mode of vibrating disruption. Rather, I'm suggesting function, not form. By this I mean to say music is often *used* by listeners as a means of protest, and in so doing listeners imply utility that supersedes the musician's intent (which listeners cannot fully know anyway). Furthermore, there is a folk wisdom quality to the use of music that entails a signifying and application of signs and symbols. In a sense—from a particular vantage point of transformative-disruptive

---

19. In making this argument, I have in mind Albert Camus's *Myth of Sisyphus and Other Essays* (New York: Vintage International, 1991).

potential of unlikely things—the device or technology used to present music is something of a talisman with the ability to alter perception of experience and in so doing encourage particular and fleeting existential responses that pull the individual out of themselves while also fostering deeper introspection. But the talisman has little significance without human work to accommodate the human craving for song. I hear something of this desire for song when Alice Walker says,

> When I am in a country where people still sing spontaneously, while working or even while strolling along the street, or beach, I feel comforted, and at home. I regret deeply that more people in more countries have given up the gift to others that is voluntary song. It is true many great voices have been 'captured' on machines, I am not ungrateful. But if humans lose completely our human tendency to burst into song when the spirit moves us, we will be like birds who never learned to fly.[20]

Walker's attention to location is intriguing to me. Elsewhere I've talked about mundane "place" being the location of transformation and epistemological alteration, and music only amplifies such a manipulation of time and space. There is an attentiveness, a moment of transition, that precedes and enables listening. As the hand guides the needle, moving it toward the record, there is anticipation or an affective consideration tied to a scientifically verifiable mechanics and logic: the hand moves the needle, the needle engages the grooves in the vinyl, and sound is produced—sound that disrupts the mundane nature of the moment through an intensification of memory and possibility. It invites an intersection of physical and mental geographies arranged so as to promote a wrestling over meaning in a world that seems so

---

20. Alice Walker, "Alice Walker on Writing, Dancing, and Bursting into Song," Literary Hub (October 2, 2018). Found at: https://lithub.com/alice-walker-on-writing-dancing-and-bursting-into-song/. Accessed on February 19, 2024.

meaningless, so disinterested in our concerns and aims.[21] Music, in a sense, gives substance to what otherwise remains beyond reach, and this involves both affirmation and de/re/construction of perception and experience. The stereo stacked with LPs and 45s and anchored by the turntable and the radio constituted the potential for a song, for an invitation to see and (re)imagine the world. Musical expression entailed a potentiality—both presence and absence, sound and silence.

Mindful of Walker's words and my interest in thinking of place as a type of conscious manipulation of time and space, often for purposes that run contrary to the restrictive sensibilities of the social world, I acknowledge home wasn't the only place where music marked out time and space. Yet, there was a specialness to home as a space of one's own both in and away from the world. Hence, in a certain sense, the home typically looked like us—"looked" more like us than any other space we occupied during the course of a day. It looked like us if for no other reason than because it provided familiarity through our belongings arranged as we saw fit, with places dedicated for our purposes allowing for a type of spatially organized intimacy. I wouldn't call it a "safe" space—after all, what is safe about any space, public or private, in the context of the United States in the twenty-first century?—but rather a *distinct* space, which is to say an affectively and socially distinguishable location in which, for a particular time frame, outside obligations and interactions can be suspended. It's not a place defined by alone time per se in that the creator(s) of the music (if no one else) can be said to claim presence—interacting, calling, assuring, pushing, prodding, enabling. The overlap between the social world that impacts us and the possible world(s) poetically built and described in music were encountered with fewer external distractions due to

21. See Anthony B. Pinn, *The End of God-Talk: An African American Humanist Theology* (New York: Oxford University Press, 2012), especially chapter 6.

the familiarity of home. The sense of rightful belonging cushioned our listening and served to soften the noise of a less than welcoming social world beyond the boundaries of the house. The home space, for the most part, was as we needed it to be—complete with reminders of intimate and casual connections and things that spoke a type of comfort. When it came to music, the home (particularly where the stereo or other playing device was located), became a kind of liminal space—a location of transition holding together divergent possibilities. Each new song, each new or familiar artist, offered opportunity for an encounter with liminality. Music invited and marked out a short-lived merger of experience and proposition. Although on the other side of that in-betweenness there was the world left behind, the music offered something defined by difference from "social" time. I want to believe something like this is what Earth, Wind, and Fire, for instance, meant to convey when singing,

> Every man has a place
> In his heart, there's a space
> And the world can't erase his fantasies.[22]

The music affirmed, but also challenged—pushed and prodded, informed and concealed. It plunged us into our experiences, mapped moments within our history, and put us in touch with the deep and affective structures of our reality while affirming the right to imagine something different. There is a *full*-ness to that time defined by fragile materiality, fantasy and memory that celebrated our embodied selves.

While each type of music had its own ideal setting—e.g., R&B and soul anywhere folks could gather in comfort to chill, and Hip Hop outdoors and loud (perhaps the most mobile of the genres, particularly on the West Coast and deep South, where it had to be bumped in

22. Earth, Wind, and Fire, "Fantasy," on *The Best of Earth, Wind & Fire*, vol. 1, Columbia Records, 1978.

a car)—it was all transferable. Its power wasn't localized firmly; it was simply our comfort with particular arrangements of time and space that either quieted the mind or hyped us up—whichever we believed our particular circumstances called for. It allowed for the signifying of conditions. Yet, there was also something about those moments that affirmed much of what the status quo endorsed—elemental dimensions of the American dream—but with a certain swag that loops back to the signification that exposed the downside of that dream qua "nightmare," as Malcolm X called it.[23] Each genre of Black music (which is the music of most concern to me in what follows) spoke to and about this truth in its own way. Something of this is captured, again, in Ellison's reflections on jazz:

> I had learned too that the end of all this discipline and technical mastery was the desire to express an affirmative way of life through its musical tradition and that this tradition insisted that each artist achieve his creativity within its frame. He must learn the best of the past, and add to it his personal vision. Life could be harsh, loud and wrong if it wished, but they lived it fully, and when they expressed their attitude toward the world it was with a fluid style that reduced the chaos of living to form.[24]

A WORD ON HIP HOP

Moving to the beat was involuntary—like a heartbeat, and as natural as breathing. The "right" music pulled at the self in its various dimensions—detangling and tangling intellectual and emotional

---

23. Malcolm X, "Ballot or Bullet Speech," in *Malcolm X Speaks: Selected Speeches and Statements*, ed. George Breitman (New York: Pathfinder, 1989), chapter 3.

24. Ralph Ellison, "Living with Music," in *Shadow and Act* (New York: Vintage International, 1995), 189–90.

registers—the effect of this process often announced through a simple phrase: *That's my jam!* It's the song that speaks to and about an invaluable dimension of one's self understanding. That's what Flo Rida is getting at in the epigraph that begins this introduction. It's a process of discernment and intentionality leading to a type of subjective selection on an affective level with psychological connotations framed through a simple three-word phrase—"That's *my* jam." Music named particular moments of significance and provided expression of what life might be some day. It was all genres of music—gospel, spirituals, blues, R&B, funk, rock and roll, jazz. It all contributed something to how I (and others) viewed the world and named what it meant to be touched by all with which we shared the world. Music acknowledged and amplified the "rhythm" that is life and provided a poetic means for naming that rhythm. Yet, Hip Hop was special.

There was something defiant about the music we picked—my friends and I. It spoke about the world in ways, we hoped, the elders in our family and community would acknowledge, but certainly wouldn't understand. A type of delight marked hearing one of them say, "What is that stuff you're listening to? It doesn't make any damn sense!" Of course, this was more likely the response to Hip Hop than alterations and updates to the musical genres that had guided and shaped their youth. We might have changed R&B some by making it "funky," but the basic structure rang true. But Hip Hop? That was different. My response . . . our response . . . we *are* different, and proud of it . . . dammit! Different, yes; but there was still something about Hip Hop that was familiar—if folks were willing to actually think about it.

Every phase of my development from high school through graduate school and now my professional life is marked by some type of contact and interaction with Hip Hop. It is something of a touchstone for me—helping me to see the margins of collective life and how life happens as a process of signified celebration and resistance. Grand Master Flash and the Furious Five helped to describe the affective connotations of urban decay with a phrase that resonates through the years: "Don't push me 'cause I'm close to the edge." And, more recently, Kendrick Lamar took the same dilemma and captured it through an alternate phrase of resignation and triumph: "We gonna be alright." Think of Cardi B's call to live one's best life despite all, or the implications of claiming the aesthetics of Black embodiment in Megan Thee Stallion's status as "the hood Mona Lisa."[25] These songs employ modes of poetic realism to capture social circumstances as consequential but not so consequential as to have the power to ultimately define us.

Hip Hop wasn't just music. It was a marker of the "post soul era"[26] as a time when the unfinished business of the civil rights movement was most graphic and challenged. It was the emergence and naming of a (counter)*culture*—a structure of living that captured the times and challenged them. It signified the American narrative that implicitly anchored so much US music. And in its place Hip Hop shaped a new grammar and vocabulary for describing and challenging the marginalization of "darkened" communities. However, it didn't develop in a vacuum. Hip Hop culture pulled from other musical forms, as the DJ samples from the albums that had anchored the imagination of earlier generations. The MC has something of the blues singers' posture toward the world; and others who live Hip Hop culture celebrate an aesthetic explosiveness that is reminiscent of the celebration of "style" found in so much R&B and funk. And breaking . . . well, breaking continued the tradition of transforming how bodies occupy time and

25. Grand Master Flash and the Furious Five, "The Message," on *The Message*, Sugar Hill Records, 1982; Kendrick Lamar, "Alright," on *To Pimp a Butterfly*, Top Dawg Entertainment, 2015; Cardi B, "Best Life," on *Invasion of Privacy*, Atlantic Records, 2018; Megan Thee Stallion, "Savage," on *Suga*, 1501 Certified, 2020.

26. See Nelson George, *Buppies, B-Boys, Baps & Bohos: Notes on Post-soul Black Culture* (New York: HarperPerennial, 1994).

space through movement that points to the power, grace, and supple nature of the body in motion. Breakers use movement to highlight human value reminiscent of how Blacks danced their dignity during earlier decades. Hip Hop is the culmination of a particular take on the world signified in the blues, transcended in the spirituals and gospel, chronicled in R&B, pop, and funk, and rendered rhythmic by jazz. But Hip Hop did all of this and in the process terrified and tantalized a global population by consuming and regurgitating the social world.

PUTTING IT ON PAPER

As I've moved from church to the academy what remained consistent despite that significant existential shift is the centrality of music to my thinking, doing, and general posture toward the world. From ragtime to Hip Hop is the evolution of my musical interests—an evolution I described in this introduction as a music-centered religious-theological thought experiment conducted across decades. The range of musical influences has been broad and layered—each providing a narrative and technology (here in the Foucauldian sense of the word[27]) applicable to the unpacking of experience with all its flaws and potentialities. Each offered a way to encounter the world anew. Music has provided me a sense of the social world of Black people as well as an imaginative approach to exploring and analyzing developments within that world—all captured in numerous publications over the years. In the following pages, I offer a collection of some of these writings—thirteen in all—presented initially in a variety of locations as journal articles and book chapters.

The following pages are shaped by two overarching themes—"The 'Sound' of Be-*ing*" and "Theologizing's Rhythm." The first

27. See, for example, Michel Foucault, *Technologies of the Self: A Seminar* (Amherst: University of Massachusetts Press, 1988).

thematic category is meant to say something about the manner in which music explores and challenges notions of identity, sociality, and the nature and meaning of life over against the structures of the social world. That is to say, the chapters in that first section offer some sense of the relationship between music and epistemological-ontological issues, framed in terms of the workings of embodied Blackness. The second thematic grouping ("Theologizing's Rhythm") is meant to give some sense of how music informs and influences the study of religion in general and theological conceptualizations in particular. Over the course of the years captured by these pieces, I've had an interest in exploring the ways in which music—particularly Hip Hop—challenges and changes the theological vocabulary and grammar used to name and discuss human meaning making processes. Hence, the second section of the book investigates a range of music's theological and religious studies implications.

In addition, the chapters are arranged chronologically (in accordance with publication date). It is my hope this presentation by date (1999–2021) provides a sense of how my thinking on music developed and evolved over time—for example, concepts established and repeated, and the artists/songs dominating my thinking. In this way, conceptual and content overlap is informative—giving a sense of the progression of my thought over time in relationship to sociopolitical and economic changes in the nation. Ideas and arguments build on each other—pull from and expand upon each other over the course of years. This, I believe, speaks to the manner in which particular artists and lyrics anchor my thinking and, over time, lend themselves to a variety of concerns, and ground a range of ideas and topics. Mindful of this interest in showing the evolution of my thinking, readers will also note that there is a shift in my writing from *black* to *Black* at times. Rather than correcting chapters so as to represent consistently the now standard use of the capital *B*, I have left the chapters as they were initially published in order to represent shifts in both my writing style and social sensibilities. Relatedly, readers will note that in some places, I use *African American* and in other places, *Black Americans* or *Black people*. The same is the case with "hip hop" over against "Hip Hop." Otherwise, I have made only slight alterations related to misspelling and the addition of some wording in order to mark out transitions between the chapters.

In both content and form, the aim of this book is to illustrate the centrality of music to human meaning making—the manner in which it recognizes, names and influences experience in and with the world (and its contents). Despite socioeconomic restrictions, limitations or barriers, Black people have created music that has spoken worlds through a manipulation of past and present: the power of imagination. It seems every moment of significance in the history of Black America has had its theme songs, the sonic rhythm that named the significance of the times and the nature of the struggle. The music was not only motivational, but also provided a language framing the moment. Think, for example of James Brown: "Say It Loud! I'm Black and I'm Proud," or Nina Simone's "Young Gifted and Black." There's the spiritual transformed into a civil rights freedom song "Ain't Gonna Let Nobody Turn Me Around."[28] And there's Public Enemy's "Fight the Power," which was mindful of traumas that marked Black life in the twentieth-century US and, as a consequence, held suspect "American" optimism.[29] The list goes on . . .

From the first chapter to the last, I aim to chronicle the shaping of sound as having its own materiality—that is, its own realness that touches various dynamics of life historically situated. Music, in

---

28. James Brown, "Say It Loud—I'm Black and I'm Proud (Part 1)," single, King, 1968; Nina Simone, "To Be Young, Gifted and Black," single, RCA, 1970; "Ain't Gonna Let Nobody Turn Me Around," based on the spiritual "Don't You Let Nobody Turn You 'Round."

29. Public Enemy, "Fight the Power" on *Fear of a Black Planet* (Def Jam, 1990).

a word, offers sonically arranged insight and impact across a range of issues and activities. And there is something aesthetically bespoke about this experience because each has their own musical preferences with certain selections "hitting" harder than others. But music, in a more general sense, is a pliant aural force of human creation with the ability to alter perception and experience. So, find your jam, and let it play!

Section One

THE "SOUND" OF BE-*ING*

1 RAP MUSIC AS SOCIAL TRANSFORMATION

For African Americans, the presentation of life as a multileveled reality has often taken form through musical expression. Music chronicles and critiques developments regarding the complexities of life within the Black community, with spirituals responding to the hardships of slavery and the blues addressing the paradoxical situation of African Americans in the post–Civil War era. Those familiar with the civil rights movement will note the importance of gospel songs and other musical forms for the expression of the goals and objectives of the movement for freedom. For example, the singing of "we shall overcome" held tremendous epistomological and existential significance for civil rights workers.[1] And most recently, rap music provides a discussion of contemporary Black life that actively engages issues relevant to the civil rights struggle and its sociopolitical as well as economic aftermath.

METHODOLOGICAL CONSIDERATIONS

Moving from an exploration of rap music and the workings of Black manhood, within this chapter I will explore the nature and content of

1. The brevity and focus of this chapter do not permit a discussion of the civil rights movement's musical tradition. However, those interested in this should see, for example, Jon Michael Spencer's *Protest and Praise: Sacred Music of Black Religion* (Minneapolis: Fortress Press, 1990).

rap music's lyrically expressed vision of social transformation. Attention is given to two major categories of rap music—"gangsta" rap and progressive rap.[2] As a methodological note, this exploration is in part guided by Albert Camus's notion of the "Absurd"[3] and African American models of response to oppression such as the Jeremiad tradition present within African American religious thought.[4] Concern-

---

2. My typology of rap music includes these two categories as well as the category I currently label "bravado" rap. This term is not intended to be derogatory; rather, it refers to a level of discussion within this brand of rap that does not consistently include issues of social justice, racism, etc. This form of rap is overwhelmingly concerned with personalized "quality of life" issues—dressing well, sexual partnerships, bragadocious behavior. Other scholars include additional categories within their typologies (e.g., "dis" rap as discussed by Michael Dyson). However, I argue that my triadic structure covers the essential and major distinctive rap manifestations. For other typological approaches see, for example, Ronald Jemal Stephens, "The Three Waves of Contemporary Rap Music," in *Black Sacred Music: A Journal of Theomusicology* 5 (Spring 1991): 25–40.

3. This discussion is limited to lyrical analysis of recorded rap music. I am not suggesting, however, that the musical content of rap is of less importance. Both are important components of rap's expressivity. Yet within this chapter, my goal is to point out certain connections between various forms of cultural production and visions of transformation. This can be reasonably achieved without a detailed discussion of musical content. Such a discussion is beyond the scope of this short piece. For interested readers, information on the musical element can be found, for example, in the Tricia Rose materials mentioned in this essay. In *Black Noise: Rap Music and Black Culture in Contemporary America* (Middletown, CT: Wesleyan University Press, 1994), Rose provides a critical assessment of a piece by Andre Craddock-Willis. The reader should look at Craddock-Willis's piece, "Rap Music and the Black Musical Tradition: A Critical Assessment," *Radical America* 23, no. 4 (October 1, 1989). Also see "Rap: Taking It from the Streets," in *Keyboard* 14, no. 11 (November 1, 1988) and Thomas Schumacher, "'This Is a Sampling Sport': Digital Sampling, Rap Music and the Law in Cultural Production," *Media, Culture and Society* 17, no. 2 (April 1, 1995).

4. Although more is said concerning the Jeremiadic tradition in the United States, particularly in African American thought, I would like to begin by mentioning one resource that provides historical and rhetorical context for the

ing the latter methodological consideration, attention to the Jeremiad tradition points to my recognition of a link between the cultural tools used by rap artists and those used by past generations, the former's approach entailing contemporary manipulations of the Black oral tradition—the Jeremiad, toasting, signifying, and so on, for the purpose of social transformation.

Before moving into the major points of this chapter, I would like to say a few words about absurdity as a way of denoting systemic oppression encountered by African Americans. Life for African Americans living in the United States is well captured by Camus's notion of absurdity. In the words of Camus,

> A world that can be explained even with bad reasons is a familiar world. But, on the other hand, in a universe suddenly divested of illusions and lights, humanity feels an alien, a stranger . . . exile is without remedy since humanity is deprived of the memory of a lost home or the hope of a promised land. This divorce between humanity and its life, the actor and his/her setting, is properly the feeling of absurdity.[5]

In the context of Black American life, this absurdity involves the manner in which the illusion of equality is contradicted by systemic oppression (e.g., racism/sexism as well as the byproduct of a market-driven economy), and results in a triadic alienation from self, others, and nature.

With regards to alienation from self, racism within the United States provides an understanding of "blackness"—related to physical

---

African American Jeremiad: David Howard-Pitney, *The Afro-American Jeremiad: Appeals for Justice in America* (Philadelphia: Temple University Press, 1990).

5. Albert Camus, *The Myth of Sisyphus and Other Essays*, trans. Justin O'Brien (New York: Alfred A. Knopf, 1969), 6. Gendered language contained in this passage has been altered. I am not as convinced as Camus that revolt and rebellion ultimately collapse.

bodies—as inferior, soiled, and dangerous. Consequently, many African Americans are taught to prize certain European physical traits and to hate themselves for straying from these "normative" features. This condition connotes alienation from self and leads to a collapse of self-esteem—such as poor self-image and a dwarfed sense of self-worth. The effort is made to alter oneself in order to fit the illusive model of perfection—what Cornel West calls the "normative gaze."[6] Failure to embody this "ideal type" produces self-hatred and contempt for those resembling the tortured self. It produces internalized racism.

Those who have adopted this attitude find it difficult to maintain healthy relations with other African Americans because other African Americans remind them of what they dislike in themselves. The prevalence of Black-on-Black crime points to the sense of nihilism, uselessness, and hopelessness engendered by internalized racism and how it fosters alienation from others, especially others similarly oppressed.[7] On both the personal and interpersonal levels, racism and its effects work in concert with classism and sexism to create a web-like structure of oppression.

Finally, life restricted by economic hardships creates distance between many African Americans and the world of nature—the structures of life existing outside of the asphalt and concrete world. Under such conditions, it becomes rather difficult to see one's environment as anything other than hostile. Furthermore, the quest for economic survival reduces "space" outside of one's immediate surroundings to the unknown and unreasonable. In Camus's words, the "strangeness of the world is the absurd."[8]

---

6. See Cornel West, *Prophesy Deliverance: An Afro-American Revolutionary Christianity* (Philadelphia: The Westminster Press, 1982), 53–57.
7. West, *Prophesy Deliverance*, 40.
8. Camus, *Myth of Sisyphus and Other Essays*, 14.

This alienation can result in societal if not physical death or it can foster an attitude of defiance—the effort to create meaning and value in a nonresponsive environment. One sees this effort, for example, in the civil rights struggle waged several decades ago. However, the limited reach of some gains and the reversal of others made during the civil rights movement reinforces the present absurdity experienced by members of the African American community and requires renewed combat and a new vision of transformation. In very real ways this vision differs from that posed some twenty years ago. As Nelson George wisely comments,

> In 1965 African Americans in urban centers like Watts were seeking their bit of the civil rights miracle that was transforming the South. Their needs were as much economic as social, and those needs were never addressed. Twenty-seven years later a generation has grown up that knows zip about those past hopes and views this world with precious little optimism. Crucially, the folks who wear X hats . . . and know the sound of Tech-9's better than the 10 commandments are not going to respond to racist provocation the way liberals and their African-American elders want them to.[9]

One form of this renewed defiance is found within the phenomena that originated in New York City—hip hop. By recognizing and exploring their historical and cultural roots, young hip hop artists create values by which to orient themselves, such as distinctive dress. Within the larger culture of hip hop, this sense of defiance is given

9. Nelson George, *Hip Hop America* (New York: Viking, 1998), 161–62. This quotation indicates what is not explicitly stated but is understood within the following pages: not all African Americans find rap musical appealing. However, my argument does not concern the outlining of Black Americans' various musical tastes. Rather, my goal is to outline the agenda and "style" of presentation found in rap music.

actual voice through the medium of rap music, particularly in gangsta and progressive rap.

GANGSTA RAP AND SOCIAL TRANSFORMATION

Gangsta rap emerges as a recognized Los Angeles–based musical category and large market business during the late 1980s with the recordings of NWA (Niggas with Attitudes).[10] Within this form of rap music, there is a response to absurdity and meaninglessness that suggests social transformation through the mimicking or signifying of certain ideologies and behaviors. There is the realization that life as currently lived does not meet basic needs. Gangsta rap, therefore, seeks to move African Americans away from the underbelly of capitalism. Yet, its vision for such movement does not extend beyond an embracing of the hated system. That is, gangsta rappers seek to break away from the structural defects of the post–Reagan/Bush United States by a questionable manipulation of the very principles on which it operated: the acquisition of "goods" by violent maneuvers.

> I know the game, so I'm a do the same
> Don't like when I play the same way

10. I readily acknowledge that lyrical elements and attitudes identified as "gangsta" are first present in Schooly D (1987) and the early work of KRS-One and Scott La Rock (1987) on the East Coast and Ice-T (1987) on the West Coast. However, my point is that gangsta rap is "labeled" and gains more than regional attention with the emergence of NWA. For information on rap music on the West Coast, see Brian Cross, *It's Not About a Salary . . . Rap, Race and Resistance in Los Angeles* (New York: Verso, 1993). There is much debate over the distinction between "original" or "real" gangstas and "studio" gangstas. The crux of this debate is over identity and legitimacy. My concern in this chapter is limited to the action depicted and approved in gangsta rap, irrespective of lifestyles' actualization or fictitious nature.

And say, hey, freedom got an A-K
You better call 9-1-1
The nigga 's got a gun.[11]

Such a parody of the "American system" often provides short-term benefit for the participants. One need only look at the material success of many rap artists for evidence of this. Yet there are negative consequences as well that result in a kind of violence done to other people—usually other residents of Black communities. For example, one cannot overlook the blatant exposition of negative and destructive attitudes toward women and homophobic tendencies within this music. Snoop Doggy Dogg is not alone in his objectification of and attempts to commodify women. However, few rappers have received the same notoriety for their destructive intentions. In "Ain't No Fun (If the Homies Can't Have None)," one song on his debut CD *Doggy Style*, he says,

I know the pussy's mine
I'm a fuck a couple more times
And then I'm through with it
There's nothing else to do with it
Pass it to the Homie, now you hit it.
'cause she ain't nothing but a bitch to me
And you all know that bitches ain't shit to me.

Gangsta rappers' barbarism and hostility toward women masks fear that is centered on the idea that women threaten the survival of men. Because of this fear, gangstas work to control and subdue women in order to maintain manhood and social status. Although produced a good number of years ago, the Geto Boys' *Grip It! On That Other*

11. From Da Lench Mob, "Freedom Got an A-K," on *Guerilla's in Tha Mist*, EastWest/Atlantic Records, 1992.

Level still provides two of the stronger examples of gangstas casting Black women as suspect. In the notorious "Let a Ho Be a Ho," above the '70s "hustler" sound and strong beat are the following words, which graphically account the demasculating effect of intimacy with women:

> It seems to be alot of motherfuckas blind to the fact that a ho is going to be just that.
>
> And this type of ignorance is the reason so many niggas is in the goddamn cemetery.

The fear and hatred expressed in this song are superseded by the bloodthirsty fantasy of murder, rape, and nihilism found in "The Mind of a Lunatic." It was such songs by the Geto Boys and other "hard-core" rap groups that caught the attention of the media and "watchdog" groups who sought to sanitize popular culture.[12]

Arguments against censorship and for a sense of accountability and responsibility on the part of rappers, however, ignore the complexities of the conditions from which this music emerges. Yet it must be acknowledged that rap albums "go platinum" because they echo patterns of behavior endemic to this society that have appeal outside of the Black community. Rappers, in fact, display the values and norms of the United States. In bell hooks's analysis, "more than anything, gangsta rap celebrates the world of the material, the dog-eat-dog world where you do what you gotta do to make it even if it

12. The issue of "sampling" and the ensuing legal cases has the potential to alter the production and context of rap music and, in this way, institutionalized and less overt means of "policing" rap music are realized. These institutionalized and economically coded forms of control are harder to recognize than are the attacks by Rev. Calvin Butts, Tipper Gore, and Cynthia Delores Tucker. See Rose, *Black Noise*, 90–93 and William Eric Perkins, *Droppin' Science: Critical Essays on Rap Music and Hip Hop Culture* (Philadelphia: Temple University Press, 1996). Public Enemy addresses this issue of sampling on *It Takes a Nation of Million to Hold Us Back*, Def Jam, 1988, in the song "Caught, Can I Get a Witness!"

means fucking over folks and taking them out."[13] The kind of insight offered by hooks, however, is all too rare. Not all critics of rap music have acknowledged its connections to a larger culture of violence and domination and how it reflects that culture like a carnival mirror. By addressing the abusive behavior many rap artists mimic, I do not intend to hedge or to legitimize verbal violence and degradation as devices for controlling a hostile environment. Rather, my goal is to place gangsta rap in a larger context and thereby call for a wider reading that acknowledges the problematic nature of cries to "ban 'em!" The truth is, gangsta rappers exist somewhere between the persona of the scapegoated "untouchable" predator and the victim of a cruel society.[14]

It is in relationship to this in-between space they occupy that gangsta rappers signify (i.e., indirection and manipulation of language, a strategy for temporarily controlling the more "powerful") the absurdity encountered daily.[15] One way certain gangsta rappers signify

---

13. bell hooks, "Sexism and Misogyny: Who Will Take the Rap," in *Outlaw Culture* (New York: Routledge, 1994), 117.

14. Rappers such as Queen Latifah ("Ladies First") have responded to displays of misogyny with raps that provide positive depictions of women. Others such as Salt-n-Pepa have countered the derogatory lyrics of many male rappers by glorifying female agency. That is, Salt-n-Pepa portray themselves as women of will who embrace the display of their sexuality (e.g., the song "Shoop"). Some argue, however, that Salt-n-Pepa's counterattack actually contains a form of reverse sexism and, as a result, is of little value. This is of course open to debate. Of less question is the gangsta style of groups such as Bytches with Problems and solo acts such as The Boss who mirror the abusive attitudes and behavior of many male gangsta rappers. Their "turning of the tables" undoubtedly results in female-generated objectification and debasement.

15. Signification is not limited to the lyrics of rap music; signification also involves the uses of technology in ways not traditionally approved—the manipulation of beats, etc. See Rose, *Black Noise*, chapter 3. Early versions of this chapter appear as "Soul Sonic Forces: Technology, Orality, and Black Cultural Practices in Rap Music," in *Sounding Off: Music as Subversion/Resistance/Revolution*, ed. Ron

and thereby foster protest is by maintaining the presence of Black cultural heroes—the trickster/badman figures of Black oral tradition.[16] As William Perkins observes, gangsta rap's appeal rests in its representation of an "ideology of authenticity." In a world defined by absurdity, gangsta-isms respond with a call to "keepin' it real," countering uncertain existence with visions of true ghetto existence. In this way the ghetto provides stability, but often with death and destruction as the price paid. Furthermore, misogyny, homophobia, appeals to violence, and so on, are presented as the code of authentic existence.[17] This authenticity is connected to a reclamation of the 1970s ghetto hustlers and the early twentieth-century "Badmen," all of whom are larger-than-life figures who ruthlessly fulfill their desires in almost superhuman ways. These icons provide historical grounding and context as well as epistemological backing for ghetto "realness"—portrayed through lyrics, music, clothing, *Being*. Through the emulation of these folk heroes, gangsta rappers turn life's absurdity on its head and in the process create a sense of balance, a sense of self.

Placing rap within Black oral tradition such as toasts and the blues does not, however, preclude an appreciation of rap's unique

---

Sakolsky and Fred Wei-Han Ho (Brooklyn: Autonomedia, 1995), 97–108, and "Orality and Technology: Rap Music and Afro-American Cultural Resistance," *Popular Music and Society* (Winter 1989).

16. Rose, *Black Noise*, 23–26. Robin Kelley ("Kickin' Reality, Kickin' Ballistics: Gangsta Rap and Postindustrial Los Angeles," in Perkins, *Droppin' Science*, 117–58) and Rose, *Black Noise*, 3, among others, make reference to the presence of the Badman attitude and antics in gangsta rap. And Michael Eric Dyson, *Between God and Gangsta Rap: Bearing Witness to Black Culture* (New York: Oxford University Press, 1996), 165–71 ("Public Enemy: Rap's Prophets of Rage") and others have pointed out the Jeremiad and griot traditions within certain strands of rap music. However, they have not—to my knowledge—developed these connections in the manner presented in this chapter.

17. Perkins, *Droppin' Science*, 19–20.

development in time. As Tricia Rose explains in *Black Noise*, rap's technological alterations give evidence of the ways in which all progression of Black expressivity shows both a continuance and a unique trajectory resulting from its particular context and make-up. These developments, whether raps or toasts, mark a continuation of Black expressivity as it responds to the conditions of life and presents a "unique" mode with its own complexities. This dynamic between continuity and innovation is not unusual when one keeps in mind the same sense of absurdity or meaninglessness fostered by material circumstances that gave rise to early folk wisdom and lore. Before the ghetto hustlers and Badmen there were Black folk figures who functioned like the "gangsta" persona, shaping a form of defiance through signification.

Creating stories with trickster figures such as the Signifying Monkey provided enslaved Africans with an outlet for their frustrations and fears, a means by which to indirectly respond to white abuse and dehumanization.[18] This was done through indirect confrontation through language "games." For example, in one such tale, monkey decided to create friction between the lion and the elephant by telling lion that elephant questioned his authority and talked about lion's family. The lion, as a result, confronts the elephant and is severely beaten during the exchange. At that moment, as Henry Gates Jr., indicates, the

18. The discussion of Black oral tradition presented here is limited to a brief introduction. For additional information see, for example, Henry L. Gates, Jr., *The Signifying Monkey: A Theory of African-American Literary Criticism* (New York: Oxford University Press, 1989); Alan Dundes, *Interpreting Folklore* (Bloomington: Indiana University Press, 1980); John W. Roberts, *From Trickster to Badman: The Black Folk Hero in Slavery and Freedom* (Philadelphia: University of Pennsylvania Press, 1990); Lawrence Levine, *Black Culture and Black Consciousness: Afro-American Folk Thought from Slavery To Freedom* (New York: Oxford University Press, 1977), and Langston Hughes and Arna Bontemps, *The Book of Negro Folklore* (New York: Dodd, Mead & Company, 1959).

monkey has become "king" through his clever use of language and his ability to manipulate through guile. When applied to the relationship between African Americans and the "System," signifying marks a process of exposing lies and "insulting" oppressive structures and attitudes.[19] Although indirect and of temporary benefit, signifying was an appropriate method of survival for antebellum and nineteenth-century trickster figures *and* their creators.

The subtle and indirect approach of these trickster figures is brought into question during the twentieth century because of postslavery chances for direct expression of feelings, concerns, and thoughts.[20] The changing conditions after slavery and on into the contemporary period made certain aspects of the trickster's behavior unappealing. Postslavery life did not warrant complete dismissal of the trickster's shrewdness and cunning; the artfulness with which the trickster observes human nature and the world remained relevant. Yet even small changes in society allowed for a more aggressive figure who directly confronted power structures through the exhibition of "badness." These societal changes including the attempt by many African Americans to rethink the position of African American men in family and societal life also resulted in an embracing of an understanding

---

19. Henry Louis Gates, Jr., *Signifying Monkey: A Theory of African-American Literary Criticism* (New York: Oxford University Press, 1988), 59.

20. Lawrence Levine, *Black Culture and Black Consciousness: Afro-American Folk Thought from Slavery To Freedom* (New York: Oxford University Press, 383. Theophus Smith, in *Conjuring Culture: Biblical Formations of Black America* (New York: Oxford University Press, 1994), provides an interesting study of trickster and biblical personalities within Black conjure tradition. In some ways, gangsta rappers and "root workers" both make use of powerful words and symbols to bring about social change. Hence, it seems plausible to argue that gangsta rappers also make use of the "conjurer" personality in constructing themselves and their relationship to the world. However, an investigation of this possible connection is beyond the scope of this chapter. I hope to pick up this question at another time.

of Black women premised upon domesticity arguments. This struggle for male identity also helps to explain the presence of misogynistic attitudes in twentieth-century oral tradition not as readily present in the Signifying Monkey and Brer Rabbit accounts of the nineteenth century.[21]

Badmen emerge during the early twentieth century and receive the mixed praise of many Black Americans. These figures reach their peak and even achieve some commercial success with late-twentieth-century figures such as Dolomite (Rudy Ray Moore). These bad men struck out at any time and at any one. Although they defied social norms and the power structures created by white Americans, they also wreaked havoc within the Black community.[22] The merciless activities of Stackolee (Stagger Lee or Stack O'Lee), for example, are recounted in song. Mississippi John Hurt has this to say about Stack O'Lee the Badman:

I told Stack O'Lee please don't take my life,
I got two li'l babes and a darling, loving wife.
[Stack O'Lee remarks] What I care about your two babies and
your loving, darling wife?
You done stole my Stetson hat and I'm bound to take your life.[23]

---

21. For a good discussion of Black women and these issues see Paula Giddings's *When and Where I Enter: The Impact of Black Women on Race and Sex in America* (New York: Bantam Books, 1984).

22. William Labov, Paul Cohen, Clarence Robins, and John Lewis, *A Study of the Non-standard English of Negro and Puerto Rican Speakers in New York City* (Washington, DC: Educational Resources Information Center, 1968), 335–36. Also of interest are Daryl Cumber Dance, *Shuckin' and Jivin': Folklore from Contemporary Black Americans* (Bloomington: Indiana University Press, 1978) and Mel Watkins, *On the Real Side: Laughing, Lying, and Signifying—the Underground Tradition of African-American Humor That Transformed American Culture, from Slavery to Richard Pryor* (New York: Simon & Schuster, 1994).

23. Mississippi John Hurt, "Stack O'Lee Blues," on *The Blues*, vol. 2, Smithsonian Collection of Recordings, 1993.

A similar recounting of Stagger Lee's exploits is found on the live recording from the Mississippi and Louisiana State Penitentiaries compiled by Alan Lomax. The prisoners sing of Stagger Lee's lack of concern with codes of conduct that are not in keeping with his interests and desires.[24]

Stackolee and others are not concerned with societal norms imposed by white Americans; they defiantly take "power" and apply it indiscriminately. In this way, those who "respect" these figures are able to entertain fantasies of revenge and give release to their defiant urges. The violent behavior of both Stackolee and certain rap lyrics, in one questionable sense, marks a "freeing" process of sorts, the claiming of one's rights and space, even if this is merely the right to self-destruct. The following remark by Lawrence Levine discusses nineteenth-century attitudes but is relevant to contemporary gangsta rap artists:

> Coming from the depths of the society, representing
> the most oppressed and deprived strata, these
> bandits are manifestations of the feeling that,
> within the circumstances in which they operate,
> to assert any power at all is a triumph.[25]

Nonetheless, the vision of redemption here involves obtaining of power and practicing societal principles of domination that, in the longer run, are counterproductive. The antics of tricksters, Badmen, and their late-twentieth-century imitators allow for a form of control that does not ultimately disturb the existing power structures. For young gangsta rappers, however, even this short-lived feeling of dominance has appeal; and so, they covet the opportunity to obtain voice

---

24. "StackerLee," *Negro Prison Blues and Songs* (Beverly Hills: Legacy International, n.d.).

25. Lawrence Levine, *Black Culture and Black Consciousness: Afro-American Folk Thought from Slavery To Freedom* (New York: Oxford University Press, 1977), 418.

and power, the abstract "merits" of tricksters and Badmen. Yet the exercise of defiance sought involves the destruction of Black community and self.

The careful listener and observer will notice that although some songs by gangsta rappers glory in cruel exploits, they also acknowledge and lament this destruction. During these moments, gangstas instruct through illustrations of "life gone wrong."[26] It is not all guns and glory . . . it's not "all good." And as LV and Coolio remorsefully note, "Ain't no gangstas livin' in paradise." This lamenting over the gangsta's self-destructive bent is at times complemented by songs such as Ice Cube's "My Skin Is My Sin" and "What Can I Do?" Ice Cube, in these songs, presents the connections between institutional racism and the gangsta's life. Yet even through this lament of self-destruction and recognition of societal responsibilities for economic shortcomings, the gangsta's lifestyle maintains its allure for countless young people.

PROGRESSIVE RAP AND SOCIAL TRANSFORMATION

Progressive rap, witnessed by the emergence of groups such as Public Enemy and Boogie Down Productions in the late 1980s and groups such as Arrested Development, suggests another approach. Whereas gangsta rap represents the ideology of the Badmen, progressive rap loosely represents a late twentieth-century incarnation of the Jeremiad tradition, with hints of the griot.

The term *Jeremiad* is a reference to the prophet Jeremiah who spoke of Judah's fall and the destruction of the Jerusalem temple. He argued that this devastation was a result of misconduct, misdeeds correctable in part by an adherence to the cultural and religious identity established by God. Narrowly conceived, the Jeremiad is a lamentation of

26. See, for example, Ice Cube's "Robbin' Hood (Cause It Ain't All Good)" and "Li'l Ass Gee," and Dr. Dre's "Li'l Ghetto Boy."

present conditions, the condemnation of misconduct and its resulting destruction. When extended beyond its immediate biblical context, the Jeremiad is the term denoting the dominant style of manifest destiny and "special" status argumentation expressed in white antebellum America, and the rhetorical device employed by African Americans to critique racism and pending "judgement."[27]

African Americans argued that America's assertions of privileged status, due to election by God, was not in keeping with their treatment of Native Americans and African Americans. American rhetoric and action were in direct opposition and, consequently, resulted in the rejection of God's plan for the United States.[28] Only destruction could

27. See Jeremiah, chapters 1–52. For an interesting examination of this proclamation tradition in Black thought, see Wilson J. Moses, "The Black Jeremiad and American Messianic Traditions," in *Black Messiahs and Uncle Toms: Social and Literary Manipulations of a Religious Myth*, ed. Wilson J. Moses (University Park: The Pennsylvania State University Press, 1982), 30–48. For more general information on the American Jeremiad see: Reginald Horsman, *Race and Manifest Destiny: The Origins of American Racial Anglo-Saxonism* (Cambridge, MA: Harvard University Press, 1981).

28. Several distinctions exist between current Jeremiads provided by rap music and early Black Jeremiads. One is the rejection of an "American-ness" and sense of manifest destiny by current rappers. It is clear, in Nathanial Paul, David Walker, Maria Stewart and others, that the ideals of America are not questioned; rather, it is the uneven practice of these ideals that is problematic. One does not find, in Public Enemy (PE), for example, this same patriotism. Also noticeable is a lack of attention to mainstream Black religious institutions with Jeremiads produced by rap groups such as Public Enemy. PE encounters a church that has been substantially "de-radicalized," to use Gayraud Wilmore's term (*Black Religion and Black Radicalism* [Maryknoll: Orbis Books, 1983]). In many respects Black churches are still attempting to recapture some of their nineteenth-century social and political thrust. PE and others, hence, are suspicious of Black churches that have a questionable record with respect to the fight for justice on earth. This helps to explain an attraction by the members of some

result from this rebuff of God's call to justice. Black Jeremiads, using biblical stories of enslavement and the exodus, pinpointed this hypocrisy and called for social transformation on all levels. David Walker's *Appeal* (1829) is not the only example of this Jeremiadic tradition, but it is certainly one of the most frequently mentioned because of its precise and biting tone. For example, article III of his four-article *Appeal* (Walker's critique of preachers who support the system of slavery) ends with these words:

> It appears as though they [white Americans] are bent only on daring God Almighty to do his best—they chain and handcuff us and our children and drive us around the country like brutes, and go into the house of the God of justice to return him thanks for having aided them in their infernal cruelties inflected upon us. Will the Lord suffer his people to go on much longer, taking his holy name in vain? Will he not stop them, preachers and all? O Americans! Americans!! I call God—I call angels—I call men, to witness, that your Destruction is at hand, and will be speedily consummated unless you Repent.[29]

A twentieth-century version of the Jeremiad, tempered by the realities of civil rights struggles and urban turmoil, is found in the writings and speeches of Dr. Martin Luther King Jr. Filtered through his commitment to nonviolence as the means by which to affect widespread change and create the "beloved community," King argues that time is quickly moving toward the punishment of the United States. Only justice and equality on all levels can prevent this. In King's words,

---

rap groups to non-Christian traditions first established in the 1920s and '30s in response to dysfunctional Black churches.

29. David Walker, *David Walker's Appeal: To the Coloured Citizens of the World, but in Particular, and Very Expressly, to Those of the United States of America* (New York: Hill and Wang, 1995), 43.

> The American people are infected with racism—that is the peril. Paradoxically, they are also infected with democratic ideals—that is the hope. While doing wrong, they have the potential to do right. But they do not have a millennium to make changes. Nor have they a choice of continuing in the old way. The future they are asked to inaugurate is not so unpalatable that it justifies the evils that beset the nation. To end poverty, to extirpate prejudice, to free a tormented conscience, to make a tomorrow of justice, fair play and creativity—all these are worthy of the America ideal. . . . All of us are on trial in this troubled hour, but time still permits us to meet the future with a clear conscience.[30]

Similar statements have been made by African Americans throughout the history of the United States. The necessity for ongoing articulations of the Jeremiad resulted from continued oppression. Yet Jeremiads fluctuate in tone and content. However, the unaltered essence of the Jeremiad is its exposure of hypocrisy and injustice and its call for a unified movement toward collective health and harmony—the humanist vision broadly conceived. Within this form of expression is the ability to "revise" meaning while critiquing the norms of white society—the reconstituting of Blacks as subjects rather than as objects.

Although collective memory tends to privilege the Jeremiad tradition as presented by David Walker, Martin Luther King, and others who left behind prose, expression of the Black Jeremiadic tradition extends beyond the written word. Music has often served as a Jeremiadic form of protest, such as progressive rap music. Rap groups of this genre also recognize the hypocrisy inherent in North American governmental and economic dealings and the need for strong leadership in

---

30. Martin Luther King Jr., "The Poor People's Campaign," in *Autobiography of Martin Luther King, Jr.*, ed. Clayborne Carson (New York: Warner Books, 1998), 350–51.

order to move beyond the present condition of the African-American community. In the words of Arrested Development,

> The great depression everyone is in depression
> No one knows exactly what their role
> totally confused, depressed cuz of the news
> Watch TV, more bad is what U see
> Everyone's lost and we're looking for a savior
> Everyone's blind and we're looking for a leader
> We've lost our faith so we need someone to guide us.[31]

Furthermore, these rappers speak against the ways in which such oppressive activities alienate the Black community from itself and others. A strong example of this lament over disconnection to people and the land is provided by Arrested Development. In "Tennessee" (from *Three Years . . .*), Speech, the leader of the group, takes the listener on a journey back to his roots, and by extension, the listener is urged to also make the necessary connections. Using symbols and images reminiscent of the Yoruba tradition's respect for nature and the spirits, Speech says,

> Then outta nowhere you [God] tell me to break
> outta the country and into more country,
> past Dyesburg into Ripley.
> Where the ghost of childhood haunts me,
> walk the roads—my forefathers hung from.
> Ask those trees for all their wisdom.[32]

---

31. "United Front," on *Zingalamaduni*, New York: Chrysalis Records, 1994.

32. "Tennessee," on *3 Years, 5 Months and 2 Days in the Life of . . .* , Chrysalis, 1992. Respect and appreciation for land are also highlighted on Arrested Development's second album, *Zingalamaduni*. It must be noted that Arrested Development is no longer a group. Dionne Farris and Speech have each embarked upon solo careers.

This transformative response to people and nature entails the "rupturing" of subjugated knowledge, to use Foucault's terms. That is, Arrested Development and others attempt to educate African Americans regarding their condition and the causes of their condition. One sees this, for example, in the words produced by Public Enemy (PE), often noted as the exemplar of overtly political rap music. PE, primarily through its leader Chuck D, provides an analysis of current conditions, combining philosophical inquiry, cultural criticism and hardcore rage.[33] Through a sense of cultural nationalism, which owes much to the Nation of Islam and the Black Power Movement of the 1960s and historical deconstruction, PE seeks to ground Black people in an understanding of the "U.S. of A." and its status quo. They urge people to fight for a healthy existence by acquiring and exercising knowledge, through TRUTH . . . "Fight the power" and "party for your right to fight":

Power Equality
And we're out to get it
I know some of you ain't wit' it
This party started right in '66
With a pro-Black radical mix
Then at the hour of twelve
Some force cut the power
And emerged from hell
It was your so-called government
That made this occur
Like the grafted devils they were.[34]

---

33. For additional information on Chuck D and Public Enemy see Armond White, "Fear of Language: American Media and Public Enemy," *The City Sun*, December 12–18, 1990, 25, 33–36; Robert Christgau and Greg Tate, "Chuck D All Over The Map," *Village Voice*, October 22, 1991, 12–18; James G. Spady and Joseph D. Eure eds., *Nation Conscious Rap* (New York: PC International Press, 1991) 307–86.

34. "Party for Your Right to Fight," on *It Takes a Nation*.

Within this rap, Public Enemy argues that much of what Black Americans face is the result of a demonic government that is determined to promote the welfare of a few at the expense of many. Chuck D remarks that much of the push toward Black uplift, that resulted in the governmental backlash, is traceable to the Black Power movement and the efforts of the Black Panthers. The bottom line for Public Enemy and other progressive groups is this: knowledge of oppressive plots and the value/worth of "Blackness" will result in transformation.[35]

Public Enemy's critical gaze is not restricted to "devils" outside the Black community. Addressing the absurdity of life also requires recognizing and responding to the culpability of Black people—self-critical assessments. And so, Black Americans who fail to remember their "roots" and Black Americans who harm themselves and the community in other ways are targeted for lyrical attack. For example, in "Night of the Living Baseheads" (from *It Takes a Nation*), PE denounces the trafficking of drugs within Black communities and the damage done by drug abuse.

> The problem is this—we gotta' fix it
> Check out the justice—and how they run it
> Sellin', smellin'
> Swiffin', riffin'
> And Brothers try to get swift an'
> Sell to their own, rob a home
> While some shrivel to bone.

PE also argues for self-determination—a united Black community—through a recognition of the dollar's power. Whereas Arrested

35. However, progressive rap is not free from problems. The homophobia, for example, of these rappers needs to be addressed. In this respect, progressive rap must rethink the manner in which it does do further damage to victims of systemic oppression.

Development, in the above examples, talks of Black unity in terms of cultural and epistemological connection, PE discusses this but also talks in terms of political and economic like-mindedness. That is to say, within the Black community progress is tied to businesses "giving back." To the extent this is not the operative model for businesses, PE's Jeremiad urges Black Americans to "Shut 'Em Down" (from *Apocalypse 91*):

I like Nike but wait a minute
The Neighborhood supports so put some
Money in it
Corporations owe
Dey gotta give up the dough
To da town
Or else
We gotta shut 'em down.[36]

A similar message concerning the use of knowledge as a weapon is provided by Sister Souljah, Minister of Information for Public Enemy. For her, knowledge is the key to Black regeneration; without it, Black Americans run the risk of perpetual blindness. Considered a racist by figures such as President Bill Clinton, Sister Souljah is unrelentless in her appeal to "truth" and enlightenment, such as in "The Hate That Hate Produced" (*360 Degrees of Power*):

Souljah's creating the statements I'm stating
Meant to be real never accommodating
I give it to you straight I don't water it down.
No need to debate, I don't change it around.
Well if the truth hurts, well then you'll be in pain.[37]

---

36. Public Enemy, "Shut 'Em Down," on *Apocalypse 91…The Enemy Strikes Back*, Def Jam, 1991.

37. Sister Souljah, "The Hate That Hate Produced," on *360 Degrees of Power*, Epic, 1992.

This quest for truth and righteous living also requires occasional blistering verbal correctives for the Black community. In one such attack, Sister Souljah speaks to Black women and men who participate in their own degradation—"Niggas." In a style somewhat reminiscent of the work of the Last Poets, Sister Souljah outlines apathy and pathologies in "Nigga's Gotta" (*360 Degrees*):

> Nigga's still drinking, boozing and stinking
> St. Ides big banking and nigga's not thinking
> Nigga's still smoking, gagging and choking
> Counting pennies and broke
> And still nigga's joking.

Like PE and other overtly political rappers, Sister Souljah is not opposed to violence; the freeing of Black people requires the use of numerous strategies and tools. In the oft-quoted words of Sister Souljah from "The Hate That Hate Produced,"

> Souljah was not born to make white people feel comfortable
> I am African first, I am Black first
> I want what's good for me and my people first
> And if my survival means your total destruction, then so be it
> You built this wicked system
> They say two wrongs don't make it right
> But it damn sure makes it even.

The group Arrested Development also acknowledges that the dynamics of institutional and internalized racism often make violence unavoidable. Speech, playing off the song "Everyday People," says the following concerning a day in the park ruined by the ignorance of others: "That's the story of a Black man, acting like a nigga, and getting' stomped by an African" ("People Everyday," from *Three Years* . . .).

The overall manner in which Public Enemy and others provide Jeremiads against self-destruction is echoed in the words of the song

"Self-Destruction," produced by Boogie Down Productions (BDP). In the following lines, KRS-One of BDP and Kool Moe Dee point out the illogical actions of Black people:

Well today's topic is self-destruction
It really ain't the rap audience that's buggin'
It's one or two suckers, ignorant brothers
Tryin' to rob and steal from one another . . .
'Cause the way we live is positive
We don't kill our relatives. . . .

Back in the sixties our brothers and sisters were hanged
How could you gang-bang?
I never ever ran from the Ku Klux Klan
And I shouldn't have to run from a black man
'Cause that's self-destruction
Ya headed for self-destruction.[38]

In this way, they hope to spark continued defiance of existing structures through Black unity and self-sufficiency. Tied to this notion is the oft-repeated appeal to knowledge and the deconstruction of myths and government agendas. Boogie Down Productions provides fierce commentary on this front in the song "Why Is That?" from the *Ghetto Music* CD. Herein BDP brings into question religious doctrine and stories that support false claims of white superiority and Black inferiority. Above a strong and haunting (if not sinister—a marker that suggests the uncovering of a devious plot against Black people) beat are the following words:

Yes, my brothers and sisters take this here song,
 yo correct the wrong.

38. Stop the Violence Movement, "Self Destruction," single, Jive, 1989, as cited in Michael Eric Dyson, "Performance, Protest, and Prophecy in the Culture of Hip-Hop," *Black Sacred Music* 5, no. 1 (Spring 1991): 12–24.

The information we get today is just wac,
    but ask yourself why is that?
. . . The age of the ignorant rapper is done
. . . The stereotype must be lost that love and peace and
    knowledge are soft.[39]

CONCLUSION

History is marked with efforts to negotiate life's triadic structure of alienation. Drawing on the examples of trickster and Badmen figures, gangsta rap creates meaning through the violent and often self-destructive manipulation of structures and persons. Progressive rap, extending the Jeremiad tradition, warns Black Americans about such destructive methods and aims to provide alternative ideological structures based upon self-pride, self-knowledge, and unity. In both cases, rap artists are attempting to defy the world and its restraints and, in so doing, find meaning in an absurd world. Whether their efforts will ultimately succeed is not yet evident. But, if nothing else, they have made many reassess what it means to live in and "change the world." If we are wise, we will heed their warning—see the "Badmen" and hear the Jeremiad. In a very real way, our collective life depends upon it.

39. Boogie Down Productions, "Why Is That," on *Ghetto Music: The Blueprint of Hip Hop*, Jive, 1989.

2 THE BLUES AND IDENTITY

The first chapter addressed rap music, and here I turn to another musical form—the blues—while maintaining a focus on issues of identity and transformation. For some time now I have found the blues appealing, something about the aesthetics of that genre, but also something about the general worldview that I find hauntingly tragic and attractive. Muddy Waters has captured my attention many an evening, particularly "Manish Boy." But what is this "manish boy," perhaps someone with hypersensitivity to the ways in which the body receives and gives pleasure?

> I'm a hoochie coochie man
> The line I shoot will never miss
> When I make love to a woman,
> she can't resist.[1]

To be a "manish boy," I believe, is to be positioned between adulthood and childhood—moving between assertions of responsibility to expressions of a narrow focus on strong individual want. Yet, it also involves an unfortunate attempt at invisibility, not of the body per se, but of the body's moral and ethical possibilities and obligations. That is to say, it seeks to ignore, or render invisible, the male's obligation

1. Muddy Waters, "Manish Boy," single, Chess, 1955.

to move the body in ways that are ethically and morally sensitive and productive. Within the context of the blues, this perspective is most commonly and graphically presented with respect to the libido—the body as sexual. Regarding this, one finds Muddy Waters noting,

> Now when I was a young boy, at the age of five
> My mother said I was gonna be the greatest man alive
> But now I'm a man, way past twenty-one
> Want you to believe me baby,
> I had lots of fun.[2]

While black males can legitimately claim to being oppressed within the context of the United States, maleness has also entailed certain forms of privilege including a limited ability to render the body invisible in certain regards. Granted, practices such as profiling clearly indicate that the black (male) body is never completely free from observation; yet, there remain ways in which the black male body can be moved through the world with a limited obligation to observe certain moral and ethical responsibilities, particularly with respect to interactions with black women. This ability to shadow human interactions involves invisibility.

I want to label this epistemological and ontological oddity—a type of invisibility—the "manish boy" phenomenon. It is this male relationship to the world that at least in part accounts for the positioning in negative ways of women with respect to themselves and community. Perhaps, in part, this is what Zora Neale Hurston meant when referring to black women as the "mules" of the world. And perhaps this ability to remain undetected is noticed and signified in the subtle brilliance of Alice Walker's "Mr.," on so many occasions in *The Color Purple*, simply as the identifier of Celie's husband.

In the first instance, Hurston, I believe, notes the manner in which the bodies of black women are "fixed" and understood in terms of

2. Waters, "Manish Boy."

service given (what Delores Williams might note as the meta-reality of surrogacy); while others, including black men to some degree, have bodies that are more ambiguous. Walker, who is well aware of Hurston's analysis of African American women's alterity, outlines the various ways in which even privilege within the context of discrimination (such as the benefits of maleness for racialized men) allows for the body to take on a "shadow" existence—to be somewhat ghostlike in that its "weight" is deniable. Yet, in both cases it seems clear that invisibility of the black male body allows for moral and ethical slippage. Aren't, for example, Walker's "Mr." from *The Color Purple* (sometimes Albert) and Hurston's Tea Cake (from *Their Eyes Were Watching God*) in this sense "manish boys"?

With this said, and in light of my training as a theologian, I cannot resist asking a question: What is the theological equivalent of the "manish body"? That is to say, are there ways in which this ability to disappear the black male body has shaped black theological discourse in particularly harmful ways? Put yet another way, has black (male) theological discourse, the project I participate in, acted in bad faith with respect to its moral and ethical outlook because black male theologians have conducted their work as "shadows"? The obvious, and correct, answer is yes.

I ask these questions, and provide an answer in the affirmative, in large part because of implicit and explicit lessons I have learned from Womanist scholarship.[3] Although this should be an obvious statement, Womanist scholarship urged me to recognize that I have a body, and

---

3. I refer to both formal engagement through conferences and reading (and teaching as best I can) Womanist scholarship, as well as the gracious ways in which Womanist scholars such as Katie Geneva Cannon, Cheryl Kirk-Duggan, and Stacey Floyd-Thomas have shared their insights and critique through more informal conversations. In this short chapter, however, I concentrate on my formal engagement with Womanist scholarship.

that this body is in fact gendered. In the same way that white privilege entails the ability of whites to think of only the "Other" as being raced, male privilege (even in its limited form as experienced by black men) entails a similar option for "not-ness," or invisibility (a dimension of invisibility, I should like to say, that was ignored in Ralph Ellison's *Invisible Man*). Such willful ignorance on my part, I was beginning to learn, did damage to my ability to theologize in complex ways; and it also influenced my pedagogical options.

I made certain assumptions and embraced particular unacknowledged privileges that accompany the male body—such as an assumption that one is entitled to comfortably occupy "space." And with respect to pedagogy, whether I acknowledged it or not, my physical presence in the classroom sent nonwritten and nonverbal messages to my students. My body provided information that affected the manner in which my students received and processed the knowledge I attempted to impart. But I often ignored this reality.[4]

With my first encounter of Alice Walker's definition of "Womanist," I was challenged to recognize the means by which the unacknowledged assertion of the black male body affects the manner in which black women experience the world. With respect to my scholarship, it became clear that a proper articulation and vision of "liberation" had to entail the exorcising of the black male body, the acknowledgement of its "weight" and presence. In its most pressing form this realization meant knowing that it is not enough to acknowledge sexism as a dimension of oppression experienced within African American communities.

---

4. For my thoughts on pedagogy as it relates to the body see *African American Humanist Principles: Living and Thinking Like the Children of Nimrod* (New York: Palgrave Macmillan, 2004), chapter 9. This pedagogical issue has also been highlighted in a Wabash-sponsored seminar, organized by Lynne Westfield of Drew University, in which I participated.

While black male theology of liberation has acknowledged and attempted to exorcise its more demonic (in the Tillichian sense) features, problems remain. Black theology, for example, has failed beyond a few exceptions to critique and offer an alternate to the hypermasculinity promoted in some Christian circles as a way of combating the destruction of the traditional model of familial existence.[5] By so doing, black theology fails to take advantage of an opportunity to extend its vision beyond an updated version of the cult of domesticity. There is no doubt that this epistemological stance fosters a theological posture that misreads African American communities and their "needs," the nature of their oppression, in that it views these communities through a lens of heterosexual male-centered existence. I am not suggesting the complete obliteration of "male-ness." Rather I am suggesting that there must be ways to add complexity to it, and to place it in relationship with other modes of encounter with the world.

Jacquelyn Grant's *White Women's Christ, Black Women's Jesus* and Delores Williams's *Sisters in the Wilderness*, for example, required me to acknowledge the manner in which my very being as a male entailed a certain language and grammar that in itself placed restrictions on my theologizing.[6] These limitations revolved around a tension at times, and a paradox at other moments, in that I, like my colleagues, argued for an existential theology, a black theology as a body theology. But what I typically presented was a not-body theology. As Hortense Spillers and Toni Morrison have noted with great insight, the flesh tells stories, and as Mary Douglas remarks, the body is a symbol of

---

5. Dwight Hopkin's recent work, an example of which is in *Loving the Body: Black Religious Studies and the Erotic*, ed. Anthony Pinn and Dwight Hopkins (New York: Palgrave Macmillan, 2004), pushes for a new sense of masculinity.

6. Jacquelyn Grant, *White Women's Christ, Black Women's Jesus* (Atlanta: Scholars Press, 1989); Delores Williams, *Sisters in the Wilderness* (Maryknoll, NY: Orbis Books, 1993).

the social system. I am unwilling to say that my socially constructed and reified existence as "male" means a hopelessness with respect to my position as oppressed-oppressor. Redemption is possible for even those who move through the world carrying the weight of the male body. Yet, these three theories—presented by Spillers, Morrison, and Douglas—of the body when recognized, and combined with the insights of Womanist scholars, demand a need for sensitivity to the ways in which the existence of the male body (my body) as coded, as symbol of the social system, involved a type of theological double-talk.[7]

Womanist scholars, through the development of a complex and intellectually sophisticated theological methodology and theory of experience that is interdisciplinary in nature, have challenged traditional theological formulations. This critique highlighted the manner in which black theological discourse, dominated by males, entails the passive acceptance of privilege that does damage to efforts toward liberation. This damage involves the, again passive, assumption that the black male body (keep in mind what Spillers, Douglas, and Morrison say about the body) is normative.[8] That means a certain set of symbols, signs, and a fixed grammar shape theological perspective and argumentation.

In a sense, the movement of the black body sets the proper posture for theological engagement. What results, Womanist have convincingly demonstrated, is a failure to take seriously, to really take seriously in a way that changes deeply the way in which scholarship is

7. I have given some attention to body awareness in recent publications. See my essay in Pinn and Hopkins, *Loving the Body*, and Pinn, *African American Humanist Principles*, chapters 5–6.

8. See G. M. Gonzalez, "Of Property: On 'Captive' 'Bodies,' Hidden 'Flesh,' and Colonization," in *Existence in Black: An Anthology of Black Existential Philosophy*, ed. Lewis R. Gordon (New York: Routledge, 1997) and Toni Morrison's "The Site of Memory" in *Out There: Marginalization and Contemporary Cultures*, ed. Russell Ferguson et al. (Cambridge, MA: MIT Press, 1990).

conducted, alternate modalities of experience—sexism, heterosexism, and so on.

In addition to the ways in which Womanist scholarship has surfaced (through what I would refer to as a hermeneutic of archeology) African American women's experiences as theological sources or data, there is a more theoretically and methodologically centered consequence of Womanist work.[9] This second, theoretical and methodological, challenge posed by Womanist scholarship has pushed on me a growing awareness of the incomplete status of my theological formulations, through an effort to maintain the invisibility of my body.[10] If I am sensitive to the sociocultural, psychological, and political implications of my physical presence even in the ways in which I think and teach theology, it is likely that theological formulations will take on a more nuanced, a more complex, a "thicker" meaning.

In a sense, Womanist existential sensibilities push theologians to entertain the possibility of transforming black theology into a proper body theology. In this way it moves in the direction of discourse that is genuinely concerned with the implications of existence (and meaning) present in the physical body, mining the body for its theological import. So doing involves the ability to construct theology that does not seek to avoid or ignore the body, but rather theology that is done through sustained contact with the body. This seems the theological

9. In addition to the Delores Williams text already noted, good examples of this attention to black women's experience as theological sources include Katie Geneva Cannon, *Womanist Ethics*; Karen Baker Fletcher, *A Singing Something*; Emile Townes, *Ida B. Wells*; Cheryl Townsend Gilkes, *If It Wasn't For the Women.*

10. My text on the theory of black religion, *Terror and Triumph: The Nature of Black Religion* (Minneapolis: Fortress Press, 2003), is one of my more substantive attempts to wrestle with this issue. It is an effort to develop an understanding of black religion's nature and meaning through continued awareness of the manner in which black bodies carry and shape perceptions of the world and our relationship to the world.

implication of the Womanist appreciation for "roundness" highlighted in Alice Walker's definition of the term, appropriated by black women in religious studies during the mid-1980s. Such an understanding of theology's connection to the physical world holds intriguing potential for doing black (male) theology in ways that push beyond its methodological provincialism and theoretical xenophia.

It is conceivable that black theology, following the *best* of the Womanist tradition, will give the notion of liberation greater depth and epistemological balance in that it becomes a sense of free movement that appreciates the flesh rather than simply attempting to ignore it, or assume that only male bodies matter.[11] This entails the death of the "manish boy" and the birth of a more complex and more deeply connected human—one who appreciates, in Alice Walker's words, a yearning for "survival and wholeness of entire people, male and female."[12]

---

11. This is not to say that Womanist scholarship is without its own shortcomings. I do not want to romanticize Womanist work; it has its own issues, when one considers that the debate between Cheryl Sanders and other Womanists in the 1980s remains significant (see *Journal of Feminist Studies in Religion*). Yet, within the context of this short chapter, I have in mind the limitations of black theological discourse pointed out by first-generation Womanist thinkers such as Jacquelyn Grant (see James Cone and Gayraud Wilmore, eds., *Black Theology: A Documentary History* [Maryknoll, NY: Orbis Books, 1979]) as well as women who predate the formal development of Womanist theology such as Pauli Murray (also see *Black Theology: A Documentary History*). Within the context of Black theology, Victor Anderson pointed out this problem with respect to the limiting effect of ontological blackness for a sense of "cultural fulfillment" that does require surrender of one's individual inclinations for the sake of blackness as the community unifier. See *Beyond Ontological Blackness* (New York: Continuum, 1995).

12. Alice Walker, "Womanist," in *In Search of Our Mother's Gardens: A Womanist Prose* (New York: Harcourt Brace Jovanovich, 1983).

3 WHAT HUMANISTS MIGHT LEARN FROM HIP HOP

In the last chapter music—the blues—was the backdrop for an assessment of masculinity and more productive modes of personhood; this chapter turns back to Hip Hop. Rather than how individuals might behave, or how Black men as a particular group might engage others, this chapter turns to what humanists (such as myself) might learn from Hip Hop. That is to say, humanism—as a life orientation, or a framework for meaning-making—stands to better position itself in relationship to more widely recognized life orientation—such as Christianity—by paying attention to the means by which Hip Hop moved from being the cultural production of despised young people to being an international influence.

We humanists have made our presence felt. Often our rhetoric is self-assured, and vividly displayed is our willingness to confront the theism bias embedded in the workings of the United States. Despite all this, humanist activities still appear entrenched in an apologetic mode—a significant expenditure of resources meant to say, "We are here and, by the way, we are good people." Even more aggressive forms of humanist engagement, those meant to challenge the religious and convert them through strong confrontation and mockery, betray, from my perspective, the same apologetic tone. Neither what some derogatorily call a conformist approach (i.e., accommodationism) nor the more self-righteous confrontational approach provides a sufficiently constructive and robust depiction of what humanistic orientations promote. This type of posture toward our work doesn't allow for the accomplishment of our full agenda to diminish the theism-centered discourse (and structures of interaction) guiding so many dimensions of public life. And this is because we are still playing by the rules offered by theists. That is to say, there is embedded in our approach an effort to get theists to appreciate (perhaps even like?) humanists. But why worry about that? Furthermore, is this type of regard even achievable?

It can still be problematic to embrace humanism publicly. Yet our typical approach to this situation does little to change this dilemma in that our marginality is embedded in the rhetoric of the nation—and has become tragically the grammar of the public sphere—and guided by the temperament of the uninformed. Even if this weren't the case, being liked hasn't done much to change the outlook for other marginalized groups. What it can produce is paternalism, patronizing attitudes that actually stymie advancement and inclusion. Perhaps we might aim to be disliked, but respected? Yet, what does being respected entail for us? What's the look, the texture, of this respect and what does securing and keeping it require of us?

HELP FROM AN UNLIKELY SOURCE: HIP HOP

Needed at this point is more attention to the construction of an alternate grammar of life along with new modalities of ethical/moral insight and practice that speak to the benefits of humanistic thinking and doing. We have demonstrated some creativity in generating this message, but still seem a bit stuck and in need of inspiration. Mindful of this, I want to propose a source of assistance worthy of consideration—Hip Hop culture.

What I have in mind extends beyond an appreciation for the outstanding work of humanist Hip Hop artists, and instead includes attention to the pedagogical possibilities offered by the larger cultural movement. So, no need to worry; I'm not asking you to turn your baseball caps backward, or forget about your sensible shoes and conservative clothing choices. I'm not calling on humanists to become Hip Hop advocates or fans. Rather, I am suggesting that Hip Hop provides a particularly compelling heuristic. My aim is to encourage recognition of Hip Hop as an interpretive tool by means of which we might learn how to better do what we say humanism is all about—and to do so in ways that appreciate the creativity lodged in our relative marginality and despised status.

A link between humanism and Hip Hop is not as absurd as one might initially think, not when one considers a common epistemological root marking much of the thinking undergirding both. That is to say, both humanistic sensibilities and Hip Hop culture share a human-centered and earthy ontology, both stem (although there are nuances to this) from a similar perception of evidence-based free thought and a signifying of supernatural claims and transhistorical assertions. Furthermore, in US culture, both humanists and members of the Hip Hop community are labeled marginal, and as problematic figures whose activities/beliefs fly in the face of normative moral and ethical structures of life.

I propose an embrace of this epistemological connection and attention to what can be learned from the successes of Hip Hop culture. While it has its problematic dimensions—elements of violence, homophobia, misguided materialism, and so on borrowed from the storehouse of American culture—there are ways in which this cultural force has offered important challenges to the "American way of life." It has outlived calls for its demise and pronouncements of its fad-like quality. Even those who fear or dislike Hip Hop have been forced to recognize it and address life in this historical moment in light of it.

Lodged within the decaying infrastructure of urban life in New York City during the late 1970s, Hip Hop culture—the music, aesthetic, dance, and visual art known as tagging and graffiti—provided a mode of communication and exchange for typically disenfranchised young people. Hip Hop is not the first cultural form to wrestle with the existential and ontological difficulties and limits marking the (post)modern period. Yet, it does so with a type of rawness and through imaginaries that push thought about and experience of the world beyond affected representations. The traumas and angst of the world are expressed in graphic form. In certain ways, Hip Hop culture offers a new language, an alternate grammar and vocabulary for articulating the nature and meaning of life. In other words, the various genres of rap—what might be described as status rap, socially conscious rap, and gangsta rap—offer perspectives on this basic arrangement: How does one make life meaningful within the context of an absurd world? Within rap music there are strong representations of this absurdity, with perhaps the most compelling being death. Humanists are well aware of death; we know the science behind it, and are quite reasonable and logical with respect to it. Yet, we live in cultural worlds that are not fully explained by means of scientific formulas. Our living toward death requires a particular cartography, a peculiar map that marks out the cultural contours of our existence. And for this, we should turn to Hip Hop in that there are ways in which it promotes significant attention to the tensions and paradox associated with efforts to map out life structures within a context marked by the look, feel, and smell of death. It offers a compelling way of describing and addressing the grotesque dimensions of our demise much too graphic for most polite, humanist conversations.

Through a creative signifying of dominant strategies for life and more graphic modes of expressing life meaning within the context of absurdity, Hip Hop marks a demand for visibility in a world more comfortable with invisibility. It has offered a way of speaking about and speaking to the tragic nature of human existence, without surrender to the nihilism that theistic intellectuals like Cornel West fear.

Instead, it provides comfort with paradox and an imagining of marginality as place for transformation.

Whereas Hip Hop has turned status as a despised and troubling but short-term fad into a powerful tool for shaping cultural worlds across a global geography, humanist movements have not been as fortunate in their effort to create status and more transnational influence.

A HIP HOP POSTURE FOR HUMANISTS

Humanists are trying to fix this situation through public conversation and praxis, and through organizational infrastructure expanding beyond North America. However, there is a flaw in this approach in that such effort tends to involve strategies tied (at least loosely) to the methods and logic associated with the civil rights movement of the mid-twentieth century. These methods and this logic require acceptance of an assumption that moral outrage made visible constitutes the means for advancement. There is in this arrangement belief that progress is somehow linear and human history purpose driven. I am not pushing for rejection of the civil rights movement and, of course, humanists aren't alone in appealing for inspiration to this process and this particular moment of struggle. After all, some important shifts in policy resulted from that movement. Yet, there are ways in which appeal to mid-twentieth century techniques may not be the best strategy for the godless. For instance, popular imagination around the civil rights movement is overwhelmingly (but not of necessity) connected to a romanticizing of certain communities of struggle—for example, churches. And the rhetoric used to articulate that civil right struggle draws from the language of those particular communities. In addition, left in place after the civil rights movement is an ethical posture toward the world based on a privileging of supernatural claims and assumptions, a spiritual ontology, as well as an accompanying sense of sanctity afforded theism that humanists fight. Why maintain an approach to transformation of thought and quality of life that historically has privileged some of the very things humanists hope to eliminate?

Instead, humanists might take seriously as a source of information and strategy the best of Hip Hop's framing of and posture towards sociocultural and political struggle. And, this process might begin with several considerations related to our posture toward the nature and meaning of the humanist movement as well as its self-understanding and its work. I'd like to offer these examples of this rethinking.

Example One: "Thick" Diversity

Hip Hop culture has demonstrated an impressive ability to trouble rigid cultural boundaries of nation-states and in this way promote diversity of expression, opinion, and so on. To speak of Hip Hop is to mention an array of racial and ethnic groups—each with celebrated contributions to its development. There is a depth and thickness to diversity as modeled by Hip Hop culture—despite some of its shortcomings. And while humanists voice an interest in diversity—and in certain ways promote it—such effort tends to produce what I will call *performative diversity*. By this I mean symbolic appreciation for "difference" as a marker of strength. It produces more *visible* "minority" communities of humanists, but this does little to change decision-making and the array of concerns promoted within these movements, and how these concerns are arranged and ranked. Yet, as Hip Hop culture has demonstrated, more substantive diversity requires production of an organic system of symbols and signs that draw from the sensibilities of a wide-ranging group of participants. Adherents, so to speak, have to see themselves reflected in the workings of movements, see themselves as having real potential for involvement (e.g., leadership positions that shape the form and content of movements), and having the humanist movement lexicon reflect their language of life. Getting to this point requires changes to our internal workings and also our recruitment strategies.

In some cases, direct confrontation has increased our numbers; however, the assumption that such tactics work in every context is a type of arrogance and disregard for cultural nuance. Not many African Americans, however, leave churches because of direct confrontation. To think so shows ignorance concerning the late-twentieth-century patterns of growth for black churches—patterns that have little to do with theological commitment and more to do with networking opportunities and cultural connections. Simply denouncing and ridiculing Christian theology and belief does little to persuade: What do we offer as alternate sources of networking and cultural community? The assumption reason can trump theology also fails to recognize the manner in which theology mutates and theism (e.g., Christian churches) transforms itself. Its contemporary manifestations are less rigid than the pre-Enlightenment theologizing we tend to target in our critiques. Talk of the end of religion also fails to acknowledge regional differences, and ignores new (and successful) religious formulations such as the Prosperity Gospel and the megachurches adhering to it. These churches do not fall victim to our typical critiques in that the most glaring examples of bad thinking are softened, and instead they highlight the Bible as a tool for advancing one's economic goals.

Theism is flexible, and does not die easy. While attempting to dismantle it, we must also recognize the short-term need to work in ways to lessen the negative impact it has on quality of life. If you think I'm wrong, think again. The "look" of the typical humanistic gathering and the perpetual asking of the "how do we recruit people of color" questions do more than suggest I'm right. Deconstruction of theism's flaws is required, but that must be followed by constructive projects and conversations that actually offer alternatives. Smash the idols, but replace them with deeply human and compelling meaning-making opportunities and platforms.

Our approaches have suffered from an underlying assumption that there is one way to promote humanism, but this is wrong because people are messy, and communities are difficult to capture. And so, we should think in terms of multiple approaches to our work—an array of strategies that mirror the complexities of our social arrangements. Thinking this way and acting in light of such a philosophy of engagement might also cut down on the amount of infighting we experience on occasion. But again, this requires an organic language—a vocabulary and grammar robust and descriptive enough to capture the imagination of humanists across various lines of tactical difference and constructive enough to translate to those outside our groups.

Example Two: Significance of the Ordinary[1]

It is often the case that we, in order to expand our presence and counter the foolishness of theistic orientations, highlight the unusual, the atypical and grand figures and moments within the history of our movement. Or, when the ordinary is highlighted, it is juxtaposed to what we consider the markers of greatness. I would suggest such a move does not serve us well. We, instead, should give more attention to the significance, the invaluable importance, of the mundane and the ordinary. I am not suggesting we fail to ritualize major life developments and challenges; rather, I am arguing even these rituals must remain committed to the importance of the mundane, and in this way provide means by which to appreciate (as individuals and in communities) the wonders of everyday life. This is one of the strong contributions we make to social existence—an unwillingness to look beyond the stuff of mundane existence, an unwillingness to demand the extraordinary as the only valuable marker of importance. This has been one of the lasting contributions of Hip Hop to the construction

1. Attention to the ordinary presented here draws from the *End of God-Talk: An African American Humanist Theology* (New York: Oxford University Press, 2012).

of cultural worlds. It is preoccupied with the ordinary, with the everyday and mundane patterns and moments of life; and it seeks to provide a lexicon for discussing and moving through those moments. In this way, it tackles head on the moments of discomfort, of paradox, of uncertainty that trouble—and by so doing it provides means by which to address the complexities of life. What such a move might allow is an earthy basis for our ethics. And, Hip Hop teaches valuable lessons—both positive and negative—concerning the people involved in these efforts and the sociocultural arrangements through means of which these people move through the world.

Bodies are real in that they live and die, and humanistic ethics should be concerned with the consequences and connotations of this realness. Our message, borrowing some cues from Hip Hop, might be the beauty of our ordinariness, the value of simple moments and events—and the need to appreciate this dimension of our existence—as individuals and in relationship. Doing so will trouble some humanists in that it means forgetting about some of the images of our godless liberalism. For example, on too many occasions, nontheists will proclaim that they do not see race; they do not give attention to difference in that way. They wear this proclamation like a blue ribbon—not realizing it is a statement representing a problem, not a solution. Antiblack racism and other modes of embodied discrimination aren't challenged and fought by ignoring them, as if difference must be cast as a problem. Rather, Hip Hop's approach to difference is much healthier, much more realistic in that Hip Hop culture understands difference not as a dilemma to solve but as a benefit that serves to enhance creativity, expand knowledge and perspective and shape cultural connections in healthier and productive ways. So, see race. We gain nothing by pretending not to see "colors." This illusion expends a lot of mental energy, generates a lot of social anxiety, and doesn't impress "racial minorities" (. . . minorities only if we fail to think globally).

Example Three: Measured Realism

In place of outcome-driven systems, a humanist ethical outlook might locate success in the process.[2] That is to say, we continue to work. We maintain this effort because we have the potential to effect/affect change, and we measure the value of our work not in terms of outcomes achieved but in the process of struggle itself. Regarding this, I am in agreement with ethicist Sharon Welch, senior fellow with the Institute for Humanist Studies. There is no foundation for moral action that guarantees individuals and groups will act in "productive" and liberating ways, nor that they will ultimately achieve their objectives. Therefore, ethical activity is risky or dangerous because it requires operating without the certainty and security of a clearly articulated "product."[3] This is a more sober—some might argue a less passionate—approach to ethics. It understands that human relationships (with self, others, and the world) are messy, inconsistent, and thick with desires, contradictions, motives, and a hopeful hopelessness.[4]

Humanistic ethical engagement should mirror the complexity and layered nature of the issues at hand. But as it currently stands, we, and traditional theists, share an unfortunate and unsupported posture of optimism. The reason for the optimism differs for these two camps: God for them and science/reason for us. I am not pointing to the equation of God and forms of scientism (although this type of poor depiction of science does exist). Rather, I am suggesting that both traditional theists and humanists assume beneficial efforts to our

---

2. Some material in this section draws from the discussion of perpetual rebellion found in *Terror and Triumph: The Nature of Black Religion* (Minneapolis: Fortress Press, 2003), 153–54.

3. Sharon Welch, *A Feminist Ethic of Risk* (Minneapolis: Fortress Press, 2000).

4. Michel Foucault, *Ethics: Subjectivity and Truth*, ed. Paul Rabinow (New York: The New Press, 1997), 319.

actions—for them this is based on the balancing work done by the divinity; and for us it is premised on the assumption of science and reasonable thought as slow but steady resolutions to our problems. Isn't it in part because of this assumption so many humanists proclaim the demise of religion and the reign of reason? Both positions are too optimistic; but, Hip Hop culture offers a more balanced perspective—something I have on many occasions referenced as measured realism.

Hip hop culture provides important lessons on the need for measured realism—a sense that human progress involves a paradox: advancement within a larger context of pain and misery. There must be awareness that human progress is not victim free, and it is not inevitable. That is to say, leave certainty to the theists; let their mythological protectors espouse overly optimistic pronouncements of future glory. We should be in a better position than they to see the world as it is and to undertake a much more mature posture toward our work in the world. We have not yet met the challenge, but we should: What is the look of ethical conduct when our efforts are just as likely to fail as to succeed? Hip Hop provides a way of thinking about this question, of moving through life without guaranteed outcomes. Like Hip Hop culture, we might learn to embrace the tragic quality of life and take from it a sobering regard for both our potential and our shortcomings. From this approach we might just come to a better and deeper appreciation of our humanity.

FINALLY...

Some readers will disagree with my assessment, and some will resist giving Hip Hop such a prominent role in our thinking. Even this disagreement, if seriously engaged and interrogated, might just point us in the direction of new and creative approaches to our humanist thought and efforts. My goal is merely to suggest the importance of a particular conversation, to point out the weak spots in our mechanisms for understanding and acting out our humanism.

4 ZOMBIES IN THE 'HOOD

The last chapter identified a problem, one related to the need for humanists to reimagine humanism in ways that foster a more organic relationship with the dynamics and challenges of the social world they seek to influence. I suggested the raise and growth of Hip Hop culture offered something of significant pedagogical value. In this chapter, a different problem is addressed.

W. E. B. Du Bois frames as a "problem" the presence of African Americans in the United States, and he maps this out in terms of the color line defining the twentieth century. African Americans, as he observes, struggle to maintain in tension two dimensions of themselves: they are African and American, and only their determination and "dogged strength" keep them from being (ontologically) torn apart.[1] In this chapter, I want to extend the notion of African Americans as a problem, but I have in mind the manner in which African Americans have been made to reflect the question of death. In this way, I maintain the idea of African Americans as constructed in relationship to a discourse of anxiety, but I propose they are constructed as a resolution to this anxiety over death.

---

1. W. E. B. DuBois, *The Souls of Black Folk* (Chicago: A. C. McClurg & Co., 1903).

I address in numerous places African Americans and the meaning of physical death, but here I intend death as the end of meaning, or meaninglessness—as an ontological and epistemological rupture in its most graphic form. My basic argument is this: African Americans are positioned as the very embodiment of death—or meaninglessness. As such they have been rendered epistemologically and ontologically the un/dead—zombies.[2] Yet, my argument does not end there. I also suggest this remaking of African Americans has not gone unchallenged and, in these pages, I outlined ways in which rap music seeks to address the "zombification" of African Americans.[3]

THE NATURE OF DEATH

I share a question with Sharon Patricia Holland—"What if some subjects never achieve . . . the status of the 'living'"? Holland frames the question in light of Toni Morrison's brilliant *Beloved*, and raises the specter of some existing with the dead, being "at one with the dead."[4]

---

2. Much of the anxiety in the United States in recent decades revolves around the threat of infection, of contamination, whereby death imposes on the grand narrative of privileged life and meaning. Globalization imposes this potential for meaningless by pointing out the porous and vulnerable nature of USA modalities of protection—economic superiority, educational status, political certainty (i.e., a certain positioning of democracy as ideally "American"). And on the domestic front, public advancement of African Americans (perhaps best represented in/by the presidency of Barack Obama) heightens fear that African Americans may not be so easily captured and reified as zombies but rather have range and a modality of life long denied.

3. It is the case that I attempt to describe zombies and zombification in numerous ways in the first few sections of the chapter. And, while this puts me at risk of redundancy, these two concepts are essential and, therefore, it is vital that readers have clarity regarding what I have in mind.

4. Sharon Patricia Holland, *Raising the Dead: Readings of Death and (Black) Subjectivity* (Durham, NC: Duke University Press, 2000), 15; Toni Morrison, *Beloved* (New York: Vintage, 2004).

For Holland, African Americans are perceived as ghosts.[5] Not so for me. I suggest, they, African Americans, do not achieve this status of the "living" because they are categorized not with the dead—the ancestors for instance—but rather they are the un/dead. They are neither fully objects nor fully subjects. They occupy an in-between space of sorts. That is to say, the dead must also be "alive" —present, ever present—if meaning is to have meaning. But they can't be so present as to cause epistemological and ontological discomfort on a fundamental level for those (e.g., advocates of white supremacy) depending on this particular arrangement of the dead. The logic of life, in fact, is death. To talk about death—to understand it on some level beyond its most superficial dimensions as confrontation of the senses—is to talk about life. This, nonetheless, is a reality fought on a variety of fronts.

Again, this is a different theorizing of death. Death, within the context of this chapter, is not primarily a marker of biological boundary and more importantly it is not a material condition primarily. It is a way of thought and of structuring reality. It is not the end of vital functions such as heart activity or brain activity that I have in mind. Nor do I mean the end of soul-*full* vitality in a traditional religious-theological or "spiritual" sense. This is not death as a physical or "spiritual" condition, but rather death more fully as an ontological positioning and an epistemological rupture. It is the loss of meaning more generally as opposed to the particular ending of a given person's mattering.

As I also note in chapter 11, the physical body—the bio-chemical reality whose functions end—can be ritually addressed upon death. It can be mourned, represented in a variety of ways, and then set apart from the living in a clear and "final" manner. It can be presented and available to the living—for example, cemeteries and urns—but still

5. Holland, *Raising the Dead*, 23.

at a safe distance from the living, confined, managed, epistemologically docile.[6] It, the dead, must be apparent, in place, exposed to life so as to differentiate it from that which isn't meaninglessness. In this regard, practices related to the material body are fairly sure across cultures and social dynamics. For example, white Americans and black Americans make use of a shared legal structuring regarding what can happen with bodies, share use of professionals who prepare bodies for presentation and ritualized goodbyes, and so on. Not so, however, with the cultural constructed body that is death—that presents the physical body as a symbol of this death and that renders a particular ontology of death normative in order to maintain sociopolitical arrangements.

African Americans are made zombies epistemologically and ontologically in that there is great effort put into controlling their presence in order to avoid total destruction of the logic of social organization and relationships. What takes place in the construction of African Americans as death is meant to avoid contamination and to preserve the dominant population's ways of being, of thinking, of doing.

WHAT IS A ZOMBIE?

Others have noted the manner in which some bodies defy traditional or normative configurations of life due to sociocultural and other factors. Elizabeth Hallam, Jenny Hockey, and Glennys Howarth, for instance, have written about the vampire as a category of body that resists easy classification as alive or dead. This is because such bodies have markers representing both categories, resulting in a unique configuration as non/being.[7] Unlike the zombie, the vampire, however,

---

6. See Gary Laderman, *Rest in Peace: A Cultural History of Death and the Funeral Home in 21st Century America* (New York: Oxford University Press, 2003).

7. Elizabeth Hallam, Jenny Hockey, and Glennys Howarth, *Beyond the Body: Death and Social Identity* (London: Routledge, 1999), chapter 1.

is superhuman—a creature with the capacity to hunt humans (e.g., higher on the food chain) and without mortality. It is a heightened self, but a nonreflexive self (e.g., no image in the mirror). The "mirror" serves as a reminder to humans that our days are numbered. To see oneself captured in this manner makes visible the fragility of the body as it changes over time.[8] However, again, vampires are not subject to such reflection.[9] In certain regards the vampire marks extreme or radical life—feeding on the liquid of life, with an infinite existence once certain practices are in place (and some of these such as exposure to sunlight can be sidestepped). Furthermore, the vampire is still sensitive to, in certain respects bound by, the markers of authority recognized within the context of social existence. Religion, the symbols and signs of faith and the strictures on conduct meant by religion, still hold sway over vampires. Think in terms of the discomfort caused vampires by exposure to holy water or a crucifix held by a believer. And in this regard, there are ways in which vampires are social creatures, as they are also communal creatures ("living" in the context of communities of the non/being). Like vampires, zombies do not age and therefore do not experience some of the markers of physical existence, yet the similarities beyond this are difficult to locate. For instance, vampires can extend their "gift" to others in a way desired and sought—not so much the case for the zombie, the un/dead, with its aesthetic of decay and its clumsy movement through the world. With respect to encounter with zombies, the stance for the living is awareness, visual contact, confinement, and distance. African Americans, hence, have not been cast as a type of vampire

8. In some ways, the same could be said of the portrait as in the case of Dorian Gray, particularly as Gray's effort is to stop this process of fragility. See Oscar Wilde, *The Picture of Dorian Gray* (Franklin Park, IL: World Library Publications, 2009)

9. Hallam, Hockey, and Howarth, *Beyond the Body*, 2 and 31–33.

unleashed upon the world, but rather as zombies bent on consuming the content and meaning of human life. With the zombie there is the absence of personality still held by the vampire, the absence of contact with humans that isn't destruction and death dealing.

Putting aside the vampire as a proper conceptual paradigm for understanding the imposed relationship of African Americans to death, Russ Castronovo's intriguing notion of "necro citizenship" also fails to fully capture what I mean to represent in this chapter. His sense of a citizenry rendered docile, disengaged, corpse-like, entails some of the consequences associated with the ontological-epistemological death of African Americans but I also have more in mind, more than the sociopolitical spheres of life. For Castronovo, there is something about recognition of morality as political capital that says a word about the "democratic existence within the state." Social death, also discussed by Orlando Patterson, defines the position of enslaved Africans and positions death—metaphoric and biological—as a point of significance within US democracy.[10] The corpse—the body—for Castronovo can be dead, or can be reanimated through particular shifts in political ideals, practices, and sensibilities. This sense of death, of the final disembodiment, understood within the context of "necro citizenship" has something to do with the sense of privatization that so many have understood as the modern turn regarding the dead, while the political is public. This separation isn't certain and it isn't fixed, when, for instance, one considers the political importance of the social death of enslaved Africans. Furthermore, Castronovo argues US democracy enjoys nonresponsive citizens—African Americans—who do not react to political developments, who are passive and still—who are . . . corpses.[11]

10. Russ Castronovo, *Necro Citizenship: Death, Eroticism, and the Public Sphere in the Nineteenth-Century United States* (Durham, NC: Duke University Press, 2001), 1.

11. Castronovo, *Necro Citizenship*, 4–5.

While not the same idea, my sense of death shares something with Castronovo's depiction of death as it does with Patterson's sociological discussion of social death.[12] However, I also mean something more fundamental by epistemological and ontological death over against the "dis/embodied experience, social position, and political metaphor" intended by Castronovo and Patterson. The death I describe is not the physical or social death over against political freedom. Rather, it is the structuring of knowledge about black bodies and the very meaning of black bodies that undergirds these other historical patterns of individual and collective life. It, death so conceived, is one reason we can talk about bodies mattering.[13]

Finally, when I argue African Americans have been constructed as zombies, I don't have in mind the zombie of the movies, or of the religious traditions growing out of West Africa. Those about which I speak are not religio-theological zombies in a strict sense. While understood in part through the absolutes undergirding what we might call theological formulations, zombies as I understand them are also epistemological and ontological in nature in a way that cuts against and across this more limited sense of the zombie found in film, stories, and religious arenas. It isn't a process, orchestrated by a (religious) bokor or (spiritual) ritual expert, of placing a person in a limbo space of ego docility through incantations and chemicals (as Wade Davis suggests[14]). No, zombies as I discuss them are created to maintain the basic framework and logic of life writ large. As Albert Camus notes, humans wrestle with meaninglessness—both trying to destroy it while

12. Orlando Patterson, *Slavery and Social Death: A Comparative Study* (Cambridge, MA: Harvard University Press, 1985).

13. Russ Castronovo, *Necro Citizenship*, 10, 40–44.

14. Wade Davis, *The Serpent and the Rainbow: A Harvard Scientist's Astonishing Journey into the Secret Societies of Haitian Voodoo, Zombis, and Magic* (New York: Touchstone, 1997).

reinforcing it—a dilemma for sure. The construction of the African American as zombie—the un/dead representing meaninglessness rendered external to "human" life—is meant to address this dilemma. The zombie becomes residue of a "Unity," to borrow another concept from Camus. I am referencing his sense of the human desire or hope for conclusion, for wholeness, cohesive and certain value—for a unity of ideas.[15]

WHY ZOMBIES?

This fixing of zombies serves to push human life closer to, more in line with, the ultimate "Unity" of life. In a word, the presence of the zombie helps to authenticate a fundamental and expansive meaning (either theological or ideological in nature matters little), something greater—a greater "good"—and more significant than any particular person and her wants or needs. This "good" that demands zombification of African Americans as its safeguard might entail the substance of religious salvation or the beauty of democracy. Either way, it pulls at humans for obedience and complacency.[16]

The zombified African American marks the absence of substance, the complete destruction of social sensibilities and communal connection. One might think of the zombie as the symbolic and ideological container for all that is despised and feared, for the loss of meaning as waste. It is both despised (***un***) and needed (***dead***). Put another way, African Americans were constructed as enfleshed *vanitas* through which meaninglessness is abated, and the fragility of "life" captured (or controlled) in time and space. Doesn't this capture the "New World"

15. I read this meaning in numerous of his works such as those referenced throughout.

16. Albert Camus, *Resistance, Rebellion, and Death: Essays* (New York: Vintage International, 1995), 222.

as the laboratory for the construction of raced bodies as "other" bodies both similar but epistemologically and ontologically distinct? Yes, as the zombie constitutes the substance of another's fear of death, of meaninglessness—as if meaning and meaninglessness can be so easily separated. But still the effort is made, and the presence of life devoid of death so understood remains a fantasy over against the real. Such a move is centrifuge.

Finally, it is not the case, nor need it be, that all agree to the merit of African Americans so constructed. The manner of structuring African Americans as such isn't dependent upon consensus. It only needs to become the dominant logic, with people benefitting directly and indirectly from its normativity. So, the presentation of this logic must be compelling or at least presented in light of a shared need, and with time it will become the unspoken reality, the assumed condition of life. It, to borrow and apply in a different context a phrase from Camus, entails "solidarity against death."[17] The cause of the zombie phenomenon is hidden in the larger narrative, but this is its power: it doesn't need full conversation, but rather must have ritualized consent. And those given authority—either religious or secular—are best positioned to prophesy the need for this structuring of reality. Both sermons (religion) and speeches (politics) have the capacity to explain and fix this logic, to make appealing—in other words, establish deep need—the structuring of reality that confines African Americans.[18] They, sermons and speeches, can numb the mind, slow critical thinking, enhance emotion, and make more difficult

17. Camus uses the phrase in reference to the logic behind capital punishment—the death penalty. Speaking against the usefulness of it, he argues "capital judgment," rather than aiding, actually harms our most fundamental human solidarity, that against death. Camus, *Resistance, Rebellion, and Death*, 222.

18. These are categories of exchange mentioned at times by Camus. See, for instance, *The Plague* (New York: Vintage International, 1991).

counterargument.[19] Those who oppose it, once this solidification occurs, are noted as the odd ones, the troublemakers, un-American mobs seeking to destroy the very fabric of collective life.

Zombies, African Americans, are because they are. Undergirding this is a prior epistemologically grounded and ontological move: zombies are needed in order for meaning to be and to be lodged in the "life" of the nonzombies. Within this narrative of meaning, the zombie is a cautionary tale suggesting the importance of accepting the dominant structuring of individual and collective existence—of safeguarding against contamination. Letting one's guard down in the presence of zombies can only result in destruction of social existence as vital, vibrant, and humane. Death is meaninglessness in that it restricts one's life force to memory. That is to say, it subjects one to the caprice of others, to the will of others who determine to what degree one has presence. One becomes, through death, easily shifted and changed. It is to be without human will that "matters." One's ontology, through death, is warped, and one's social relationship involves confinement and destruction.

Zombification involves more than *other*-ing, of rendering African Americans objects. It is important to note that, while objectification is vital, zombification marks recognition that the work of objectification can't be finished as such. African Americans can't be rendered, in a strict sense, objects—without impact on subjects. Nonetheless, if death could be confined, marked off, quarantined so to speak, life—the meaning of the dominant population—could be safeguarded somewhat. The history of the United States suggests the response to this prospect was always at least, "it's worth a try."

19. Keep in mind, for instance, the content and description of sermons given by the priest Father Paneloux, in *The Plague*.

MAKING ZOMBIES

As I've worked to establish above, African Americans weren't simply positioned as the personification of evil, but rather their construction and placement meant they were meaninglessness (e.g., death or demise) grasped and harnessed, to the extent it can be handled in this manner. Personification of evil would mean African Americans became a way of addressing the sociology and economy of enslavement and modern discrimination. The latter, construction as meaninglessness/death, however, draws attention to a more fundamental challenge: elemental and ontological meaning in the "world" humanity both does and doesn't create. This problem would have been in place without enslavement. It would have found another form of expression, and it would have required another way to externalize death. In other words, we know this process in the Americas vis-à-vis race and racism, for instance, but it is not simply a matter of racial or even gender, sexuality, or other constructions for that matter. Put differently, this focus on death informs racial dynamics but it is not confined to that particular structuring of human interaction.

Still, the very construction and presentation of black bodies already and always hints to death, or meaninglessness.[20] Death is

20. My earlier work, particularly the idea of "rituals of reference" found in *Terror and Triumph: The Nature of Black Religion* (Minneapolis: Fortress Press, 2004) speaks to the realization that African Americans have been "othered." That is to say, the auction block and lynching pointed out to African Americans that they were not perceived to have the same ontological importance as white Americans. There are ways in which this current discussion of death is an extension of that earlier discussion. Hence, what rituals of reference might be said to affirm for African Americans is the manner in which they are zombies: they are ontologically and epistemologically dead. In latter work, I plan to further unpack this relationship between the terror and dread of rituals of reference and my current sense of zombies.

never unassociated with difference. Put another way, antiblack racism, as philosopher Lewis Gordon names it, was modernity's virus rendering people of African descent ontological and epistemological zombies—those whose being is unfinished, unfulfilled, and therefore marked by a bizarre rendition of death and life.[21] As zombies African Americans give conceptual and metaphorical clarity to a necessary dimension of the life and meaning of white Americans; hence African Americans are alive, a presence. Yet, they also house the fear of meaning lost; hence, they also connote death: they are the un/dead. That is to say, sociocultural structures tied to race and racism are not meant to destroy death, to wipe out death as a threat, but rather to confine death into something more manageable—to confine death in time and space in ways that take away its "sting." The threat is the uncontrolled zombie that hungers for human flesh and brains (body and mind).[22]

This is not simply a statement regarding alterity—the other as a "presence" to be recognized and addressed. Such cannot be the case when African Americans are ontological and epistemological zombies. This difference in being won't be addressed by simply recognizing the other or having the other recognize the dominant mode of humanity. Even the aesthetic representation of African Americans from zip coon to Trayvon Martin, for instance, offers yet another way in which the African American as marker of death, as zombie, is represented in and by the cultural frameworks and imagination of the

---

21. Lewis Gordon, ed., *Existence in Black: An Anthology of Black Existential Philosophy* (New York: Routledge, 1996).

22. My assertion here runs contrary to many others who claim there is an effort within society to destroy death. See, for example, Clive Seale, *Constructing Death: The Sociology of Dying and Bereavement* (Cambridge: Cambridge University Press, 1998), chapter 1.

general public.[23] It is in thinking African Americans along these lines, and presenting them in this fashion, that white Americans over the course of centuries have been able to envision themselves as alive, or invested with meaning—to be subjects moving and arranging their world. In this way, over against zombies, they have meaning within a world marked by no central and consistent meaning.[24]

Everything about African Americans as death has an underlying function of affirming as right this grand narrative of white American life and meaning. There is a warped assumption that through zombification the zombie makers are able to harness reality, control it through a mode of prescience.[25] This is the lot of the African American as undead, as zombie. African Americans are constructed as the

---

23. Think about this in relationship to Trayvon Martin and George Zimmerman. Trayvon was a zombie attempting to be human, and to extend itself beyond the confines of death and it had to be resettled within its proper epistemological and ontological geography. Zimmerman's action—the killing of Martin—was an effort to restore a bizarre and damning sense of meaning—to embody death—in ways that safeguarded white Americans with protection from death. Killing sought to confine death by protecting a particular unity of ideas around the nature and meaning. On the surface this was the protection of white privilege, but on a more fundamental level it was the restoration of death's confinement by disciplining a zombie. Martin is not the first, nor will he be the last, graphic example of how fissures in zombification are addressed. So important is the work done by the classification of zombies that the United States, among other societies, will kill (bodies, ideas, meaning) to maintain it. The strategies of "law and order" provide the justification as well as outline the most product techniques.

24. Albert Camus, "Fourth Letter," in *Resistance, Rebellion, and Death*, 28.

25. See Lizette Alvarez and Cara Buckley, "Zimmerman Is Acquitted in Trayvon Martin Killing," *New York Times*, July 13, 2013, http://www.nytimes.com/2013/07/14/us/george-zimmerman-verdict-trayvon-martin.html. Accessed on December 21, 2013.

embodiment and discourse of danger, destruction, and disorder whose very efforts to produce meaning result in contamination and chaos that must be controlled by naming it death—a push against ultimate meaning, against ultimate Unity.[26] Yet, oddly enough, this process is not without its weak points. For instance, to the extent African Americans cannot be forgotten, the African American is immortal; dead to the extent projected as without meaning, but perpetually alive to the extent the memory of him/her/they is essential for the safeguarding of the American narrative.

HIP HOP'S INTERVENTION

Some have recognized such weaknesses, and have worked to exploit them. From my perspective this is the case with hip hop culture in general, and rap music in particular. Those who carry the bodies of symbolic death speak in haunting tones of their demise and what it means for the larger structures of existential concern within the context of the United States.[27]

More precisely, hip hop culture is an intervention of sorts, marking a cultural shift—a change in the grammar and vocabulary of living in a way that acknowledges the presence of death's shadow. In this situation, meaning is ***me***(an)***ing***—tension between the individual and frameworks of communality played out through and in the fragility of life. In some respects, hip hop recognizes the manner in which African Americans have been produced as zombies—the un/dead—and it works to address and dismantle the nature and meaning of

26. Genesis 10–11. See Anthony B. Pinn and Allen D. Callahan, eds., *African American Religious Life and the Story of Nimrod* (New York: Palgrave Macmillan, 2008).

27. This statement could be read through the work of various rap artists, such as Ice Cube, "My Skin Is My Sin," on *Bootlegs & B-Sides*, Priority Records, 1994.

this creation by giving the zombie new ontological arrangements and significance. In what follows I provide an example of rap music's push against zombification. I argue artists such as Kanye West damage the Unity that supports and justifies zombification, and in the process consume death and thereby disrupt its deep ontological under pinning.[28]

The Destruction of Zombifications "Unity"

Tupac Shakur, through his personae of "Black Jesuz," recast ethics and morality in a way that privilege the behaviors rejected by the larger society and in this way creates space to reconsider what the larger society has created and constituted.[29] Kanye West's ontological claims pushing beyond more traditional theological anthropology will come up numerous times in this volume, but for now suffice it to say that his thinking on ontology challenges the notion of a "distant" God—the grounding for creation—by fostering a different set of expectations and markers of meaning that privilege the un/dead and that reconstruct them as those with the most importance, the most value, and the most meaning. In short, West rejects zombification by claiming fundamental authority over life and death. He is one of them, the zombies as the dominant narrative of life in the United States argues, *and he is a god.* (Jay Z does this as well, but without the same sustained attention to the impact of this move, when reminding listeners that they are in the presence of a god, or at the very least

---

28. I give this normalization of death more attention in "When It's Over: Humanism, Rap Music, and the Culture of Death," in *Humanism: Essays on Race, Religion, and Cultural Production* (New York: Bloomsbury Academic, 2015).

29. I offer a discussion of Tupac Shakur in relationship to notions of death in another piece: "The End: An Essay on Humanist Theology, Rap Music, and Death," in "Secular Theologies and Theologies of the Secular," ed. Whitney Bauman, a special issue of *Dialog: A Journal of Theology* 45, no. 45 (December 2015): 347–54.

he feels like, Jesus, the Son of God . . . or maybe a prophet of a new reality.[30]) Hence, West won't be represented (solely) as death, and captured through the logic of the dead. This ontological shift is important as a type of prophylactic against zombification, even when, as for Kanye West, the transformation ("I Am a God"!) is motivated by a rather mundane concern—access to Fashion Week activities.[31] Think about it: Shouldn't access to the matrix of beauty, to the logic of aesthetics draped on bodies, be sufficient motivation for deification as opposition to zombification?

I don't think I am making too much of this proclamation of divinity. The screaming and movement marking "I Am a God" is not the marker of zombification embraced as inevitable. In a particularly haunting and telling way, rap music as represented by the likes of West seeks to humanize the zombie, to transform the zombie, by a simple proclamation that serves as an antidote: "I am . . . until *I* say *I* am not."

The artist has become the grounding for reality, the source of all meaning and, in this way, addressed meaninglessness through the institution of a new overarching Camusian unity of meaning. This becoming god does not push into another world, a different realm of meaning, but instead harnesses itself into the present in robust ways. For West, being a god involves the ability to make demands—whether for food,

---

30. Jay Z, "Crown," and "Heaven," on *Magna Carta*, Roc-A-Fella Records, 2013.

31. West argues his song "I Am a God" was motivated by his experiences at Fashion Week. See Ben Westhoff, "The Enigma of Kanye West—and How the World's Biggest Pop Star Ended Up Being Its Most Reviled, Too," *Guardian*, July 25, 2015, https://www.theguardian.com/music/2015/jun/25/kanye-west-glastonbury-festival-2015-worlds-biggest-pop-star; Kia Makarechi, "Kanye Wests's 'I Am a God' Inspired by Fashion Week Diss," Huffpost, June 24, 2013, http://www.huffingtonpost.com/2013/06/24/kanye-west-i-am-a-god-fashion-week-diss_n_3490688.html. Accessed on January 29, 2014.

goods, or services.[32] This doesn't wipe out consideration of something else (a most high), but the historical and practical consequences of this consideration aren't worth much discussion on his part. Kanye West as "Yeezus," as a "god." The created un/dead becomes the creator.

KRS-One ruminated on the divinity of the rap artist years ago, arguing the artist is godlike by means of creating worlds with words.[33] West seems to have something else in mind. It is not simply the development of new structures but recognition of the problematic nature of the logic undergirding old structures. KRS-One seems to substitute black gods for white gods using the old logic; West disrupts this logic and exposes its flaws. For the former, KRS-One, it is the old world controlled by new authorities; and for the latter, Kanye West, the unity of the old world and its ways are exposed, signified, and epistemologically mocked. In this way, West offers an alternate ontology of life and death, while simultaneously working to dismantle even this new ontology: the songs "New Slaves" and "I Am a God" are two sides of this process held together as/by Yeezus.[34] The first speaks to the constraints of black life, the manner in which African Americans are aware of their predicament; and, the second speaks to an effort to circumvent that predicament. For West, then, African Americans are both dead and alive—the productive of a particular Unity (i.e., zombies) and the presence of a different authority (the substance of a new unity of ideas). A despised black embodied body claims metaphysical superiority in a sense, by claiming status as a god. The rejected becomes, in this manner, the desired.

The future of human existence is captured in the trauma of the present. West kills in this regard much of what "god" has meant.

32. Kanye West, "I Am a God," *Yeezus* (New York: Def Jam Recordings, 2013).

33. Readers will find his Temple of Hip Hop on YouTube of interest: https://www.youtube.com/@TheTempleofHipHop1996.

34. Kanye West, *Yeezus*, Def Jam Recordings, 2013.

Passion with which this song ("I Am a God") and others on his 2013 album *Yeezus* have been critiqued suggests there is little (beyond the vocabulary itself) that is recognizable to those who lodge their futures in the existence of a metaphysical "Other." In placing himself alongside God, West provides a push against this troubling construction of the un/dead by wiping out the metaphysical authority for it. This being the case, those demanding the presence of zombies, the un/dead, have to acknowledge that the authority for this construction is human: if they reject West's claim, they open themselves to other constructions of divinity. If West can't stand next to God what validates their status as next to God in knowledge and power? His act of rebellion exposes the larger system of corruption and the rather mundane justifications for the framing of the un/dead.[35] Through this epistemological turn a new self is produced, and it is one that pushes against and beyond the framing of the zombie. Even when West announces the "New Slaves," they are self-aware and with the capacity to affect a reaction from those around them.[36]

This is more than the expansion of the self, the ego, alone; but instead, it entails a connection to others that is grand and determined outside the confines of what the zombie can achieve. "I know that *we* the new slaves." It is a statement of a collective present. There is something substantive (and perhaps rebellious?) in West's proclamation, "I know we're the new slaves." They aren't simply zombies; they are more dangerous to the status quo than that because of their knowledge—familiarity with the structuring of the dominant narrative of life and meaning—and their actions (i.e., pushing against boundaries) even within the context of their condition. It's lucidity—awareness—of a kind. Turning to cultural critique of Albert Murray,

35. Albert Camus, *The Rebel* (New York: Vintage International, 1991), 55.
36. West, "New Slaves," on *Yeezus*.

what he projects as the task of the blues is also present, I would argue, in certain modalities of rap music. One, for instance, could understand "New Slaves" and "I Am a God" in this way, in light of Murray's discussion of the blues:

> That kind of musical statement is a basic existential affirmation. And the musicians counterstate their problems; they counterstate the depression, despair, despondency, melancholia, and so forth. Blues music is a ritualistic counterstatement.[37]

This isn't a push for liberation advocated by liberation theologians such as James Cone, nor is it the ethical approach championed by other advocates of theologies of liberation; but it is awareness of the geography and structures of life meaning.[38] It takes seriously movement possible within the world—a world that both needs and despises zombies. Perhaps there is something related to this framing of life and death and the dismantling of the dominant narrative's Unity in Jay Z's questioning of what the church can do for people and whether or not Jesus can actually provide salvation. "Empire State of Mind" provides the answer: no, life is somewhere outside the confines of the church's vision.[39] Chuuch!

By extension and implication, there are ways in which religion tries to cover up this process of zombification, to redirect attention, through the assurance of an eternal logic and truth; but the flaws in religion's efforts are noteworthy and exposed: little can we gain, and

37. Albert Murray, "An All-Purpose, All-American Literary Intellectual," in *From the Briarpatch File: On Context, Procedure, and American Identity* (New York: Pantheon, 2001), 195.

38. James Cone, *A Black Theology of Liberation* (Maryknoll, NY: Orbis Books, 1989). See, for instance, Gayraud Wilmore, *Black Religion and Black Radicalism* (Maryknoll, NY: Orbis Books, 1973).

39. Jay Z, "Empire State of Mind," on *The Blueprint 3*, Roc Nation, 2009.

nothing is certain in that there is no overarching Unity binding all together. "No Church in the Wild," right?

West and Jay Z aren't necessarily promoting atheism as the proper response to the structuring of reality qua death (i.e., zombification). Instead, they maintain the meaning of certain theistic symbols but destroy their ability—their authority—to fix nihilism and end absurdity; and they do this in a way that exposes the violence embedded in the process. In a related fashion, the epistemology associated with Tupac Shakur's thug life, for instance, is tied to ethics and ontology of marginality that recognizes death as a dimension of life. For instance, the thug life code contains this: "All new jacks to the game must know: 1) He's going to get rich; 2) He's going to jail; c) He's going to die."[40] What we can say is this: a shift in the ontology promoted by artists such as West (as well as Jay Z and Tupac Shakur) removes the potentiality of transcendence as a safeguard against death. They expose as faulty the assurance of a type of transcendence based on rendering a particular population the epistemological and ontological—the metaphysical—sign and substance of death.

West puts in place new terms of meaning and life. He consumes death in life through new ontological arrangements that blur the line between the zombies and the source of the zombification. If Kanye West is a god (and this statement on his part seems to have struck a nerve), one must ask, Who are the zombies? If a zombie controls the terms of creation and organization, what is a zombie? This is not the deification Camus fears and rejects, in that it leaves space and does not offer the certainties and resolutions he opposes.[41] It is celebration of moderation. It is the framing of limitation as both central and

---

40. "Code of Thug Life," Tupac.be, https://tupac.be/en/his-world/code-of-thug-life/.

41. Albert Camus, *The Myth of Sisyphus and Other Essays* (New York: Vintage International, 1991); and *The Rebel.*

as the defining mode of value and epistemology. It is a taming of grand claims to control over life and death. Hence, this deification is a move necessary to break the logic of zombification and to establish humanity. Through this move, death is swallowed up, but not as the biblical Christ intends through an embrace of misery as redemptive, but rather for West this is accomplished by naming deception—naming the construction of zombies—as nonessential and subject to being dismantled.

The zombie's construction is recognized through West's proclamation as a matter of ontological dissonance held in place by epistemological prestige (i.e., trick or illusion). In short, if West is a god, zombies don't exist, at least the logic for them is dismantled; but humans falsely labeled as such do live. What remains after this process, however, and to what some of the critique of West points, is the establishment of a more useful means for living life aware of death. Dismantled are the epistemological and ontological processes and ideals fundamental in the construction of African Americans as zombies. What does it mean to be fully human, an African American, within a world still capable of ontological and epistemological crime? West demands control over the constitution of life in order to undercut the justification for constituting African Americans as zombies.

Maybe there is something of Camus's "rebel" in the likes of Kanye West? Perhaps there is something of Camus's claim (to differing degrees but present nonetheless) in the lyrics and activities of West and other artists like him? "The rebel," Camus writes, "obstinately confronts a world condemned to death and the impenetrable obscurity of the human condition with his demand for life and absolute clarity."[42] What the rebel, the rap artist, seeks to achieve disrupts the norm. According to the popular narrative, the will-less, non-self-aware

42. Camus, *The Rebel*, 101.

zombie can't want what nonzombies want; can't demand what they demand; and can't do the type of damage or destruction they can do.

Efforts to counteract this narrative typically collapse, but even so, there is something appealing, something reflective of the rap artist as critic of zombification in Camus's words regarding the work of the rebel. "Rebellion," he reflects, "is the refusal to be treated as an object and to be reduced to simple historical terms. It is the affirmation of a nature common to all men, which eludes the world of power."[43] The fact that artists like West do this while fostering such discomfort and dissonance only amplifies the process of signification, reversal and recasting of African American life.

And here's the philosophical analysis offered by Camus that speaks, I believe, to the new Unity of ideas sought by these artists—the analysis that explains the demand to be a god. He writes, "If the rebel blasphemes, it is in the hope of finding a new god."[44] And, what does Kanye West, for one, claim to be? A god! However, if Camus is followed, the end of this rapper's work takes it away from rebellion to the extent it surrenders to nihilism by demanding absolutes, unities.[45] I, however, am not convinced these artists collapse into nihilism, but instead continue in a way more in line with Camus's sense of the absurd, the rebel of the absurd. That is to say, for instance, West's claim to be a god borders on a quest for a new absolute, but it maintains a sense of the absurd in that it is meant to de/center assumptions of an absolute that sacrifices African Americans. That is to say, death is still in place but the logic allowing it to be isolated and confined to one population is damaged.

For artists like Du Bois there had to be closure, fulfillment, and resolution of the goal. "Every human endeavor," writes Camus, "finally obeys this unreasonable desire and claims to give life a form it does not

43. Camus, *The Rebel*, 250.

44. Camus, *The Rebel*, 101.

45. Camus, *The Rebel*, 102.

have. The same impulse, which can lead to the adoration of the heavens or the destruction of man, also leads to creative literature, which derives its serious content from this source."[46] For certain rap artists, however, there can be no final resolution and they are "ok" with this. As Camus says of another figure—Sisyphus—we must believe the rap artist to be "happy" in this situation; and, happy to the extent the situation is something of the artist's own effort and creation.

Back to Being People

Running the risk of redundancy, let me say this in way of summation: figures such as West trouble the configuration of zombie's precisely by exposing schemes of absolutes and unities of ideas—the stuff of which zombies are constructed and maintained. By so doing they seek to dismantle African Americans as death by exposing the logic of death (as a structuring of reality). Death is pulled out of a particular materiality—that is, embodied African Americans—and is resettled as a dimension of life rather than a type of meaninglessness that can be ontologically and epistemologically projected. It is a structuring of reality still, but not one dependent on a particular host. The logic of the zombie is damaged and, in its place, emerges the reestablished African American. Again, whether it's Tupac Shakur on a cross, or West claiming to be a god who constructs truth and demands a certain system of ethics, rap artists have at times and in significant ways troubled the logic of death that holds in place the nature and meaning of the African American as zombie. This work is important but it is far from unproblematic because what remains intact is the ability (if not desire) to create other zombies, to reconfigure other groups through a similar logic and structuring of reality.

The function of the zombie is to isolate misery and suffering, to isolate decay, and position it over against life as represented by the

46. Camus, *The Rebel*, 262.

population of "humans." Within the narrative offered in certain rap music quarters, this practice is challenged on a variety of fronts. Pain and misery are rendered human, not some type of epistemological and ontological virus, but rather dimensions of reality inseparable from living into death. In this way, rap music has the potential to disrupt this construction project by maintaining the presence of death as human—that is to say, endemic to all humanity and not the structuring of any one group made for the purpose of warehousing death as meaninglessness, or in a sense history.

Through an altered ontology some artists encourage ways of thinking about life in death so as to hold them in creative tension, to recognize the contradictions but also similarities between them as markers of life's interior and borders—its exterior edges and interior spaces. This is a comfort with middle spaces, the vantage point from which both life and death are visible and blend into a common horizon.

Some do not like what these artists have to say, the narrative of life presented, in part because it often lacks hope—the type of easy, blind hope that appeals to those who fear death and exercise dread over the instability of meaning. That type of hope makes no sense to the artist who has pulled the cover off the illusion of a structuring of death as confinable and against which one can defend oneself. Such hope requires a willingness to overlook, to ignore, the conditions of life. And that is not the perspective, not the posture toward living into death, one finds in "I Am a God," and a host of other tracks that question conforming hope over against confronting the very logic of zombification.

Poetic representation and interrogation, in a broad sense, are what these artists have available to them. Perceived as "entertainment," even those considered zombies are allowed them. By these means, culture and cultural production, the artist challenges the making of zombies.[47]

---

47. Camus, "The Myth of Sisyphus," in *The Myth of Sisyphus*.

5 THE REALISM OF KENDRICK LAMAR

From the embodiment of death as discussed in the last chapter, attention here is turned to the nature of the (black) body read through a certain brand of realism. The artist presented in relationship to this interrogation is Kendrick Lamar.

Advocates (e.g., academics, journalists, and fans) have probed and prodded hip hop culture for what it might tell us about the nature of life meaning within the context of our social-political arrangements, and so on. Some of this effort involves a repositioning—transfiguration of the despised, of scapegoats, into heroes, if not salvific figures. This, as I note in various places in this volume, has meant at times casting hip hop artists as social embodiment of contemporary tricksters, prophets, and other exceptional entities who manipulate words in order to forge new worlds—or systems of meaning through appropriation.[1]

Consistent with such metamorphoses, Kendrick Lamar's vision of life for many positions him an "anointed" one—an existential hero. In discussing similarities between Alex Haley's *Roots* and Kendrick

---

1. Artists have embraced this on some level; think, for instance, of their own proclamations of divinity for them and by them—Tupac as Black Jesuz, Jay-Z as Hova, Kanye West's assertion "I am a God," Lil' B as the "Based God," and the list goes on.

Lamar's art, Natalie Graham makes a statement that has some bearing on what I want to highlight here:

> While Lamar is no stranger to dramatic effect—even to the point of deeply orchestral sentimentality—a central tension in his songs often has to do with the limits of language and storytelling, as Lamar is confronted by a listener's inability to understand or his own inability to tell. The whole story cannot be told, in part because his prose, and the underlying embrace of paradox and contradiction, brings into question the plausibility of unity or "fullness." This insistence on fragmentation also resists romanticizing resistance in the face of mutilation or annihilation and provides a space for nontraditional or antiheroic figures to emerge as central.[2]

POSITIONING KENDRICK LAMAR

As scholars have highlighted, Lamar's lyrics have been used recently to articulate disruption of dominant political-social discourses, and from within the context of discursive struggle offer an affirmation of life. This, as Siebe Bluijs suggests, is one way to interpret the persistent chant "we gon' be alright" from Lamar's *To Pimp a Butterfly*. "The song," writes Bluijs, "has given a voice to a 'we' that feels itself the target of a polarized debate about race and identity politics: a discourse that explicitly creates an identity in opposition to the 'we' of Lamar's song."[3] Furthermore, as Bluijs and others have noted, there is an overtly autobiographical element to Lamar's lyrics—including

---

2. "What Slaves We Are: Narrative, Trauma, and Power in Kendrick Lamar's Roots," *Transition* 122 (2017): 123–32, at 125–26.

3. Siebe Bluijs, "From Compton to Congress: The Barbarians inside the Gates—an Exploraiton of 'Black Subjectivity' in Kendrick Lamar's To Pimp a Butterfly," *Thamyris/Intersecting: Place, Sex & Race* 32 (2017): 72–87, at 73.

the manner in which theological commitments rub against barriers to fulfillment, as he reflects on the religious sensibilities of family members over against the existential realities of urban life.

In expressing this tension, he highlights a reflexive quality to his life vision connected to an earthy and somewhat "raw" set of affective-ethical orientations. For example, there are layers to Kendrick Lamar's *DAMN*, particularly the track "DNA."[4] Here, with this track, the essential information determining, shaping, arranging, and producing life is for Lamar defined by contradictory realities that impinge and press against and ultimately disrupt traditional sensibilities and challenging normative moral-ethical frameworks. Ranging from commentary on affective-psychological qualities, to social arrangements and network identifications, to historical lineage, to bio-chemical markers of embodied personhood, to metaphysical assumptions, *DAMN* as a whole, and the lyrics of "DNA" in particular, chronicle the thick and contradictory nature of "blackened" existence.[5] That is to say—and this serves as the organizing concern of this chapter—Lamar, through an embrace of the "grotesque," chronicles and critiques metaphysical assumptions regarding black life, when 'blackness' is something of a social fiction used to restrict and control a population of which he is a part. For instance, comparing his lyrics to scriptural pronouncements, according to some, Lamar offers an urban epistemology couched in the sights and sounds of Los Angeles.[6] His is a secular religiosity in that it doesn't point away from humanity and materiality, but rather

4. Also known as deoxyribonucleic acid.

5. Rolling Stone named *DAMN* of the best albums of 2017: "50 Best Albums of 2017," *Rolling Stone*, November 22, 2017, https://www.rollingstone.com/music/lists/50-best-albums-of-2017-w511763/kendrick-lamar-damn-w511815.

6. Brian Hiatt, "Kendrick Lamar: The Rolling Stone Interview," *Rolling Stone*, August 9, 2017, at https://www.rollingstone.com/music/features/kendrick-lamar-on-humble-bono-taylor-swift-mandela-w496385. Accessed on January 11, 2018.

commits to the "raw" (i.e., base experiences and their meanings without the mediating effect of untested theological claims) and haunting magnetism pulling toward historical realities. Lamar celebrates earthy existence, not the failsafe of transcendent possibilities beyond the restrictions of bio-chemical materiality—chronicled through stories of deep angst recognized and confronted. In this way, the rawness noted above has a synergistic relationship with openness—that is with embodied life exposed and penetrated without the prophylactic effect of religious mystery trumping historical encounters.

As a matter of context (a conceptual bridge of a kind) for my discussion of *DAMN*, I briefly turn to James McLeod, who referenced *To Pimp a Butterfly* as an existentialist turn in rap music—by means of which death is addressed straightforward and without surrender to the terror of the "end."[7] And while there is something to this claim of existentialism, to the extent the lyrical content of Lamar's music opens to a wrestling with the existential arrangements of life and does so privileging existence over essence, McLeod misstates its genesis. Prior to Lamar, the Geto Boys chronicled an existentially driven living into death within an inhospitable world through tracks such as "Mind Playin' Tricks on Me," and Scarface continued his confrontation with the comic-tragic nature of life through tracks such as "Mind Playin' Tricks on Me 94."[8] This said, my interest isn't historiography of existentialism within rap music in general; rather, more to the point, I am concerned with the manner in which existential questions and

---

7. James D. McLeod Jr., "If God Got Us: Kendrick Lamar, Paul Tillich, and the Advent of Existentialist Hip Hop," *Toronto Journal of Theology* 33, no. 1 (2017): 123–35. I give attention to death and dying in hip hop culture in *Deathlife: Hip Hop and Thanatological Narrations of Blackness* (Durham, NC: Duke University Press, 2024).

8. Geto Boys, "Mind Playing Tricks on Me," on *We Can't Be Stopped*, Rap-A-Lot Records, 1991; Scarface, "Mind Playin' Tricks on Me 94," on *The Diary*, Rap-A-Lot Records, 1994.

concerns play out in Lamar's *DAMN.* Furthermore, while McLeod seeks to read Lamar through a theological lens, I would suggest Lamar builds on a preexisting philosophical turn in hip hop represented by earlier artists such as Scarface and aligned with thinkers including W. E. B. Du Bois, Albert Camus, Richard Wright, Nella Larsen.[9] Put another way, rather than the certainty and unifying aim of theological discourse, Lamar, like several before him, turns in the direction of moralism—a philosophical stance concerned with critical engagement of circumstances without the preconceived answers typically associated with theological reflection. As such, Lamar's prose points out a posture toward the world, like that of Du Bois, Wright, Larsen, and Camus, comfortable with paradox and with the unresolved quality of human wrestling for meaning.

Bluijs suggests what Lamar offers in terms of subjectivity connects to the "barbaric" persona[10]—perhaps just as the blues musician chronicled the significance of the trickster and "bad" man. It, the barbaric, constitutes a framing of life, a process of encounter in and with the world, marked by a certain type of defiance read by structures of authority as chaotic and dangerous. Yet, there is a particular type of "flatness" to the imaginary of the barbaric—to the extent it assumes something of the integrity of the normativities under attack. For Lamar there is an affective-ethical turn meant as a lucid embrace and safeguarding of (metaphysical and) existential meaning.[11] Rather

9. Camus did not understand himself to be an existentialist. Rather, he understood himself to be a moralist.

10. Bluijs, "From Compton to Congress," 73.

11. Adam Wert provides an interesting read of Lamar through Paul Tillich, and through this read he highlights the existential and ontological tensions and dualism at work, particularly as this plays out through the self-world dualism. See Adam Wert, "Tension and Ambiguity: Paul Tillich and Kendrick Lamar on Courage and Faith," *Toronto Journal of Theology* 33, no. /1 (2017): 113–21.

than the barbaric persona, which does not interrogate sufficiently the illusionary nature of boundaries and confinement but instead simply attacks restriction, I argue Lamar promotes the open body as a fundamental challenge to confinement and boundaries as it highlights the porous and complex nature of embodied meaning. By this I mean to highlight the manner in which Lamar privileges vulnerability, the ways in which our embodied existence is exposed to material-psychological circumstances and altered by those arrangements of time and space. For Lamar, there are no clear and undeniable boundaries or mechanisms of restriction (e.g., belief systems, political frameworks, social codes, material geographies) that safeguard against social-historical dis-*ease*. As his prose suggests, we are exposed to and by the world. We are confronted with a world and circumstances in that world beyond our ability to control or orchestrate. Hence, we are vulnerable. We are exposed. We are open.

Moving back to Bluijs, the barbaric may create a certain level of metaphysical dissonance, yet it leaves in place too much pretense of legitimacy surrounding the structures of disregard that impinge upon the quality and quantity of black life. The barbaric is read over against normativity. Contrary to this, Lamar, through recognition of openness and recognition of a quality of "rawness," offers insights that push against normative structures through the persistence of contradiction and complexities of perception and meaning—as well as the failure of social expression—while also reinforcing these structures. By so doing, Lamar exposes the barbaric as inadequate and "made" by the discourse of the "normal." His sense of openness, and a quality of rawness, seeks to go underneath this discourse. What is more, through performance of the body as disruption—as open, porous, and hence able to signify the strictures of dominant social worlds—Lamar points out a type of sociocultural "necrophobia" played out by whites in various forms of racial disregard—and at its most extreme in the effort to control death through death. And in addition to pointing out this process of metaphysical and existential confinement, Lamar promotes the porous nature of bodies in time and space, the flexibility of these bodies as they are constantly confronted with the dynamics of living into death. Put differently, Lamar promotes recognition of bodies as complex signifiers that are already and always impacted (and to some degree defined or known) by the material and discursive arrangements of life. It is not a particular type of body that is open, rather it is a certain socially coded (e.g., white) body that is allowed the pretense of closure—of having boundaries that are real and firm. I make much of this framing of Lamar in light of his album *DAMN.*

DAMN AND THE GROTESQUE

DAMN promotes a hip hop inflected version of Mikhail Bakhtin's grotesque realism[12] and the track "DNA" in particular speaks to what Bakhtin positions as the grotesque body—the body porous and open to the world.[13] Furthermore, Lamar offers a psycho-ethical response to the human encounter with the world framed by complex embodied

12. I use Mikhail Bakhtin (*Rabelias and His World*), Du Bois (*The Souls of Black Folk*), and Camus (*The Myth of Sisyphus and Other Essays* [New York: Vintage International, 1991]) in much of my recent work. In particular, I use them to develop a theoretical approach to the nature of religion and description of things at work within religion. My most substantive framing of this work is *Interplay of Things: Technology of Religion, Art, and Presence Together* (Durham, NC: Duke University Press, 2021).

13. Small portions of this essay were initially written for an online publication, *Marginalia Review of Books*, as a response to conversation (and Louis Rolsky's "Black Millennial Music, Critical Studies of Religion, and the Gravitational Pull of Kendrick Lamar") regarding a book I coedited with Monica Miller and Bun B—titled *Religion in Hip Hop* (London: Bloomsbury, 2015). I decided not to publish it through that venue.

meaning as a type of grotesquery, and marked out by a mode of black moralism.[14]

In African American culture, grotesque realism emerges with the earthiness of the blues, and reaches its high point in the Bronx (NY) with the cultural revolt of the despised we have come to call hip hop. It does not involve "folk" practices one might associate with carnivals celebrated by Bakhtin—such as signifying civic and religious authority through song and costume, relieving oneself in public, and so on—but instead hip hop entails a similar posture toward the world, a similar performance of history and being over against structures of restriction. Modes of authority are exposed and challenged. In Bakhtin's analysis this is expressed in part through the rejection of theologically justified distinction, authority and social difference. What Bakhtin points to is the manner in which carnival turns the sociopolitical and cultural arrangements (or boundaries) of life against themselves. Carnival displays bodies in such a way as to trouble the codes of collective life meant to provide boundaries between classes, and to enforce distinctions between private activities (e.g., defecating) and public activities. The stranglehold of discursively arranged restrictions is broken and their mechanisms of enactment are signified. Through this performance, the mechanism and discourse of power are disrupted to the degree markers of authority—civic leaders and church officials—are mocked and manipulated through play. And with hip hop it is graphically promoted through a restructuring of collective values. In a general sense,

14. As I note a few lines from this note, I have in mind W. E. B. Du Bois (see Pinn, *The Interplay of Things*) and Albert Camus. One need not be an atheist to embrace this modality of moralism. Instead one must simply struggle/live without denying the material connotations of life and the nature of the absurd. That is to say, Lamar, as a theist, can embrace moralism to the extend he struggles to live without hope born of absurdity denied. See: Camus, *The Myth of Sisyphus and Other Essays*.

then, like carnival for Bakhtin, hip hop for Lamar entails dismantling of established, rigidly binary ways of thinking and being.

Hip hop's artists (and fans) consent to this openness between "things" (including bodies) and to the challenging of rigid binaries—all metaphorically played out through performance. One hears this in the music—the work of the DJ involving the manipulation of various musical sounds—scratching and cutting by means of which music is altered from its original intent and "sound" and put to a different service. The DJ, in this sense, uses the open nature, the porous quality of music through the manipulation of records, and so on.[15] The MC manipulates language and uses the mouth to tame structures of disregard and restriction by painting new worlds out of a gritty vocabulary and grammar of life. In this way, by extension, the MC uses the mouth as Bakhtin celebrates—as encounter with the world—out of which protrudes the sound of thought and doing.[16] Artistic expression within hip hop culture also plays on the porous nature of aesthetic expression through the placement of "art" in unanticipated places—such as trains and walls. In so doing the inside/outside of the art world is signified. When hip hop–influenced art moved into established spaces, graffiti forced the traditional art world to rethink its philosophy and practice of artistic production.[17] Furthermore, dance within hip hop culture arranges the body in time and space in ways that seem to defy gravity and that position the body in unlikely ways.[18] This is all to suggest

---

15. See for example, Tricia Rose, *Black Nose: Rap Music and Black Culture in Contemporary America* (Middleton, CT: Wesleyan University Press, 1994).

16. Mikhail Bakhtin, *Rabelais and His World* (Bloomington: Indiana University Press, 1984), 281, 317, 325.

17. A prime example of this is the neo-expressionism of graffiti artist turned art world figure Jean Michel Basquiat.

18. See, for instance, Joseph Schloss, *Foundations: B-boys, B-girls and Hip Hop in New York* (New York: Oxford University Press, 2009).

the manner in which hip hop culture speaks the value of openness, to the porous quality of life. Hip hop is fundamentally a poetic demonstration of the grotesque (as Bakhtin names it) of life circumstances over against the illusions of containment, social cleanliness and cultural fixity. The grotesque and open body is a complex and contradictory body—for example, the structure of experience—as porous, or open to various arrangements of encounter. It is penetrated by the world and it penetrates the world—defying in the process any easy description and truncated coding of meaning. Put differently, this open body—the African American—is marked by structures of being that are layered, thick, complex and that defy restriction.

In addition to Bakhtin, I suggest Georges Bataille offers insights into the performance of openness of some value here. Still, it is perhaps too much to read through Bataille Lamar's pronouncement of the contrary nature of black life, in that *DAMN*, for instance, doesn't exactly read life as most forceful and "human" within "the cesspool of the heart."[19] Bataille entertains "decomposition," a process of performance within despised activities, which is not of particular concern to Lamar. Lamar's dreams and fantasies outlined in his work are not the dreams spoken of by Bataille.[20] Lamar, for example, isn't concerned with the appeal of despised body fluids as is Bataille, but rather Lamar explores and signifies a more general bodily existence and disruptive playfulness. Both speak of death—Bataille in relationship, at times,

19. Georges Bataille, "The 'Old Mole' and the Prefix *Sur* in the Words *Surhomme* [Superman] and *Surrealist*," in Bataille, *Vision of Excess: Selected Writings, 1927–1939*, ed. Allan Stoekl (Minneapolis: University of Minnesota Press, 1985), 41.

20. I would argue one finds something more along the lines of Bataille's thinking in the work of controversial artist Tyler, the Creator. See for example, Tyler the Creator, "Yonkers," OFWGKTA, February 10, 2011: https://www.youtube.com/watch?v=XSbZidsgMfw. Accessed on January 20, 2018. I give attention to the connection between Bataille and Tyler, the Creator in *Deathlife*.

to an erotic regard for the cadaver and Lamar as a condition into which one is already living. Yet, disregard for the moral ideals of the dominant society offers a touch of robust presence, but without the dissension advocated by Bataille. Rather, Lamar's is more akin to degradation (i.e., referring to the horizontal or earth-based and material realm of existence) as promoted by Bakhtin. In a word, he presents the grotesque body—a body that opposes objectification but also demands more than the reifying boundaries associated with "American" subjectivity. It is, in a sense, "flesh and blood"[21] as disruption. Presentation of this "flesh and blood"—this grotesque body—chronicled in the stories woven through the album seeks no resolution—no denouncement of certain codes of living and embrace of others so as to foster moral and ethical boundaries of existence.[22]

THE "POLITICS" OF BEING—OR, "REAL NIGGA CONDITIONS"[23]

From framing of circumstances grounded in the interplay of life and death found with "BLOOD," the first track, *DAMN* moves to "DNA." Initiated with circumstances under which one lives, the album moves to fundamental make-up—to the nature of embodied life and the material "markers" of meaning that shape values and

---

21. "Introduction" in *Modern Art and the Grotesque*, ed. Frances S. Connelly (New York: Cambridge University Press, 2003), 8.

22. In early feedback regarding this topic, it was noted that "more evidence for this point may come in the form of Lamar rereleasing the album in reverse order": Christopher Hooton, "Why Kendrick Lamar Just Re-released DAMN. in Reverse," *Independent*, December 8, 2017, http://www.independent.co.uk/arts-entertainment/music/news/kendrick-lamar-damn-album-collectors-edition-backwards-reverse-back-to-front-explanation-why-twitter-a8098561.html

23. "Real nigga conditions" is a line from "YAH" on *DAMN*, Interscope Records, 2017: "I got so many theories and suspicions; I'm diagnosed with real nigga conditions."

postures toward the world. Lamar—in the track "DNA"—is defined by a blend of what society would call contradictory influences—"antisocial, extrovert" as he names it. He is penetrated and penetrates (as the line goes, "I don't compromise, I just penetrate") the world in a manner that signifies the dictates and moral boundaries imposed by the social world.[24]

He is lucid to his make-up, his social-psychic meaning, and in this way, Lamar is aware of the illusion of authority—the effort to simplify existence so as to tame it. He resists the lure of a metaphysics pulling away from earth, and instead "what happens on Earth stays on Earth" as is recounted in the intro to "ELEMENT," track number 4 on *DAMN.* Lamar privileges the horizontal interactions of life—and finds meaning in earthy interplay. If the album begins with a question of life or death, Lamar selects the former. In this regard, he highlights life within his "element" or what Bakhtin might note as life within the circumstances of degradation. In both instances, what dominant social authority would position as negative and devalued, Lamar highlights as the productive domain of materiality and historically situated interplay. Within his "element" life is "real"—and even the harsh demands of the world he handles with grace, without remorse—or as he puts it, he "makes it look sexy."[25] Historical circumstances of our existence recognized can generate lucidity marked by the lack of "hope" for a firm and 'different' future reflected in lines such as "I feel like it ain't no tomorrow, fuck the world" ("FEEL"). Yet, this shouldn't be read as surrender; it isn't a mode of nihilism. Rather, it is rejection of illusions of continuity and unity of purpose—a dismissal of final resolution. God language is still present in his lyrics, but all seems to bow to the realities of material existence.

---

24. The proper response to circumstances on some level involves human accountability and responsibility—forged through mutuality and commitment.

25. "ELEMENT" on *DAMN.*

While remaining "religious," Lamar suggests dismantling of reifying theological authority when in "Yah" he proclaims, "I'm not 'bout a religion"—hence, distancing himself from a particular scheme of regulation and confinement. Instead, his priority is to historical placement and its social ramification. The social construct of race—"don't call me black no mo"—gives way to his intuition and persistence over against religious-theological pronouncements justifying disregard.[26] One might say religious abstraction is tamed by the pull of material existence within embodied bodies—or, in other words, by "truly human relations . . . experienced." This is an earthy, materially related presence.[27] Put yet another way, it is reasonable to argue Lamar remains "religious," but this is a religiosity that rejects religion to the extent it is less concerned with the "content" of religion and more concerned with the mechanisms of language and the poetic quality of expression afforded through the theological language games attached to religion. Hence, he is an Israelite—which allows a historical disruption of black life as confined to the markers of servitude (i.e., "not black no mo") and the discursive creativity of the age of exploration and conquest. Black in this regard is a socially orchestrated attempt to forge boundary between substantive being as a subject of history and passive existence as an object of history. He, Lamar proclaims, is not black; rather his being disrupts historical and epistemological arrangements as a type of confinement. But little about his engagement with his status as Israelite suggests a firm commitment to the enactment of this signifier as a life discipline. Flesh matters as performance of his chemical-metaphorical DNA, the configuration of potentiality out of which all issues—life, death, and all the pleasures and pain in between the two. Through attention to chemical-metaphorical DNA, Lamar brings life into and through the body.

26. Kendrick Lamar, "YAH."

27. Bakhtin, *Rabelais and His World*, 10, 18–19.

Social codes don't determine the arrangement of and values associated with life—rather it is the body in time and space that mark out the cartography of life. This embodied performance is not disconnected from the embodied experience of others but reflects even in its nuance something of that shared existence within social arrangements that despise black being, a sentiment demonstrated through effort to reduce "blackness" (if not end it). Yet, Lamar speaks against such effort as long as he proclaims the complexity of his being—the multitude of meanings shaping his fundamental self. This does not deny the biological nature of the self, but Lamar's work places this self within a larger arrangement—people who share his sensibilities and placement in time and space—for instance the "Israelites" framed in terms of the materiality of life.[28] Reference to the history of the Israelites isn't simply a theological pronouncement. It is also historical, dealing with their placement, hence his placement, within time and space and within a larger "ancestral body." This marks yet another moment of grotesque realism—the moment when the individual body connects to the body "of the people."[29] Instead of articulating the place of blackness vis-à-vis sociopolitical circumstances, Lamar, in the track "DNA," explores the manner in which complexity or interplay mark out life at a more fundamental level—the symbolic significance of genetic structure as the geography of existence—and as a matter of relationship between biology and sociality.

Again, Lamar isn't about a religion, as he states, and through this clarification he pushes against theological abstraction, against effort to promote vertical explanations (e.g., theodicy) and relationships and instead, to borrow from Bakhtin, he gives high regard to horizontal relationships—to earthy, historically situated, experience in and with

28. Flesh matters as the performance of his chemical-metaphorical DNA, the configuration of potentiality out of which all issues—life, death, and all the pleasures and pain in between the two.

29. Bakhtin, *Rabelais and His World*, 367.

the body.[30] As Bakhtin asserts, life projects a "system of values" communicated through a variety of mechanisms.[31] In this regard, *DAMN* can be understood as an expression of values projected and configured anew. And within *DAMN* these values first expose the illusions projected by the dominant society and its cultural codes. Lamar signifies the social structures normalized and instead promotes alternatives that embrace what is typically despised—for example, social contradiction, political complexity, existential anger, and black desire. The cultural construction of life often involves a pretense of closure—of codes and regulations that keep things arranged "rightly." That is to say, the assumed proper arrangement of individual and collective interactions that constitute the structuring of life involves the ability to bracket off, to isolate, and limit. Boundaries, in this sense, constitute self-understanding and security of being. Institutions and systems of authority produce and encourage anxiety over boundaries as to maintain "control" over circumstance and bodies. Yet, the constitution of his embodied body speaks openness, or a mode of transgression that exposes the body to the world by means of which both are engaged and altered. This body, the grotesque body—the exaggerated body—storied by Lamar extends beyond social boundaries and "exceeds everything we view as normal."[32] This is certainly one way to read his rejection of "black" as a substantive marker of identity.[33]

"DNA" AND THE OPEN BODY AS GROTESQUE

In the track "DNA" Lamar makes light of his protagonist—outlining the deficiencies of his chemical-metaphorical DNA over against the

30. Bakhtin, *Rabelais and His World*, 395.

31. Krystyna Pomorska, "Foreword," in Bakhtin, *Rabelais and His World*, viii.

32. Ola Sigurdson, "The Grotesque Body," in *Heavenly Bodies: Incarnation, the Gaze, and Embodiment in Christian Theology* (Grand Rapids: Eerdmans, 2016), 492.

33. Kendrick Lamar, "YAH."

vitality and importance of Lamar's chemical-metaphorical DNA and its implications. The difference: Lamar's chemical-metaphorical DNA is oppositional to the status quo and embraces openness ("I just penetrate"), messiness ("war and peace"), complexity ("power, poison, pain and joy"); and the officer's chemical-metaphorical DNA speaks acquiescence to authority, an embrace of confinement. The levity, the laughter associated with this signifying constitutes a moment of conquest in that "terror is conquered by laughter."[34] Through lucid complexity, the track "DNA" signifies, thus damages, the social structures of distinction that are meant to reify African American being into a truncated meaning—that is, object for use, consumption, disposal. The "black" body is open, porous—penetrated by bullets, attacked by social codes, arranged and stored in prisons, but also penetrates the world through a persistent refusal to die unnoticed. It is an exaggerated body, whose make-up (i.e., chemical-metaphorical DNA) expands its reach and impact while deflating the value of traditional systems of value—of equal value, for Lamar, is the assumed "negative" register of experience.

One might say what Lamar offers in the track "DNA" is more than the double consciousness chronicled by W. E. B. Du Bois, which is perhaps one of the more compelling depictions of exposure provided during the twentieth century, in that it isn't defined so easily by "a peculiar sensation . . . this sense of always looking at one's self through the eyes of others, of measuring one's soul by the tape of a world that looks on in amused contempt and pity. One ever feels his twoness,—an American, a Negro; two souls, two thoughts, two unreconciled strivings, two warring ideals in one dark body."[35] It is not a

34. Bakhtin, *Rabelais and His World*, 336.

35. W. E. B. Du Bois, *The Souls of Black Folk*, ed. Henry Louis Gates Jr., and Terri Hume Oliver (New York: W. W. Norton & Company, 1999), 11. Even in Du Bois's depiction of the dilemma of existence in blackness, there is a bracketing

friction between two neat social identities—neatly arranged although tenacious in the damage done. In fact, "DNA" rejects double consciousness to the extent it rejects the idea of "warring" ideals; instead embracing complexity and tension, and thereby denying the discourse that would normalize the boundaries sought by whiteness. He accepts nothing of the boundaries desired by the larger framing of life and instead he embraces the ability of "black" being to mark out penetration, imposition, difference, and same-ness simultaneously: "See, my pedigree most definitely don't tolerate the front. Shit I've been through probably offend you, this is Paula's oldest son." Even Lamar's attire in the video to the track "DNA" speaks to this type of fluidity and challenges even the aesthetics—movement between what one would think of as an outfit perhaps made aware to African Americans through kung fu films (and exemplified by the Wu Tang Clang's celebration of kung fu cultural markers) to the more traditional T-shirt and jeans more keenly associated with hip hop culture.[36]

Lamar's "mood" channels that of the blues: a lucidity with respect to circumstances that doesn't seek to reduce tension but rather embraces competing components—allowing meaning to entail slippage and interplay between them. This is the nature of Lamar's self-understanding—the reality of being, the meaning of his movement through time and space, or, "real nigga conditions." Through a rejection of despair and melancholy, of angst and fear, regarding

---

of dimensions found distasteful according to the social norms of the day. In a word, Du Bois seeks to depict African Americans consistent with the assumed best of American life—striving for inclusion, although such efforts, as *Souls of Black Folk* points out, ultimately fail to deliver. For Du Bois the existential and social challenge faced by African Americans is superficial, that is to say it isn't an inherent dimension of how they are but rather how they are positioned within the cultural matrix of life post-Reconstruction.

36. See Kendrick Lamar, "DNA," Kendrick Lamar, https://www.youtube.com/watch?v=NLZRYQMLDW4. Accessed January 21, 2018.

circumstances, Lamar tames the discourse of disregard and, like the trickster, turns arrangements upside down by embracing what is despised—maintaining openness to the world as he knows it—and pushing for recognition of the grotesquery of life. As he proclaims, "Realness, I just kill shit 'cause it's in my DNA."

Meaning isn't determined by subtracting from circumstances and conditions but rather through an embrace of entanglement, through lucid reflection on one's existential surroundings. But then again, when has hip hop ever assumed the normativity of dominant codes of being? When has it ever assumed meaning is restricted to what is opposite of blackness? When has hip hop not involved a certain modality of the grotesque as posture toward the circumstances with which one is confronted?

Hip hop, in significant ways, then, is a strategy, a means by which to confront the absurdity of life—action in the face of death. Put differently, hip hop culture is one of the most robust moralist stances available in African American life and letters. It, along these lines, gives response to the challenges surfaced by Camus, Du Bois, and others, and in the process accepts what the former notes as an "invitation to live and to create, in the very midst of the desert."[37] Revolt—as hip hop—is to live without assurances and without surrender to fixity of an imposed blackness (i.e., Lamar's rejection of "blackness" as more than a color and therefore not a description of meaning). Revolt is a lucid push against the boundaries imposed so as to distance the force of absurdity. Hip hop troubles neat framings of life, and instead endorses complexity, messiness, and—in the Bakhtian sense—degraded life. Dualism—tension—remains a means by which to articulate social life for African Americans; but it becomes the noting of something inherent—not to be overcome, but rather recognized and embraced.

---

37. Camus, *The Myth of Sisyphus and Other Essays*, v.

By rejecting efforts to fit in, to accommodate the discourse of inclusion promoted by the "powers that be," Lamar takes a different existential and metaphysical path. The "DNA" video depicts such defiance: Beginning with the track "YAH" fading out, Lamar is in what one might assume is a police station, undergoing a polygraph test—perhaps a metaphor for structures of authority's effort to monitor compliance.[38] However, the tables turn, so to speak, and his complexity of existence—the contradictory components of his essential being—"contaminates" and disrupts normative discourses of continuity. Lamar, despite the wishes of authorities, is not reduced, not confined. By stating his complexity—his defiance or revolt—Lamar maintains the vitality of the grotesque and subverts normative discourses of wholeness as bounded conformity. His refusal to deny any dimension of his psycho-ethical make-up is substantive and disruptive—and marked by comfort with paradox, complexity, tension, and uncertainty.

It is in this way the track "DNA" opposes the effort to confine and reify black meaning. The narrative of his chemical-metaphorical DNA points to the embodied body in all its complexities, and codes that inform movement through the world. The chemical-metaphorical DNA, in this sense, encompasses the geography of life, and in the context of Lamar's track "DNA" this geography plays off but also informs social existence—to *be* is to *resist restriction, to defy*. In the video the symbol of authority—the police officer—mocks this openness but in so doing exposes the essential nature of this openness and the artificial nature of efforts to deny and restrict it. There is harmony between these various elements of being. They are not at war because, in a significant

38. The fading out of "YAH" as the video for "DNA" begins speaks to the existential connection between the "real nigga conditions" marking the former, and the constitution of being in the world referenced by those conditions, which situates the latter.

manner, Lamar is unwilling to assume the normativity of more linear and closed-off modalities of social/psycho-identification and ethical impulse. This is exemplified through his reversal of the police interrogation played out in the video for "DNA". The officer, who initially belittles Lamar's social placement and meaning, is exposed and signified. The false distinction, the illusionary ability to bracket off and distinguish "blackness" as problematic, is exposed, challenged, and conquered. Open being can't be policed and quarantined. To deny an element of this complexity is to bend to the will of the status quo, to the social norms and standards that dwarf and fix black life—positing African Americans, by extension, as of limited consequence. Lamar signifies this by embracing that which cultural codes tell us to reject. Elements of ethical positioning the larger discursive frameworks of life in the US suggest we find morally problematic, he embraces with the same energy within which he accepts the more morally normative postures. Evil in his heart seems just as acceptable to Lamar as the markers of hard work and the "American Dream" that also lurk as the stuff of his chemical-metaphorical DNA.

Like Bakhtin's depiction of carnival and its exposure of what is considered private, Lamar's turn to the despised involves a marker of complex meaning. There is similarity here in that in both cases those marginalized in social life are given center stage through a signifying of the very markers and models of authority that once served to sanction their reified status. On some level what Lamar chronicles can be read as a shallow reference to history—to the greatness of a past extended deeper and beyond the workings of enslavement. Yet, there is more than a romanticizing of an African past; Lamar points to the intrinsic nature and expression of being as tied to complexity, messiness, and porousness—not a linear path to a grand African past. He goes beneath the rhetoric and symbolic structures of social codes governing life and points to the sense of open and complex being that technologies of power work to conceal. Power dynamics are altered and Lamar—the despised one—speaks through the symbol of the status quo—the police detective working the polygraph machine. Roles are signified and shifted. Lamar isn't simply chronicling an easily deciphered sense of the good life over against the tragic. The nature of blackness—the grotesque nature of blackness—is intrinsic, and more fundamental than the "blackness" as color imposed by the status quo. It is intimately tied to the very meaning of black life—chemical-metaphorical DNA. Hence, it is to be acknowledged, not worked to resolve.

There is no melancholy, nor is there any effort to be other than open to the world—to exist within the intersections of competing possibilities. He critiques adherence to strategies of normalization, of the patterns and boundaries of accepted social coding. There is a modality of interplay, of interaction between assumingly opposed postures that frames life within the track "DNA" that signifies the assurances and that come from life understood as unilateral and "clean"—that is, lived within proper distinctions. Identity, then, involves not the unification of meaning without contradiction; but rather it entails a creative tension and penetration of varied and deemed contradictory markers of presence. The (black) body, the (black) being, celebrated by Lamar flaunts its complexity and announces its disregard for social boundaries.

Still, Lamar doesn't denounce all forms of authority, and in some ways embraces a tradition marked by standards of isolation and theologized boundaries. Rather, he tames such modalities of authority by tying their merit to materiality and the workings of human history—all for the benefit of social being recognized as complex and vibrant. He announces a horizontal set of relationships grounded in the material workings of the world, along the lines of complexity as celebrated marker of metaphysical significance, purpose and function—chronicled through the intricacies of his chemical-metaphorical DNA. He, as grotesque realism encourages, celebrates what social norms and dominant cultural coding would denounce as "tainted," "dangerous," and without proper containment or confinement. Lamar maintains as vital and vibrant the contradictions of social existence the larger social system of meaning would have him (and us) reject.

What now? Openness, celebration of the grotesque, entails what? Promotes what? And, offers what with respect to the nature and meaning of individual and collective life? This openness, this adherence to grotesque realism, prompts a sense of being in line with an altered framing of the heroic. That is to say, the track "DNA" highlights layered revolt as the proper posture toward authorities confining one's place *in* and encounter *with* the world. Or, as Lamar proclaims, "I got, I got, I got . . ."

Section Two

THEOLOGIZING'S RHYTHM

6 CONVERSION IN HIP HOP

The last chapter explored ontological issues by reading Kendrick Lamar through a mode of realism understood in connection to the thought of figures like Albert Camus and Mikhail Bakhtin. This chapter also examines issues related to being, but this time over against a theologically articulated naming of experience. That is to say, here an effort is made to re-examine what it means to be religiously committed as posed by the religious rhetoric and activities of certain rap artists. Traditional notions of religious engagement lodged, for example, within the rhetoric and structures of black churches are called into question by the religious rhetoric and existential posture of artists who claim a relationship with the divine, in this case the Christian God, but whose activities on the surface might suggest a lack of the ethical posture one might assume such a commitment might entail.

The thoughts contained in this chapter in no way suggest a fully formed theory of conversion within the context of Hip Hop culture. Rather, it is a thought experiment—an effort to begin a process of mining rap music for the manner in which it might enrich theological discourse. That is to say, rap music in particular and Hip Hop culture in general might offer a paradigm shift, a conceptual alteration of African American theological reflection, one that promotes a turn toward a fuller arrangement of organic source material. Having suggested such a move in other publications, I turn attention here to the conceptual challenge to the theological language (and ethical ramifications) of conversion within African American religious thought.

By examining the religious rhetoric of rappers, this chapter gives attention to the troubled relationship between religious language and perceived religiously motivated activity, and in the process offers an alternate means by which to access the nature and meaning, the accompanying framework of religious experience. In this way, rap music—particularly the synergy between talk and action promoted—is used as a problematic by which to encourage attention to prevailing theories of religious experience promoted as normative by African American Christian studies. In a word, I use the religious rhetoric of commitment to the divine housed within the lyrics of certain rap artists as an example of the utility of an understanding of African American religion as quest for complex subjectivity and African American religious experience as the framing, or acting out, of this quest. In this way, theoretical and methodological challenges are posed to the normative manner in which the authenticity of African American religious commitment and experience are gauged and verified.

Theories of religious experience, or conversion, concerned with African American Christianity tend to highlight and privilege such experience as explicitly marking a transformation suggesting a new posture toward existential commitments and realities as well as a refined sense of one's ontological connections and resulting obligations. This, I would argue, is the basic meaning of African American Christian proclamation of religious experience, particularly conversion, as a "new" person, one whose thought and practice are guided by a surrender to Christ augmenting certain moral and ethical arrangements. Religious experience so understood involves the affirmation and attempt to perpetuate the substance of conversion as marked by (1) confrontation with one's spiritual (and related mundane—such as moral missteps) shortcomings; (2) wrestling with old postures and perceptions over against possibilities of a new consciousness; and (3) new consciousness and related ways of being in the world.[1] Taking place within this context of conversion is a disassociation from the secular, an epistemological tenderness resulting in an attempt to step "lightly" through the world and in this way avoid its contaminants and provide a proper example of moral and ethical correctness.

One's newly recognized and accepted ontological significance and merit (i.e., revitalized image of God) is matched by a new posture toward the world in line with a community of the like-minded. In the words of the spiritual,

> You say the Lord has set you free
> You must be loving at God's command.[2]

Through this posture, African American Christian workings of religious experience, again with particular attention to conversion, suggest the weight of transformation revolves around both a new posture toward the world—for example, an altered perspective on the manner in which bodies occupy time and space—and, more importantly, a set of rather reified ethical and moral norms drawn in large part from a rather traditional read of the Hebrew Bible and the Christian Testament:

> Therefore, if any man be in Christ, he is a new creature: old things are passed away; behold, all things are become new.[3]

In significance ways, religious experience involves the body (while also pointing beyond the physical). It entails the placement of certain

1. For information on how I ground and develop this idea, see Anthony B. Pinn, *Terror and Triumph: The Nature of Black Religion* (Minneapolis: Fortress Press, 2003), chapter 7. My thinking in this chapter draws from and builds on my thinking in that earlier text.

2. "Give Me Your Hands," https://tinyurl.com/2wcadr8a.

3. 2 Corinthians 5:17 (KJV).

bodies in new contexts, a new matrix of interactions, recognition, and exchange whereby bodies are both "in the world" but "not of the world."

Thick relationship with Christ, surrender to the plan and will of God as African American Christians might name it, involves a new experience of the body—one through which it becomes an interactive vessel promoting and contributing to the will of God. The body continues to change over time, yet such mundane and existential alterations are now viewed as secondary significance to the transcendent connection to God through Christ. In this respect, religious experience involves a re-envisioning of the body through an appreciation, tenuous as it may be, of the body while also seeking to place the physical in proper context. While never fully able to jettison the dualism of body versus soul, African American religious experience of the Christian variety involves a contestation won—the mundane, the physical body and its environ, monitored and controlled to some extent by the mechanics of the soul force (i.e., the divine and its will). Albeit a marriage of practices never perfected, there is a continual recognition of and sensitivity to spiritual failure and its historically arranged ramifications, as well as a push toward "perfection" in one's behavior.

African American Christian denominations will differ with respect to the emphasis placed on the ability of humans to live out "perfection" in one's commitment to Christ. The Holiness Movement, and its various denominations, connotes debate over this issue. Some, as the Church of God in Christ, argue doctrinally for the possibility of a "clean" life through sanctification and the presence of the Holy Spirit as the internal guiding force or compass for life decisions and arrangements. However, African American Methodist and Baptist churches tend toward more doctrinal flexibility concerning the manner in which conversion results in rigidly transformed life arrangements. Nonetheless, all seem to agree on a basic assumption that conversion involves at the very least a new epistemological posture toward and sensitivity to how one "moves" through the world. This is because religious experience, again conversion as a prime example, involves a perpetuated arrangement—a continual maneuvering—marking a tension between the draw of "this world" and the promise of better possibilities. It is, in a word, a thick and multidimensional evolution.

Much in popular culture bears out this African American Christian sense of religious experience as extension of conversion; yet, there are ways in which it is challenged by other modalities of popular culture. I have in mind certain lyrical developments in rap music. That is to say, many understand African American religious experience as related to the thinking and living out of conversion in ways that shape the perception of the body and how it occupies time and space—shifting both thought and action along rather rigid ethical and moral standards and frameworks. Rap artists such as Tupac Shakur, for instance, suggest another way of arranging religious experience. For such figures, conversion involves a more committed and uncompromising posture toward the world—a shift in one's approach to the world that connotes sensitivity to one's presence. In this way, for such figures, conversion does not require a change in behavior or interest, but rather a deeper awareness of self, of one's value, and one's "weight" within the world. Such thinking renders useless a typical black Christian pronouncement: "We are in the world, but not of it."

The church-based testimonial during which the dynamics and mechanisms of conversion are displayed publicly is replaced by Hip Hop, or rap music in particular, most commonly by lyrics. Such a shift in location acknowledges the manner in which Tupac Shakur frames his work: "My music is spiritual, if you listen to it. . . . It's all about emotion; it's all about life."[4] Tupac frames the exposing and unpacking of the spiritual dimension of his existence in ways, like African

4. Quoted in Michael Eric Dyson, *Holler If You Hear Me: Searching for Tupac Shakur* (New York: Basic Civitas Books, 2001), 138–39.

American Christians, that recognize the absurd nature of existing. He notes the difficulties of life, the ways in which socioeconomic and political arrangements—the real and raw nature of life—impinge upon efforts to survive, if not thrive: "You know they got me trapped in this prison of seclusion. Happiness, living on tha streets is a delusion."[5]

Again, in both instances, for the Christian and for Tupac, the world represented a troubled and troubling location—an arrangement of tense relationships. However, the response to such a predicament differs in these two cases. Whereas for Christians the transformation of such circumstances involves a conversion—a reconstruction of self—that resolves the world by problematizing engagement with it, Tupac's response involves transformation of self into the "Thug." In this way, conversion does not mean disengagement from the world, or an effort to purge the signs of worldly involvements, but rather a more energetic engagement with the world. The thug does not reject the world. Instead, the mark of transformation into the thug involves a new posture toward the world, a more sensitized embrace of the world, an epistemological shift resulting in clearer vision concerning the possibilities embedded in the complexities of life. For Tupac, it appears, conversion need not point beyond the world, but to a greater recognition of the beauty within the grotesque. Such a stance, as cultural critic Michael Eric Dyson remarks, has theological and moral consequences. Images of life and visions of existence promoted in rap that run contrary to the dominant Christian ethos "produce competing views of black selfhood and the moral visions they support." Furthermore, "if such visions of black selfhood imply a spiritual foundation, then a conception of God is not far away. It is easy enough to detect the divine in hip-hop communities that value traditional expressions of religious sentiment. But what of thug culture."[6]

---

5. Tupac Shakur, "Trapped," on *2Pacalypse Now*, Jive Records, 1998.

6. Dyson, *Holler If You Hear Me*, 210–11.

The epistemological posture, existential entanglements, and ontological assumptions that guide traditional African American Christian notions of conversion are not embraced by Tupac. Conversion does not involve a rejection of worldly arrangements and mechanisms of life, but rather recognition of the divine in even the despised—or thug—modalities and aesthetic of life. For the Christian, conversion amounts to a sustained push toward a Christ-like existence. This is also the case for Tupac, but it is the "Black Jesuz" who shapes life transformation vis-à-vis conversion. Such a religious move does not entail surrender to absurdity, a morphing into an unrecognizable connection to the absurd. Rather, Tupac suggests conversion as something different. In this way, the convert's posture toward the world involves the movement of the trickster, not the traditional Christ. The trickster recognizes and signifies life arrangements that trouble most—pushing for a more vibrant existence that does not fear the world. Tupac, like the African American cultural figure of folktales, Br'er Rabbit, or the thug as convert, calls the roughness of the briar patch "home." The story goes this way: Br'er Rabbit is in trouble for taking an item that did not belong to him. And as punishment he is given the option of being thrown into the briar patch or in fire:

> Some say to th'ow him in de fiah, and some say th'ow him in de brierpatch. Br'er Rabbit, he don't say nothin'. Den, Br'er Fox say, "Br'er Rabbit, which one you ruther us do?" Br'er Rabbit, he say, "Th'ow me in de fiah, please, Br'er Fox; dem old briers jest tear my eyes out, if you th'ow me in de brierpatch." So dey tuk him and th'owed him in de brierpatch. And Br'er Rabbit, he shook he'se'f and jump way up on de hill and laugh and say, "Thank you, Br'er Fox. I was bred and born in a brierpatch."[7]

7. Annie Reed, "Br'er Rabbit and the Briar Patch," in *Talk That Talk: An Anthology of African-American Storytelling*, ed. Linda Goss and Marian E. Barnes (New York: Touchstone Book, 1989), 31.

Like Br'er Rabbit, some rap artists signify and improvise in such a way as to make difficulties of life, existential challenges, a place of relative comfort.

It is true that Tupac denounces "thug life" when interviewed in 1995 by *Vibe Magazine*, but isn't it possible that what he moves against is a certain formation of the thug, one that gives little attention to the deeper shades of existence?[8] Perhaps this is similar to Howard Thurman's rejection of the form and fashion of Christianity while committing himself to the religion of Jesus? It might, then, be the case that Tupac rejects a modality of the "thug" that does not reflect authentic conversion to the ways of Black Jesuz. In his words,

> All I can say is I always try to be a real nigga in my heart. Sometimes it's good, sometimes it's bad; but it's still us. It's never to hurt nobody. I'm not gonna take advantage of you or bully you. I'm on some underdog shit. And I truly believe I've been blessed by God, and God walks with me. Me and my niggas are on some Black Jesus shit. Not a new religion or anything, but the saint for thugs and gangstas—not killers and rapists, but thugs. When I say thugs, I mean niggas who don't have anything.[9]

Such a perspective is not void of moral and ethical sensibilities; rather, Tupac offers an alternative narrative or paradigmatic structure for conversion—one that embraces the world as the arena of proper existence. Conversion does not suggest a posture of opposition to the world. "I feel like Black Jesus is controlling me," says Tupac. "He's our saint that we pray to; that we look up to. Drug dealers, they sinning, right? But they'll be millionaires. How I got shot five times—only a saint, only Black Jesus, only a nigga that know where I'm coming from, could be, like, 'You know what? He's gonna end up doing some

8. See Kevin Powell, "2Pac Shakur," *Vibe Magazine*, April 1995, 50–55.

9. In Rob Marriott, "Last Testament," *Vibe Magazine*, November 1996, T7

good.'"[10] Such a resolution mirrors the workings of the Black Jesuz, rendering Tupac and those like him—thugs—followers of Jesus who, through their actions in the world, live out the precepts of their faith: "They say Jesus is a kind man, well he should understand times in this crime land, my Thug nation."[11]

It is this Black Jesuz, this icon of life in absurdity who provides the parameters of life, who monitors and informs life transformed:

In times of war we need somebody raw, rally the troops
Like a Saint that we can trust to help to carry us through
Black Jesus, hahahahaha
He's like a Saint that we can trust to help to carry us through
Black Jesus.[12]

There is no ontological revolution brought about through conversion—no it involves a fuller sense of one's presence in the world, a realization of the complexities of one's movement through the world. In this respect it does not entail a suspicion toward the world, nor a new set of moral and ethical guidelines—no metaphysical realities revealed. No special status secured. To the contrary, conversion here involves a greater worldliness, and with this comes a certain modality of accountability: "I play the cards I was given," Tupac writes, "thank God I'm still livin'."[13] When interviewed in prison in April 1995, Tupac spoke to this worldly accountability: "The excuse maker in Tupac is dead. The vengeful Tupac is dead. The Tupac that would stand by and let dishonorable things happen is dead. God let me live [after being shot

10. In Rob Marriott, "Last Testament," *Vibe Magazine* (November 1996): T7

11. Tupac Shakur, "Blasphemy," on *The Don Killuminati, The 7 Day Theory*, Interscope Records, 1996.

12. Tupac Shakur, "Black Jesus," on *Still I Rise*, Interscope Records, 1999.

13. Tupac Shakur, "Definition of a Thug," on *R U Still Down? (Remember Me)*, Jive Records, 1997.

5 times] for me to do something extremely extraordinary, and that's what I have to do."[14] This is not to say, however, that Tupac gives no attention to notions of heaven.

I shall not fear no man but God
Thought I walk through the valley of death
I shed so many tears (if I should die before I wake)
Please God walk with me (grab a nigga and take me to Heaven).[15]

Yet, reflection on heaven does not replace, for Tupac, a deep sensitivity and commitment to full encounters with the world. What is more, heaven does not entail of necessity a radical shift from the mechanisms of life on earth. In Tupac's words, "If I die, I wonder if Heaven got a ghetto."[16] The answer appears to be yes, in that the geography of heaven involves "no shortage on G's."[17]

Conversion, hence, involves a turn inward, an embrace of one's connections to the world. This is certainly one way to interpret the illusions to the Black Jesuz in "Hail Mary." Conversion, a push toward the center of meaning and existence, does not require a suspicion concerning life's joys and pains. There, consequently, is no need to epistemologically arrange one's existence in ways that problematize the body's continued longing for the mundane. Connection to the divine through the transformative tone of conversion means a more refined integration of one's self to the world. "And God said," remarks Tupac, "he should send his one begotten son to lead the wild into the ways of the man."[18]

14. Kevin Powell, "2Pac Shakur," *Vibe Magazine* (April 1995): 52.
15. Tupac Shakur, "So Many Tears," on *Me against the World*, Jive Records, 1995.
16. Tupac Shakur, "I Wonder If Heaven Got a Ghetto," on *R U Still Down?*.
17. Tupac Shakur, "Only Fear of Death," on *R U Still Down?*.
18. Tupac Shakur, "Hail Mary," on *The Don Killuminati, The 7 Day Theory*, Interscope Records, 1996.

Snoop Dogg (aka Calvin Broadus) provides a more traditional conception of the divine. There is no Black Jesuz in his theology, simply a proclaimed devotion to the Christian God. "I'm a child of God," Snoop Dogg remarks, "doing God's work."[19] Growing up within Trinity Baptist Church, Snoop Dogg argues his mother offered an epistemology of life deeply connected to Christian commitment; and he embraced it. Put more forcefully, she "planted a seed that took deep root in my life" he assures the readers of his autobiography.[20] He does not recount the traditional surrender to Christ, the outcome of great struggle of self against the divine, suggesting instead conversion entails a sharpened perspective on the world—clear vision concerning the world's offerings. Yet, he speaks of life guidance as stemming from relationship with the divine and, in this way, he eludes to a conversion-based orientation. When questioned concerning the manner in which he secures his life orientation, Snoop Dogg remarks, "I ask for God's help and let him guide me and give me the strength."[21]

In his self-description, there is sensitivity to the workings of divine influence, to providence, and the manner in which transcendent realities impinge on human existence. Hence, "I've got a responsibility to God," Snoop Dogg, recounts. "He put me here. He'll take me down in a heartbeat the minute I start tripping on myself and how great I must be because of all the people telling me all the time."[22] He speaks, when reflecting on his youth, in muted tones of church involvement, sermons and youth groups; yet, such insular activities do not define for him the life properly lived—the core sentiments of the life devoted (converted?) to God. There is a direct relationship between allegiances

19. Snoop Dogg, with Davin Seay, *The Doggfather: The Times, Trials, and Hardcore Truths of Snoop Dogg* (New York: William Morrow and Company, Inc., 1999), 1.

20. Snoop Dogg, *The Doggfather*, 13.

21. Margena A. Christian, "Rap Star Snoop Dogg Talks about Fame, Fatherhood and Family," *Jet Magazine* (May 22, 2000).

22. Snoop Dogg, *The Doggfather*, 2.

to the divine and "quality" of life. However, whereas it is typically the case in Christian conversion and consequent life arrangements that such a recognition places restrictions on one's engagement of the world, for Snoop Dogg such devotion is best represented through a mature and focused gaze on the world in the manner of representing through word and action the realities of the streets: "I tried to keep it real, never to sell the truth, but always to tell the truth. And if there's one reason why you know the name Snoop Dogg and I don't know yours, it's because telling the truth has given me the props I need to carry out God's purpose and plan."[23] It appears that for Snoop Dogg, history is teleological in nature, unfolding the inner workings of divine intentions. Large and small events alike suggest this arrangement: "God used football to teach me about life, and not even so much the game's strategy and discipline and teamwork—that shit any brother can use to improve himself. What I'm talking about is the faith to believe in yourself, to know that God is on your side and that He cares about you trying the best you can, no matter who you are."[24] He, like Tupac, never offers a defining moment during which the allegiance to the divine is initiated. There are clear moments of struggle that suggest the need for divine intervention; but there is no clear and abiding alteration of behavior marking a turn. Rather, there appears a hermeneutically arranged shift, a new perspective on the workings of life through which the presence of divine intention marks all life activities, regardless of whether or not that fits traditional frameworks of "proper" moral and ethical outlook.

Traditional Christians with their focused conversion are, in comparison, religious savants. That is to say, they are gifted within a small range of religious activities—prayer, church practice, and so on—yet engagement with the world in other ways is more troubling, showing

23. Snoop Dogg, *The Doggfather*, 3.
24. Snoop Dogg, *The Doggfather*, 32.

a rather limited flexibility and an awkwardly demonstrated ability to engage. Epistemology through the tradition conversion, again in comparison, is limited and poorly combines with "worldly" activities. Put yet another way, discussion of traditional African American Christian conversion suggests an effort (while not always successful) to create "flat" realities, two-dimensional persons who see conflict between transcendence and the world, and attempt to embrace the former while denouncing the latter. A clear sign of the traditional Christian convert as religious savant might be the troubled relationship between soul and body that marks the conversation and workings of the erotic within African American Christian communions—an inability to foster synergy between the nurturing of the soul (or metaphysical concerns) and addressing mundane wants and desires.

This chapter is not concerned with judging the "quality" of religious experience in traditional Christian modes over against what is presented by these two rappers. On that score, there are various ways in which both groups would be found wanting. Rather, the concern here is with the manner in which attention to rap music urges attention to the theoretical assumptions that tend to guide African American religious studies in general, and notions of conversion and religious life in particular. The examples of Tupac Shakur and Snoop Dogg pose a challenge to traditional conceptualization of religious conversion and experience. And, we are left to make a decision. One can embrace the grammar and vocabulary of religious conversion/experience that privileges certain formations of Christian frameworks. Or, one can see these examples as useful ways to think through the complex nature of religious engagement. I chose the latter. Mindful of this, I suggest Tupac and Snoop offer a corrective to formations of religio-theological discussion of conversion and religious experience that frame them in terms of progress that assumes a certain sense of freedom or liberation. That is to say, more traditional formulations assume conversion entails exposure to resources enabling a push beyond the troubling frameworks of life—a God-over-against-world paradigm. In this way, the convert is expected to think and live in ways that model this over against the world posture.

The religious narratives offered by Tupac and Snoop, however, call this into question and instead suggest that conversion and religious experience involve a certain posture toward life whereby the quest for greater life meaning and being is harvested not over against the world but through the world. In this respect, conversion involves a hermeneutical shift, an alternate way of viewing the world whereby proper morality and ethics is premised on the "realness" or "authenticity" of one's actions and not the manner in which they fit neatly into doctrinal structures. Troubled through this alternate hermeneutical posture is a rigid determinism and focused range of "accepted" signs of religiosity as lived. Rebuffed are efforts to define religious engagement in terms of formal commitments to an array of relationships that seek to jettison life lived within the world as it is. Embraced is a commitment to a religious posture that accepts and works through mundane wants and needs, and views life not through a hermeneutic of escape from the world, but rather through a hermeneutic of style whereby the movement of bodies in time and space (i.e., the world) as a matter of creative impulse and sensibilities has vital value and allows for a full range of life arrangements (e.g., being a thug) that entail the converted life. And as is the case with the traditional Christian conversion, these rap artists express the tone and texture of their religious experience to articulate the dimensions of their new life, using a specialized language.

As I have argued elsewhere, in all cases, one might think of African American religion as the quest for complex subjectivity, the urge toward a fuller sense of one's meaning and importance within the context of community.[25] This theory of religion assumes that religiosity

25. See Pinn, *Terror and Triumph*, chapters 7–8.

involves in part a response to dehumanizing forces (e.g., racism, race-based discrimination) faced by African Americans across centuries of life in the Unites States. While this chapter is not the place for a full explication of this theory, allow me to suggest again that such an understanding of religion should entail recognition of religious conversion and life as marked by this inner urge toward full meaning framed by a triadic structure: (1) confrontation by historical identity noted through existential pain; (2) wrestling with old consciousness; and (3) embracing new consciousness and new modes of behavior affecting relationships with community. At stake through conversion is a marked shift in orientation—a matter of difference. This, however, does not assume a certain moral arrangement of difference—just an altered perspective, new insight into the arrangements of life involving simple resistance to irrelevance, or ontological and existential destruction. My inclination, as a constructive theologian, is to assume such a stance; yet, certain forms of popular culture (in this instance rap music) challenge such an assured perspective.[26] Of further note, however, I am not suggesting accountability be discarded. Hence, rap artists remain, even within a discussion of this type, accountable for the more troubling dimensions of their artistic production. Such attention to misogyny, unabated materialism, and so on remain problematic, but the presence of such problematic attitudes and behaviors do not offer final judgment, the last best criteria, for assessing the nature and meaning of conversion in that conversion involves a change in posture that may not be fully realized in terms of output.

I have noted this elsewhere, and the importance of this modification is made more manifest through a theo-religious exploration of rap music, even though my interests in certain modalities of liberation lurk in the shadows: "This elemental feeling and new consciousness can be interpreted and acted on in a variety of ways, some less

26. Pinn, *Terror and Triumph*, 159.

progressive than others. In all cases, converts in community understand themselves to be working toward liberation, but the outcomes of this effort do not always manifest this attitude."[27] Yes, I would continue to hold that conversion as religious experience involves a push against reified meanings and dwarfed life meaning—the outcome of this push is not so easily judged. What it means to have a proper sense of self, of one's "fullness," is not reified through talk of conversion, but remains open to debate and framed by the particular existential-cultural context of the convert and the community of converts. This communal dimension is vital, yet it does not suggest a certain ethical stance in that conservative African American Christians constitute such a community pushing for more life meaning, as do the "thugs" Tupac speaks for, or the "homies" of vital importance to Snoop Dogg and marked by constitutive aesthetics, practices, and beliefs. As Snoop Dogg notes, "The truth I tell comes from the streets, where every day is a matter of life and death, where what matters is family loyalty and honor in the 'hood and a code of survival that can't be betrayed."[28]

Subverting the process of dehumanization, the convert seeks new arrangements that might involve simple signification of their circumstances without producing a radical shift. Yet, they are religious conversions in that they speak to a more substantive yearning for more

---

27. Pinn, *Terror and Triumph*, 175–76.

28. Snoop Dogg, *The Doggfather*, 5. Studies related to the attitude of fans to rap vary to some degree. However, some studies suggest that Snoop Dogg's desired outcome is realized to some extent. See, for example, Rachel E. Sullivan, "Rap and Race: It's Got a Nice Beat, but What about the Message?," *Journal of Black Studies* 33, no. 5 (May 2003): 605–22. Sullivan notes, "Not only are rap music and hip-hop culture a potential form of resistance, they may also have broad-reaching implications for identity development and maintenance. Although many may see music as a passing phase, it is often a source of information about one's group (or other groups), and it can also be a (re)affirmation of one's identity." (616)

life meaning that does not simply rest in the workings of political-economic frameworks. Such considerations, based on the nature of dehumanization in the United States, must play a role—but they are placed in context, within the framework of a more expansive quest. As Jeffrey O. G. Ogbar remarks, "Many rap songs grapple with issues of contention in society, imploring listeners to assume higher levels of moral and spiritual consciousness, as well as social responsibility."[29] Again turning to Snoop Dogg:

> I paid the price to get myself free, from drugs and violence, from incarceration and intoxication, and from fear and death of every description. I paid the price so that maybe you don't have to, so that maybe when you read this book you can take a lesson from me, avoid my mistakes, and share my success. Like I said, I'm about elevating and educating. What I can teach comes straight out of my life. What you can learn goes straight into yours. We're here to help each other. God taught me that.[30]

One might raise questions concerning issues of authenticity and the significance of selective memory that plague personal narrative and our ability to access such stories. For example, Snoop Dogg speaks of inner-city realities as the paradigmatic structure for his work and life, but his lived context as a wealthy artist involves existential arrangements only impacted by such gritty realities to the extent he chooses. Yet, I am not convinced we, when speaking in terms of religious experience vis-à-vis conversion, can provide nonshifting and grounded responses. It is at this point the pragmatic alternative is useful: religious

---

29. Jeffrey O. G. Ogbar, "Slouching toward Bork: The Culture Wars and Self-Criticism in Hip-Hop Music," *Journal of Black Studies* 33, no. 2 (November 1999): 167.

30. Snoop Dogg, *The Doggfather*, 3–4.

conversion and experience has merit as such at least in part to the extent the convert understands it as such.

Whether or not it is admired, suggested in the autobiographical reflections of Snoop Dogg is a particular way of life. In this regard religious conversion and consequent life involve a certain mode of performance, a certain and articulated posture toward the world acted out upon the cartography of physical existence. Tupac Shakur and Snoop Dogg, to a lesser degree, critique and jettison notions of religious conversion that require adherence to staid moralism through an embrace of doctrine with, at best, minor questioning and correction. In this way, religious conversion exposes the thick and often troubling dimensions of life without simple consolation and comfort. This is a posture foreign to many, and deeply troubling to most. But, those in the rap world for whom it is their posture might respond by signifying a popular scriptural reference: the ways of God are foolishness to humans. Or, drawing directly from Scripture, "For it is written, I will destroy the wisdom of the wise, and will bring to nothing the understanding of the prudent." Such a perspective, however, does not amount to moral relativism in a strict sense, in that religious conversion for Tupac and Snoop includes an awareness of the dilemmas and dangers of their undertakings.[31] In other words, although I am not convinced that gangsta rappers such as Tupac and Snoop offer only a modality of nihilism writ as good, De Genova raises an interesting point: "Gangster rap can be found to transcend the mere reflection

---

31. The scripture reference is to 1 Corinthians 1:18, and the quotation is 1 Corinthians 1:19 (KJV).

On this point, Nick De Genova provides a useful reworking of nihilism within the context of rap music that, using Richard Wright, pushes for a utility and productive dimension of this posture toward the world: "Gangster Rap and Nihilism in Black America: Some Questions of Life and Death," *Social Text* 43 (Autumn 1995): 89–132.

of urban mayhem and enter into musical debate with these realities, without sinking into didacticism or flattening their complexity."[32]

While somewhat formulaic, this structure does not stipulate ethical and moral arrangement in a fixed fashion. Rather, it suggests an altered perspective, a new posture toward the world that can involve a variety of possibilities—including more traditional Christian models as well as the less "orthodox" processes hinted at by certain rappers. Such an array of possibilities is assumed within my earlier work, but here such assumptions are pushed to the fore and made vibrant through the framers of cultural production. For Tupac Shakur and Snoop Dogg this push for greater life meaning does not necessitate an awkward turn from the world, as is the case in many traditional African American Christian circles. Rather, it involves an embrace of the world, and thereby a signifying of dehumanization through an embrace of the very things despised. This move resembles, I believe, what cultural critic Albert Murray means by "ritualistic counterstatement." That is to say, like the blues—a forbearer of rap—rap music as represented by figures such as Tupac Shakur and Snoop Dogg involves not so much commiseration, but rather affirmation. In Murray's words: "You discover that it [the blues] is a music of affirmation; it is not a music of commiseration. It's out of that affirmation that you get all of that elegance. . . . That kind of musical statement is a basic existential affirmation. And the musicians counterstate their problems; they counterstate the depression, despair, despondency, melancholia, and so forth. Blues music is a ritualistic counterstatement."[33]

When critically examined for their take on religion and experience in the form of religious conversion and religious life, rap artists force theoretical complexity and methodological comfort with tension.

32. De Genova, "Gangster Rap and Nihilism in Black America," 114.

33. Albert Murray, *From the Briar Patch File: On Context, Procedure, and American Identity* (New York: Pantheon Books, 2001), 194–95.

These rappers express this desire for a fuller sense of meaning through the felt reality of their bodies, as they take up time and space, as they force their recognition. It is through this forced recognition—involving a certain hold on the world—that they express the renewal of self that marks religious life. This involves the religious nature of existence. Traditional Christian conversion and religious life, as noted in the first part of this chapter, oft involves a dualism of vision—the gaze backward toward a spiritual legacy connecting the convert to God through Christ, and so on, and a gaze toward the future in which the kingdom of God is proven. For rappers like Tupac Shakur or Snoop Dogg, the primary preoccupation is with the salvific nature of the present when properly understood and embraced. In part this involves a shift in religious aesthetics in that the look and workings of the body—from clothing to tattoos, and so forth—are recognized as vibrant, beautiful, and a mark of wholeness.

Furthermore, popular culture, in this case rap music, as a terrain for the articulation of religious struggle and conversion, forces a re-examination of the assumed cartography of religious engagement. It makes easier theological recognition of the historical nature of religion and the manner in which religious conversion and life are worked out not within nontroubled space, but rather within the midst of absurdity and angst. What is more, to encourage challenge to staid notions of the locus of religious conversion and the shape of religious life, such attention to rap music also troubles all-too-easy depiction of the form of cultural production as degenerate and of no serious concern. In the language of rap, those bound to such reified notions of both religious experience and rap music "betta recognize. . . ."

7 | THEOLOGY, POPULAR CULTURE, AND RELIGION

The previous chapter used Hip Hop's lyrical content as a way to raise questions concerning particular elements of traditional theological formulations of experience related to radical transformation, or what some might reference as conversion. This chapter raises more fundamental questions through an effort to correct for what I consider the troubled relationship to popular culture (i.e., signs, symbols, behaviors, postures, and frameworks recognized by and used to express meaning and place in expansive contexts and communal arrangements) that over the years shaped black religious studies in general, and black theological discourse in particular.

The discussion in this chapter was sparked in part by (and is part of a larger project meant to explore) my growing interest in dialogical models of engagement and the exploration of similarities and difference between peoples who represent geographies of and engagements with the *anti*-ness forged during the slave trade and the growth of empire. How do we communicate across these cultural lines? And more to the point, what might popular culture offer our understanding of religion and its function across these cultural lines? And so, while music might function differently for various groups, music matters—and this chapter adopts a posture that recognizes the theoretical and material importance of popular culture, of which music is a huge component.

Unlike the previous chapters, however, what follows represents one of my efforts to approach the importance of music not in terms of direct appeal to lyrics, but rather to understanding music (as a significant element of popular culture) as offering a particular hermeneutical possibility—a posture toward exploration of signs and symbols, experiences and patterns of thought. It affords a particular take that raises questions and offers alternate ways of seeing and naming our embodied movement in (and against) our social world. One gets a hint of this in the previous chapter with the ways in which, for example, music in general and Hip Hop in particular encourage a different means by which to name our encounter with the world so as to bring into question theological assumptions concerning conversion. Or, how, in earlier chapters where music offers a more relational interpretation of masculinity and a more "earthy" and critical discussion of US cultural assumptions about death. Here this hermeneutic is implied as a way to rethink what one might actually learn about religion through engagement with popular culture.

The corrective proposed involves a change in conceptual posture revolving around the significance of religious "cartography" as a plausible theoretical framing of the study of religion. In addition, I will also give some attention to thinking through this proposed reframing in light of dialogical possibilities between African American and Latino/a scholars of religion. As context for this constructive work, I begin with a few descriptive thoughts on the purposes of African American cultural production.

THE CHANGING PURPOSE OF POPULAR CULTURE

Classic works by African Americans during the early formation of the United States are marked by an effort to address existential and ontological discomfort through apologetics in the form of expressive culture. One might explain in this manner the eighteenth-century sermonic-like prose of Jupiter Hammon, an early literary figure seeking to understand the presence of Africans in North America, but in ways that did little damage to the religio-political and white supremacist paradigm used to structure the new nation.[1] Cultural production in this case sought to make sense of a rather absurd situation through the tools available. This eighteenth-century literary apologetic, a verbal alchemy, usually discounted (or, at the very least did not adequately recognize) the significance of black bodies and the rights of those bodies to occupy with comfort and freedom this space called the United States. Poetry and prose framed a process of alchemy to transform into a meaningful existence by creative manipulation the terror and dread that marked the realities of the death and rebirth of life as chattel. African Americans made use of their historical memory and the culturally derived materials available in order to do this work. An apologetic, yet one more self-assured and assertive, is present also in the nineteenth-century autobiographical writings of Frederick Douglass. Such is also the case with the visual arts during the late nineteenth century as provided by artists like Henry O. Tanner, whose "Banjo Lesson" (1893), for instance, portrays the humanity of African Americans to an American audience that held suspect such a possibility.

Following the tracks of the "Great Migration" and other historic developments after the socioeconomic and political reckoning called the Civil War and Reconstruction, the psychosocial posture of African Americans changed radically, particularly after the first decade or so of the twentieth century. That is to say, the emergence of the twentieth century was marked by a change in perspective—a movement

1. Jupiter Hammon (1711–1806): in Stanley Austin Ransom Jr., ed., *America's First Negro Poet: The Complete Works of Jupiter Hammon of Long Island* (Port Washington, NY: Kennikat Press, 1970).

of both bodies and ideas—expressed in significant ways through the growingly unapologetic language of cultural production.

While expression of cultural sensibilities has always served as an outlet for African American reflection on pressing existential questions and dilemmas, the twentieth century involved a shift in this work based on a new ontology—what Alain Locke noted as the emergence of the "New Negro." Locke traced the rise of this new consciousness, this new personhood, via the cultural self-expression dotting the landscape of African American communities. This "New Negro," representing more than simply a cosmetic makeover, marked a changed relationship between African Americans and themselves, and African Americans and the larger population of the United States. "The migrant masses, shifting from countryside to city, hurdle several generations of experience at a leap," wrote Locke in *The New Negro*, "but more important, the same thing happens spiritually in the life-attitudes and self-expression of the Young Negro, in his poetry, his art."[2] There is something to be said for the paradigm shift noted with such brilliance by Locke: it represented a new cultural period and, like a Category 5 hurricane, it cut an impressive if not systematic path through the landscape, forever changing what could and would grow on the exposed cultural soil.

LOCKE'S RENAISSANCE: THE TEXTURE OF CULTURAL EPISTEMOLOGY

What Locke speaks to is a change in the nature of cultural production within African American communities, marked in substantial ways by a move from apologetics, say, in literature to realism—an appeal to the full range of emotions, thoughts, and activities framing

2. Alain Locke, "The New Negro," in *The New Negro*, ed. Alain Locke (New York: Atheneum, 1986), 4–5.

African American life. For the purpose of this chapter, of paramount concern is the manner in which this cultural creativity informed and was informed by the religious sensibilities, the religiosity of African Americans. Locke gave attention to the manner in which African American cultural production spoke to an alternate, defiant, and proud shaping of the geography of American life in spiritual terms. That is to say, "gradually too," according to Locke, "under some spiritualizing reaction, the brands and wounds of social persecution are becoming the proud stigmata of spiritual immunity and moral victory." African Americans, as of the early twentieth century, Locke continues, are "at last spiritually free, and offer through art an emancipating vision to America."[3]

Harlem, for Locke, was during the early twentieth century a "prophetic" place, a special geography, marking cultural energy and creativity from the African diaspora. It is in New York, Locke reflects, that African Americans have built "fuller, truer self-expression" beyond the confines of the racial status quo. Yet, this has not simply involved the reconstituting of individual self-recognition and understanding on the part of African Americans *for* African Americans. Rather, this renaissance—the period of this profound artistic growth—marking the intellectual terrain of African American communities, involved the "enrichment of American art and letters and in the clarifying of our common vision of the social tasks ahead."[4] It called forth a re-envisioning of American life, one that recognized without flinching and as a matter of psychocultural realism the full-range of life activities, of group promise and foibles.

There developed during the early twentieth century an alternate aesthetic by which African Americans understood the maturation of their sociopolitical, economic, and cultural selves as a project

3. Locke, "Foreword," in Locke, *The New Negro*, 53.

4. Locke, "The New Negro," 10.

of "wholeness" and beauty. It exposes beauty embedded in "raw" life episodes rehearsed, celebrated, and at times lamented. And the dimensions of this aesthetic were presented in the various layers and levels of African American cultural production. Thereby African Americans began a transformation with deep ontological and existential consequences, one that marked a revised sense of self and self in relationship to community and world.

No wonder Locke comments near the end of his foreword to *The New Negro* that "negro life is not only establishing new contacts and founding new centers, it is finding a new soul. There is a fresh spiritual and cultural focusing. We have, as the heralding sign, an unusual outburst of creative expression."[5] And those coming of age during the period of which Locke speaks are credited with ushering in a new ontology and a radicalized reworking of existential themes and categories; full "with arresting visions and vibrant prophecies; forecasting in the mirror of art what we must see and recognize in the streets of reality tomorrow, foretelling in new notes and accents the maturing speech of full racial utterance."[6] The shattering of old notions of African American life undertaken through these cultural developments spoke in graphic terms to the depth of the yearnings within African Americans for a fuller sense of meaning and "space." And, this shattering and reconstitution of life is based on a deep feeling for and expression of the world as encountered by African Americans *and* as recounted for the benefit of African Americans.

THEOLOGICAL IMAGINATION AND POPULAR CULTURE

Scholars of African American literature and history, for instance, have mined African American cultural production, and particularly

5. Locke, "Foreword," xvii.

6. Locke, "Foreword," 47.

the developments stemming from the two waves of the "Harlem" renaissance and the cultural geography of New York City. And, the significance of cultural production for an understanding of the religious yearnings and experiences of African Americans has not been lost on theologians and other scholars of African American religion. One finds particularly intriguing examples of this recognition within theological discourse, beginning in the late 1960s, known as black theology of liberation. In fact, this modality of theological discourse lists as a primary resource for the doing of theology the culture and cultural production of African Americans. In an effort to move beyond European theological models, as well as an effort to deconstruct American theology's relationship to the status quo, African Americans began asserting theological independence and seeking alternate modes of construction. Such a move involved a process of introspection—a searching through the "stuff" of African American life.[7]

James Cone penned *The Spirituals and the Blues* after joining the Union Theological Seminary (New York City) faculty during the early 1970s. Within this text, his third major publication, Cone responded to critics who argued his first two books failed to specify a theological framework that was deeply connected to and grown out of the intimate details of the African American experience. That is to say, critics lamented the lack in those books of a deeply recognized

7. The genealogy of black theology has been rehearsed in various publications and there is no reason to present that material again here. Readers interested in that information should see Anthony B. Pinn, "Black Theology in Historical Perspective: Articulating the Quest for Subjectivity," in *The Ties That Bind: African American and Hispanic American/Latino/a Theologies in Dialogue*, ed. Anthony B. Pinn and Benjamin Valentin (New York: Continuum, 2001), 23–35; James H. Cone and Gayraud Wilmore, *Black Theology: A Documentary History*, vols. 1–2 (Maryknoll, NY: Orbis Books, 1993); Dwight Hopkins, *Introducing Black Theology of Liberation* (Maryknoll, NY: Orbis Books, 1999).

"blackness"—cultural and otherwise—as the organizing principle of theological discourse. According to his brother, Cecil Cone, James Cone's theological formulations were much more indebted to the neo-orthodoxy of Karl Barth than to the theological formulations found implicitly and explicitly in African American religious culture. For Cecil Cone, black theology during its early phase carried the imprint of European cultural and religio-theological sensibilities deep in its organizational matrix, in its "soul." Hence, a question: What is "black" in/about black theology?

The apparent theoretical and methodological genealogy of black theology, the critique went, made the religious sensibilities and outlook of white Westerners the lens through which the world was viewed. Consequently, white supremacy in the realm of religious reflection was reinforced. This move, from the perspective of critics, was odd considering James Cone's broad appeal to African American culture as a major source for the doing of black theology. For Cone black culture is "the creative forms of expression as one reflects on history, endures pain, and experiences joy. It is the black community expressing itself in music, poetry, prose, and other art forms." And, he continues, in order to be organic to the black community, black theology had to take seriously black cultural production because "black culture . . . is God's way of acting in America, God's participation in black liberation."[8]

With the critique made and its legitimacy recognized, Cone attempted to reverse this theological trend by turning attention to musical production—the spirituals and the blues, seeking to mine from them the theological insights and liberation agenda of the African American community prior to the development of formal modalities of theological inquiry (e.g., churches). It, according to Cone, was

8. James H. Cone, *A Black Theology of Liberation*, 2nd ed. (Maryknoll, NY: Orbis Books, 1986), 27–28.

through these musical forms that African Americans expressed their theological and religious sensibilities and presented an alternate ontology and epistemology. While Cone gave little attention to the visual arts for their theological insights, music and literature of various kinds served to enliven Cone's presentation of a black theological epistemology. Moving from the spirituals and the blues as modalities of theological discourse, Cone gives attention to literary genres such as the slave narratives, autobiographies, folk wisdom, and other "texts" outlining African Americans' relationship to world and the divine. Yet, there are ways in which Cone's attention to music offers insight into a particular posture toward the study of religion—a particular interpretive device for exploring and assessing. I believe it is safe to say, attention to culture as a hermeneutical device, a theological tool, implicitly informs the scholarship of those working within the tradition Cone establishes.

James Evans, for instance, has given considerable attention to the theo-religious qualities and pronouncements of African American literature.[9] More recently, Evans's work has branched out to include issues of theoretical framework and methodological sensibilities informing black theology. Furthermore, Cone's student Dwight Hopkins, at times to the exclusion of other vibrant source materials, has given consistent attention to an explication of the cultural sources (e.g., slave narratives) for black theology.[10] Like Cone, Hopkins

9. See for example James Evans Jr., *Spiritual Empowerment in African American Literature* (Lewiston, NY: Edwin Mellen Press, 1988).

10. James Evans Jr., *We Have Been Believers: An African American Systematic Theology* (Minneapolis: Fortress Press, 1992); Dwight Hopkins and George Cummings, eds., *Cut Loose Your Stammering Tongue: Black Theology in the Slave Narratives*, 2nd ed. (Louisville, KY: Westminster John Knox, 2003); Dwight Hopkins, *Shoes That Fit Our Feet: Sources for a Constructive Black Theology* (Maryknoll, NY: Orbis Books, 1993); Dwight Hopkins, *Down, Up, and Over: Slave Religion and Black Theology* (Minneapolis: Fortress Press, 1999); Dwight Hopkins, *Being Human: Race, Culture, and Religion* (Minneapolis: Fortress Press, 2005).

argues the basic dimensions and characteristics of black theology as a formal enterprise are found in the nascent theological discourse of African Americans housed in their popular expressions and modalities of engagement. Hence, according to Hopkins, contemporary black theology in part must concern itself with mining early sources and thereby building a theological discourse that mirrors and is consistent with the development of the African American community. In this way, Hopkins seeks to promote the doing of theology as a community-committed and community-responsive—a reflexive—enterprise.

At times, Hopkins's work implies a connection between African American cultural production and theological discourse so intimate and strong that no real distinction need be made: cultural production *is* theological discourse. Literature and other forms of the arts become simple carriers of a particular cosmic message. I believe this link is made, for example, because of slippage between popular culture and popular religion found in some of his work. That is one way to interpret the following statement by Hopkins: "If religion suggests a sacred, comprehensive, and integrated style of being for all reality and culture suggests the site of popular religious dimensions of black experiences, then black theology claims its God-talk and God-walk from the popular religion of the folk's total way of life."[11]

On one level the above approach runs the risk of doing precisely what Cone warns against: an equating of human words and wants with divine will, or in the language of Karl Barth, a neglecting of the infinite and qualitative distinction between God and humans.[12] On another level, it seeks to limit to one dimension (i.e., the institutionally and doctrinally recognizable as "religious") the range of African

11. Dwight Hopkins, "Black Theology on God: The Divine in Black Popular Religion." This essay is in the "Theologizing with What's Popular: Theology and Popular Culture" section of Pinn and Valentin, *The Ties that Bind*, 99.

12. Cone, *Black Theology of Liberation*, 27–28.

American creative responses to existential conditions and metaphysical questions. Based on certain religious assumptions held by black theologians of liberation, this is most commonly articulated in terms of the Christian religiosity celebrated in popular culture. At the very least, it is a (mono)theistic read that privileges notions of a loving and liberative divinity. This issue is depicted in Riggins Earl's reading of folk wisdom accounts of "Br'er Rabbit" in which he sees nascent forms of contemporary liberation paradigms. Regarding "Br'er Rabbit's Hankering for a Long Tail," for instance, Earl interprets the story as possessing a clear moral: "God in the primal act of Creation had given the oppressed the necessary intelligence for its own preservation."[13] However, lines such as the following might suggest an alternate read, one that is more concerned with a type of religious naturalism than with traditional notions of a transcendent divinity. In what follows, Br'er Rabbit has completed all the tasks required by God in order to secure the long tail he desires. But rather than an exercise of divine power resulting in the growth of the desired appendage, he is first ignored by God, then almost struck by lightning, and finally he receives this word: "You are so smart get your own long tail."[14] The actual story, as summarized here, suggests other alternative readings, ones that do not privilege a positive take on theism. While Earl paints this as a story of the resources for survival God provides and God's great wisdom in denying certain forms of assistance in order to foster human growth, the story also allows for religious naturalism as the proper read. Attention to this story is not meant as an apology for a particular read of Br'er Rabbit as religious devotion. Rather it is

13. Riggins Earl, *Dark Symbols, Obscure Signs: God, Self, and Community in the Slave Mind* (Maryknoll, NY: Orbis Books, 1993), 154.

14. Earl, *Dark Symbols, Obscure Signs*, 154; citing Abraham D. Rogers, *African Folktales: Selected and Retold by Abraham Rogers* (New York: Pantheon Books, 1983), 55.

meant to point to the potential of multiple readings of popular culture, while black theological discourse tends toward a rather myopic approach to the religious meanings of cultural production.

Studying popular culture as a theological exercise can become a way of simply establishing signposts for certain understandings of the human/divine encounter. Study of popular culture is appreciated, in such instances, to the extent it serves traditional theological reflection and religious sensibilities. This, however, can easily result in a distortion of popular culture's depth and competing robust intentions and meanings. Often when this type of read cannot be easily accomplished, popular culture is relegated to the background of theological discourse. This, for instance, accounts for the general disregard for rap music by most within black religious studies: it can be difficult to wrap the conservative (e.g., those thinking about religion in strict institutional terms) religious mind around the bald and raw depictions of life found in the music and lyrics of figures such as "The Game." In such instances when the rapper asks the epistemologically driven question—put simply "Ya heard?"—the black scholar of religion might respond "No, thank God!" This is problematic in that the scholar believes her- or himself to have opened academic exploration to the realities of popular culture, but this is done without allowing popular culture to actually penetrate and inform the academic's work.

Black male theologians are not the only scholars to engage popular culture in various ways with varying degrees of success. Unlike black (male) theology, Womanist theology is premised on a direct appeal to popular culture for its theoretical and methodological foundation. In fact, Womanist scholarship argues that black women have been excluded from the more traditional modes of power, and that they have voiced their theo-religious sensibilities through creative outlets. Cultural production for Womanists, as their name would suggest, draws its epistemological sensibilities and posture from the popular writings of Alice Walker, particularly *In Search of Our Mothers' Gardens*, where she defines and applies "Womanist" as a style of life and as a hermeneutical device for dissecting the experiences of black women in the United States:

1. From *womanish* (opp. Of "girlish," i.e., frivolous, irresponsible, not serious). A black feminist of color. From the black folk expression of mother to female children, "you acting womanish," i.e., like a woman. Usually referring to outrageous, audacious, courageous or *willful* behavior. Wanting to know more and in greater depth than is considered "good" for one. Interested in grown-up doings. Acting grown up. Being grown up. Interchangeable with another black folk expression: You trying to be grown: Responsible. In charge. *Serious.*
2. Also: A woman who loves other women, sexually and/or nonsexually. Appreciates and prefers women's culture, women's emotional flexibility (values tears as natural counterbalance of laughter), and women's strength. Sometimes loves individual men, sexually and/or nonsexually. Committed revival and wholeness of entire people, male and female. Not a separatist, except periodically, for health. Traditionally universalist, as in "Mama, why are we brown, pink, and yellow, and our cousins are white, beige, and black?"

   ans.: "Well, you know the colored race is just like a flower garden, with every color flower represented." Traditionally capable, as in "Mama, I'm walking to Canada and I'm taking you and a bunch of other slaves with me." Reply: "It wouldn't be the first time."[15]

Based on this early association of Womanist scholars in religious studies to African American literature, it was a natural move to highlight

15. Alice Walker, *In Search of Our Mothers Gardens* (New York: Harbrace Jachovanich, 1982).

for investigating the fiction (and to a lesser extent the nonfiction) writings of black women as a way of framing theological studies. Using these materials has been important from their perspective because such texts house the voices of black women, indicating "the operations of the ordinary theologies of black women's daily lives as rich sources for theological constructions, emphasizing the importance of spiritual and communal life."[16] One sees this, for example, in the early work of pioneering figure Katie Cannon, who maps out a Womanist approach to ethics using the writings of Zora Neale Hurston. In her writings, Hurston, according to Cannon, exposed the "elaborate façade of myths, traditions, and rituals erected to couch systems of injustice in America." And, while so doing, she celebrated the creative ethic and audacious ways in which African Americans express "understanding and manifestations of courageous living."[17] For Cannon, close attention to the voices of black women expressed in short stories, and so forth, can foster the formation of religious studies as a community-responsive and liberating intellectual practice.

For Delores Williams, more so than for some other Womanists, this work does not distinguish particular cultural sources as much as make available a proper hermeneutic for exploration of all source material: "Where would I begin in order to construct Christian theology (or god-talk) from the point of view of African American women?" In responding to this question, Williams recounts the following exchange:

> I pondered this question for over a year. Then one day my professor responded to my complaint about the absence of black

16. Stephanie Y. Mitchem, *Introducing Womanist Theology* (Maryknoll, NY: Orbis Books, 2002), 72.

17. Katie G. Cannon, "Resources for a Constructive Ethic: The Life and Work of Zora Neale Hurston," in *Katie's Canon: Womanism and the Soul of the Black Community* (New York: Continuum, 1995), 89.

> women's experiences from *all* Christian theology (black liberation and feminist theologies included). He suggested that my anxiety might lessen if my exploration of African-American cultural sources was consciously informed by the statement "I am a black WOMAN." He was right. I had not realized before that I read African-American sources from a black male perspective. I assumed black women were included.[18]

Mindful of this need for a pro–black woman mode of interpretation, Williams explores the unexceptional stories of black women, such as the biblical figure Hagar, for the exceptional qualities of creativity, ingenuity, and perseverance they present to the careful reader. In this way, Williams undertakes the development of a theological discourse healthy for the African American community because it takes seriously the voices of the most often forgotten.

CARTOGRAPHY OF THE RELIGIOUS THROUGH THE POPULAR: AN ALTERNATE CONCEPTUAL POSTURE

While creative and insightful, much of Womanist scholarship, like that of their male counterparts, is insular and tends to shape popular culture to fit the religio-theological sensibilities of the scholar as opposed to allowing cultural production—popular culture—to influence in a deep sense the work of the scholar of black religion. Furthermore, it seems many Womanist scholars make use of a hermeneutic of familiarity when drawing on popular culture to inform their understanding of the history, experiences, thoughts, and voices of black women. By this I mean many Womanists siphon into comfortable existential containers the "raw" material of life presented in literature, music,

18. Delores S. Williams, *Sisters in the Wilderness: The Challenge of Womanist God-Talk* (Maryknoll, NY: Orbis Books, 1993), 1.

and so on regardless of "fit." Hence, for example, Celie, from the *Color Purple*, can provide a strong critique of the traditional Christian doctrine of God and theological anthropology without it having any visible impact on the manner in which Womanist scholarship by and large understands the nature and meaning of religious experience.[19]

Furthermore, Alice Walker's panentheism is noted, at times, without it challenging existing narrow theories of religion and religious experience popular with Womanist scholars, although Walker's thought frames Womanist methodology and theory.[20] To put it bluntly, typical theories of religion within Womanist scholarship remain deeply (and often narrowly) Christian in spite of Walker's openness (in fiction and nonfiction) to a more naturalistic conception of divinity and religion.[21] Walker and characters such as Celie recognize the plurality of ways in which the significance of the universe is expressed, but many of her interpreters do not.

---

19. See for example Alice Walker, *The Color Purple* (New York: Washington Square Press, 1982), 175–79.

20. See for example Alice Walker, "The Only Reason You Want to Go to Heaven Is That You Have Been Driven Out of Your Mind," in *Anything We Love Can Be Saved* (New York: Random House, Inc., 1997).

21. More recent Womanist voices, such as Melanie Harris, who currently teaches at Texas Christian University [now teaching at Wake Forest University Divinity School], have raised questions concerning the nature of Womanist appropriations of Alice Walker. However, as opposed to the conservative and narrow christological critique offered by Cheryl Sanders in the mid-eighties (and published as part of a roundtable discussion in *The Journal of Feminist Studies in Religion*), Harris's critique is meant to enlarge the use of Walker and the religious meaning of this appropriation. She argues for an equal use of Walker's fiction and nonfiction writings as a way of exploring and embracing Walker's sense of religious pluralism, for instance, as a way of maturing Womanist thought. This argument is made in Harris's dissertation at Union Theological Seminary (NYC) and subsequent publications.

The vague shape of this dilemma is present, it seems to me, in the "Roundtable Discussion: Christian Ethics and Theology in Womanist Perspectives" published in the *Journal of Feminist Studies in Religion*.[22] In this 1989 publication, Cheryl Sanders raised questions concerning the appropriation of Walker's Womanist concept in light of its departure from traditional (read narrow) Christian theological sensibilities. This critique represented a minority opinion to be sure, but we still await the formation of a response to Sanders that offers a deeply conceptually pluralistic sense of religious experience and a comparative theological framework. While the cultural production black women offer to the world is diverse and at times contradictory, the interpretation of this material by Womanist scholars of religion is often singular in focus and teleological in perspective.[23]

Both Womanist scholarship and black male scholarship within the arena of theology in particular and religious studies in general harbor a similar problem—notable discomfort with popular culture. It is touted as a means by which to explore and unpack the depth and texture of African American religious thought and experience. However, cultural production often is handled poorly in both theological "camps" in that the deep richness and variance it represents is not fully depicted. This being the case, popular culture as a theological tool for black male theologians and Womanist scholars does not inform in a significant way epistemology of African American theological life. It strikes me that theological work has involved in large part an attempt to explain away the messy nature of existence, to make sense of complexity and paradox. It often understands history as being teleological in nature and provides a rather "flat" depiction of the African American religious landscape.

22. *Journal of Feminist Studies in Religion* 5 (Fall 1989).

23. An exception to this posture is presented by Dianne Stewart's book, *Three Eyes for the Journey: African Dimensions of the Jamaican Religious Experience* (New York: Oxford University Press, 2005).

POPULAR CULTURE

Popular culture studied within the context of black religious studies can provide thick and textured examples of the ways in which humans make meaning. In this regard, popular culture might offer an open and public discourse on the large questions of life, even when these questions are covered in nonspectacular dress such as a Jerry Springer wrestling match, *Fear Factor* feast on something decayed, or the vexing refrain of a disco-era hit. The point is not acceptance of particular approaches to questions framing life and relationship, but rather the various and messy ways in which people seek to uncover who, what, when, and why they should prove invaluable to the scholar concerned with issues of ultimate concern and orientation. Popular culture is a public and rich terrain, the space where so many find themselves. It is a varied and complex development, one about which Paul Gilroy is correct: cultural production connects social groups and communities in a web of mutuality, harboring ontological and existential concern that merits attention.[24]

The geography of human creativity and angst takes on a different look when popular culture is given serious attention. And, some of what this geography entails via popular culture is deeply religious, and the proper business of those whose professional lives are committed to better understanding religion and religious experience. Questions naturally come to mind: What are the key issues and questions one should address in the study of religion and popular culture? And, what methodological issues need to be clarified and addressed to enable increasing sophistication in advanced research in this field? I would like to combine these questions: What are some key theoretical and methodological considerations needing attention as we push

24. Paul Gilroy, *Black Atlantic: Modernity and Double Consciousness* (New York: Oxford University Press, 1995).

forward the study of black religion and popular culture? With respect to this question, I would like to offer a particular mode of framing black theological studies of popular culture by way of a metaphor. I do so because I believe a significant hindrance to such work involves the problematic nature of our theological vocabulary and grammar.

Traditional elements of black and Womanist theological vocabularies do not necessarily nor adequately address the messiness of popular culture without doing damage to it. This is certainly the case with discussions of theodicy. Furthermore, does soteriology really capture what 50 Cent might mean by "get rich or die trying"? Oh, hell no! Or, does theological anthropology as often formulated adequately address the nature of self and self-consciousness sloppily noted in shows like *The Bernie Mack Show* or *Run's House*? I doubt it. Furthermore, does our theological discourse that privileges the written word have the flexibility and creativity necessary to properly handle "nonwritten" texts?

Popular culture, say, in the form of visual arts, holds in tension material existence and nonmaterial impulses, and it brings to the mind of the viewer the presence of this nonmaterial impulse in ways that influence relationships with historical realities and materials. Like the paintings of Jean-Michel Basquiat, it has the ability to affect us by drawing into the open concealed realities, possibilities, and meanings, thereby teaching us about connections between historical developments and inner urges. Perhaps, in the area of theological and religious studies, what is necessary is a rethinking of our grammar and vocabulary in ways that allow our work to be deeply influenced by the public sensibilities of popular culture. Mindful of this challenge, I favor a multidisciplinary approach whereby the various layers, textures, and tones of popular culture are unpacked.

I suggest an alternate posture concerning this enterprise—one that involves viewing such work as a type of religious cartography. There has been spotty use of this term in some black and Womanist theologies; yet, it is typically meant to resemble a teleological depiction of black life—a charting of God's popping up in human affairs.[25] By way of a working definition, however, I mean by cartography a less Christian-specific presentation of material—an arranging and fixing in time and space of the contours and routes of meaning making. It connotes by way of relationships between various elements the parameters and shape of reality. By so doing, cartography frames our sense of ontology as well as our awareness of and response to existential situations. This metaphor of cartography might also suggest a mode of analysis, one that is comfortable with the tensions, paradoxes, inconsistencies, and often nonwritten nature of popular culture in that it allows for a visual description of the religiously centered concerns, questions, and so forth, that mark popular culture.

Novelist Peter Turchi is correct: there are ways in which the writer can be understood as a cartographer. For the "writer" involved in religious studies, this might involve using signs and symbols, words and rituals to express by charting the nature and meaning of the religious sensibilities and activities of various communities. This is a rather loose use of terminology, involving some linguistic slippage that professionals in cartography might find troubling, but I think it is a potentially important application. Religious and theological studies as cartography (combined with what I noted a few years ago concerning theology as archaeology[26]) is a vital shift in symbolism and metaphor in that the process of mapping is sensitive to the more straightforward dimensions of religious experience (such as location of rituals and doctrine). Furthermore, it hints at a corrective for the inadequacies of

---

25. See, for instance, Dwight Hopkins's passing reference to cartography in "Black Theology on God: The Divine in Popular Religion," in Pinn and Valentin, *The Ties That Bind*, 109, 110.

26. Peter Turchi, *Maps of the Imagination: The Writer as Cartographer* (San Antonio, TX: Trinity University Press, 2004); Anthony B. Pinn, *Varieties of African American Religious Experience* (Minneapolis: Fortress Press, 1998), chapter 5.

our language for capturing what I have described as the significance of religion in a more general quest for complex subjectivity—the elemental nature of religion not completely known through physical structures, rituals, doctrine. In this sense, theological and religious studies as cartography mark the known, as well as being sensitive to what is beyond our ability to fully comprehend.

PLOTTING OUT THE RELIGIOUS AND THE POPULAR

There are "blank" spots on our metaphorical map playing a role in pointing out patterns of life, arrangement of relationships. These spots correspond to activities for transformation operating outside the status quo, outside the normative structures of society; and, these developments are precisely those with which liberationists are concerned. Expressing this concern, as a liberation theologian, involves mapping the efforts on the part of the oppressed that resonate with what Rolland Paulston notes as a turn in his own work as a cartographer to a focus on "current efforts by individuals and cultural groups seeking to be more self-defining in their sociospatial relations and how they are represented."[27] Such a mapping, I believe, allows for a vital tension, an important two-way focus on both the center and periphery of meaning-making efforts—recognizing the situational nature of religious developments manifest in this case through popular culture.[28] Yet, it does so in a way that sees the significance of both the content and form of this meaning making, without trying to

27. Rolland G. Paulston, "Preface: Four Principles for a Non-innocent Social Cartography," in *Social Cartography: Mapping Ways of Seeing Social and Educational Change*, ed. Rolland G. Paulston (New York: Garland Publishing, Inc., 1996), xviii.

28. Jonathan Z. Smith, *Map Is Not Territory: Studies in the History of Religions* (Chicago: University of Chicago Press, 1993), 101.

flatten out, for the sake of consistency and uniformity, the rough terrain that is religiosity in popular culture. In this case, popular culture serves as the material for this new mapping, this detailed cartography of religion and religious life.

Signs and symbols, words and rituals, are used to chart the nature and meaning of the religious sensibilities and activities of various communities. For the scholar concerned with issues of transformation or liberation, one with a sense of the historical development of terror, this might involve mapping the tone and texture of meaning making, or sketching the geography of what Charles Long labels the crawl back through history toward the first creation of the self.[29] Such a thick analysis allows for perspective, for a framing of life in the context of our portion of the world that notes the pleasures and tensions premised on the logic of construction resulting in what we know and feel as "black" and "brown" bodies. Yet, it does so in a way that sees the significance of both the content and form of this meaning making. It involves a thick, complex, and dialogical process of recognition.

This cartography is shaped or influenced in some ways by forces that transcend the individual. Even for the ethical humanist, such a mapping premised on the rightness of naturalistic sensibilities is informed by the push and pull of the unseen, but in this case such a reality is framed by the large sense of community of which the individual is a part, but whose logic supersedes his or her own reasoning. Whereas the theist might note the need for faith as the proper posture toward this grand otherness, the humanist or religious naturalist might push for imagination, or more importantly, a sense of fantasy as providing needed flexibility when approaching the contours of our strange world. I find Peter Turchi's words a suitable framing of this process for the cartographer of religion. "It seems," he writes, "that no matter how many discoveries we make, we tell ourselves we've

29. See Charles Long, *Significations* (Philadelphia: Fortress Press, 1986).

reached the end of the knowable world. Maybe some of us are always inclined to claim we've done all we can do, while others of us refuse to rest; or maybe it's that one day we're defiant, the next we're humbled, awed by the scope of the mysteries around us."[30]

What is of fundamental significance is the manner by which exposing or rendering radically visible social boundaries through mapping allows for a questioning of their necessity, their permanence. Boundaries are chosen. What we have is recognition of the various fields of power as well as their logic. Mindfulness of this representation of sameness and difference—the ability to present comparative and complex arrangements of "realities," contested sites of knowledge and meaning, as well as competing conceptions of socioeconomic want and need—may in fact be the deep value of the cartography metaphor.[31]

THE CHALLENGE OF MAPPING TWOS

In a somewhat horrifying way, mapping with respect to the Americas is stamped on the bodies of African Americans and Latinos/as, providing the manner in which these bodies are read and regarded. Such a plotting provides an alternate, nonspoken vocabulary and grammar for the articulation of certain formations of the real, the visible, and by extension the invisible. Yet there is a tension in that these bodies have never been content with the traditional mapping, the mapping of conquest through the logic of (re)construction. Rather, they, by their very existence, propose other mappings, at times conflicting formulations, other possible directions and routes for meaning making. That is to say, the presence of African Americans and Latinos/as serves as an example of the truth of any mapping—there

30. Turchi, *Maps of the Imagination*, 225.

31. Paulston, "Four Principles for a Non-innocent Social Cartography."

are alternate possibilities and the authority of one over others is contested and must be fought for continuously.

Mindful of the above, this work is first an exercise in negative cartography—that is recognition of the limits or "lies," to borrow from Mark Monmonier, that shape the process of re-presenting reality. Or in more explicit terms, "a good map," writes Monmonier, "tells a multitude of white lies; it suppresses truth to help the user see what needs to be seen. Reality is three-dimensional, rich in detail, and far too factual to allow a complete yet uncluttered two-dimensional graphic scale model. Indeed, a map that did not generalize would be useless. But the value of a map depends on how well its generalized geometry and generalized content reflect a chosen aspect of reality."[32] In applying cartography as metaphor, Peter Turchi makes a similar remark: "How we see depends, in part, on what we want to see. . . . Every map intends not simply to serve us but to influence us."[33] While Monmonier and Turchi note the presence of "deliberate falsification or subtle propaganda in map making," I want to highlight and problematize the presence of these distortions. In short, I value a heightened skepticism concerning map making. Based in part on my appreciation for Paul Gilroy's reframing of modernity through the black Atlantic as heuristic device, I want to hold in tension, to see as the source of the problem, Monmonier's understanding of certain lies as required and his rendering of value based on how well the "lie" addresses a "chosen aspect of reality." And, I want to think this through in terms of the realities and theological mission of African Americans and Latinos/as.

Perhaps some shortcomings in mapping are unavoidable in order to adjust for scale, loss of dimension, and so on, but the general idea of deception has sociopolitical connotations, a historical context (Why

32. Mark Monmonier, *How to Lie with Maps* (Chicago: University of Chicago Press, 1991), 25.

33. Turchi, *Maps of the Imagination*, 78 and 88.

are certain dimensions of reality distorted; and what guides this process?), that give it weight and charge. This process of distortion, in other words, buttresses certain sociopolitical arrangements and sensibilities. Should one from a community that is in part shaped through such a lie written across a certain arrangement of sociopolitical, economic, and cultural frameworks see the ability to render visible and invisible, to enlarge or shrink, elements of reality any other way?

Religion in the Americas, in this case the portion called the United States, involves certain "lies," a mapping of reality that gives central importance to the "city on a hill" ideology that guided many early colonists and allowed for the use of slave labor and the destruction of indigenous populations. Even more recent mappings of life in the United States—ones that seek to be multicultural in orientations—are often drawn from older mappings, and are never completely free from the flaws that marked earlier interpretations of life and reality in the United States. Yet, this status quo mode of mapping is not the only possibility. It is not the only way to articulate and arrange the meanings of existence.

MAPPING TWOS AND STUDYING RELIGION

It was and remains clear to me that there are shared existential and epistemological realities that "children" of the New World such as African Americans and Latinos/as might discuss and utilize in productive ways—to begin a process of undertaking a more positive cartography of the US religious landscape. However, such mapping, if it is to have felt meaning, must involve more than narrowly contextual materials and insular conversations. We must face and address the silences that punctuate our collective reality, and maneuver through the uncomfortable, and at times awkward, gaps in our mutual knowledge that represent another dimension of what it has meant to be "othered." Mindful of this need, as well as an already-shared theological language and grammar, the next effort should be a reimagining of the religious landscape of the United States in part through the often-overlapping movements of popular cultural production of both groups.

There is little doubt that Latinos/as and African Americans share a similar socioeconomic and political position—related existential and ontological "spaces," a certain mapping of reality—within the United States. Both communities have undergone a certain type of "creation"—a second creation—to borrow from Charles Long, by which contact and conquest that marked the formation of the New World overdetermined and fixed their identity. In simple terms, both communities bear in their flesh even today, perhaps to differing degrees, the consequences of the travel across the Atlantic. Both wrestle against the terror and dread associated with the warping of self-consciousness, of one's sense of being, that stem from being rendered the "other." Both face destruction of their physical bodies stemming from an unequal distribution of economic resources, while both are plied with the rhetoric of politicians who recognize the significance of these voting blocs, but who offer little in the way of renewed and vibrant life options. Both groups have responded creatively to ontological and socioeconomic trauma in part through a theo-praxis of liberative cultural production.

Within this theological work of liberation there is a concern with sustained reflection on the proactive dimensions of humanity and well-being captured in both communities' religious life. In this way, theological and religious studies at their best have highlighted the manner in which African American and Latino/a religious experience and identity entail a creative tension between reaction and creativity (or initiative) within a troubled historical moment. In fact, when books and articles by thinkers within these two communities are compared, substantial similarities of theoretical framework and approach are noteworthy. But, for example, a shared sense of what it means to do theology, how one does theology, and for whom theology is done, has seldom resulted in theologians from either community initiating and sustaining deep or "thick" exchange.

Some might speak of this disconnect as the result of differing cultural sensibilities that promote, if not necessitate, insular conversations and encourage the maintenance of an insider/outsider paradigm for discourse. Yet this, even if one recognizes cultural distinctions, should not point to an inability to converse but to rich differences that might play a role in healthy and complex theological exchange. Furthermore, theologians and scholars of religion from both communities operate from a position of stability and intellectual "legitimacy" that makes possible dialogue. That is to say, the theological work of both communities is recognized in the academy—with the presence of groups devoted to both within the American Academy of Religion serving as only one example—and this provides a "space" in which to wrestle with issues of mutual concern. At its best the exchange generated by these and other questions might involve a genuine and "gloves-off" approach to exchange—the sharing of agreement and disagreement—with the intention of increased understanding and greater cooperation.

I would like to begin this process with some attention to the religious terrain marking this dialogue. Christianity dominates the religious terrain of both groups, but there are other traditions that are supple and vibrant, and very much alive. And the boundaries between these various traditions are soft, allowing for some ritual, theological, and doctrinal exchange between them. That is to say, the process of making meaning, of developing a fuller sense of humanity, that marks all of these traditions allow for overlapping intent that on some level makes some of the "soft" elements of these various traditions translatable and transferable. For example, physical bodies have religious merit and theological weight across traditions. Yet, the sense of embodiment articulated by scholars from both communities tends to be highly spiritualized or discussed in terms of the historical (i.e., sociopolitical and economic) placement of these bodies. Hence, the focus is not really on those bodies, but merely their symbolic value in relationship to spirituality and eco-political concerns. I suggest "black" and "brown" scholars have fallen short through their inability to articulate theologically the value of these bodies as both sources of pleasure (including relationship with the "divine") and as pleasured, within the context of the erotic, in a Tillichian sense. In short, I suggest complex attention to the body as both symbol and biomedical reality.

Transformation as expressed in liberation theologies done by these communities—even in its limited articulation as two-dimensional—is housed in flesh. That is to say, these two modalities of liberation theology are in fact theologies of embodiment. In this sense the body rendered visible through a certain history of race and ethnicity represents the physical world of work and pleasure, and also serves as a prime symbol of chaos. In either case, in physical terms or as symbolic representation, African Americans and Latinos/as connote something both appealing and repulsive within the historical development of North America, and "things" to be controlled vis-à-vis categorization as inferior. Hence, language used to discuss the placement of bodies serves to reinforce social sensibilities and structures. As David Davis reminds us, language has often been religious and theological, and the implications of this practice should be a part of the ongoing dialogue between these two communities. It is response to the terror and dread of this predicament that we respond to in our religions and find represented in our popular culture, and it is these various responses that we should appreciate and map in our theological and religious studies. Furthermore, the kind of dialogue we undertake ought to be sensitive to and comfortable with paradox and difference—the complex nature of relationship. Hence, we must recognize the theological weight and epistemological centrality of competing claims if dialogue is to progress in ways beneficial. That is to say, this dialogue must grow to encompass a comparative component, one that recognizes the thickness and diversity of religious experiences housed within and between these two communities.

With the above, I am pushing for a mode of discourse framed by a postapologetic form of inquiry, entailing a method of exploration that can respond to our religiously complex and shifting terrain. This is not to suggest the complete removal of liberation theologies, for instance, as a method of exploration. Rather, I am calling for the "death" of a certain illusion regarding theology's work, a deconstruction of a myopic, religiously chauvinistic, and provincial understanding of theological discourse. This entails a movement beyond theologies as general (and religiously biased) theory of religious experience, and the recognition that Christian liberation theology speaks to and about only one dimension of what it means to be and be religious. This can change. Liberationist scholarship as done in both communities has involved, to some extent, an expansion of theological language to include culturally informed nuances and alterations to categories of meaning and perception. Yet, we have maintained the same theological grammar—new theological language but the same rules of usage used to map out patterns of meaning. This can change, and popular culture may provide both the content and form of this linguistic transformation. This is because complex cartographies of religiosity using the resources of popular culture promise thickness of discourse, as well as a deeper appreciation for the varied and fluid nature of the boundaries between the ways in which we express our lives.

8 THE LYRICS OF ANGELS AND DEMONS

Finally, my brethren, be strong in the Lord, and in the power of his might.
Put on the whole armor of God, that ye may be able to stand against the wiles of the devil.
For we wrestle not against flesh and blood, but against principalities, against powers, against the rulers of the darkness of this world, against spiritual wickedness in high places.

—Ephesians 6:10–12 (KJV)

In the previous chapter, music informed an approach to the study of religion more sensitive to cultural expression—a mode of interpretation guiding my understanding of how popular culture should function in the study of religion. In this chapter there is a move away from this type of implicit interpretive strategy and, instead, music is used for what is says lyrically about the tension between "good" and "evil," between angelic forces and demonic forces.

Mindful of this, the imagery and assumed theo-existential truth of the above passage have both explicitly and implicitly haunted and guided the ethical sensibilities of the dominant modalities of African American religion in the United States—that is, African American Christian churches—for centuries. African American Christianity has drawn its vocabulary and grammar, its imagery, symbolism, and posture toward the world from the rich stories that make up the Hebrew Bible and the

New Testament. Perspectives on the complex nature and framework of human relationships are given their weight and content in large part from the workings of situations outlined in Scripture. In this regard, African American Christianity, as the above Scripture would suggest, presents life struggles as tension between physical forces and nonphysical forces, between transcendent realities and mundane presences intertwined within human history—angelic and demonic personalities.

Theological imagery and doctrinal assertions, in various regions of the United States, speak to this arrangement of synergy between celestial and mundane forces. This is certainly the case within African American evangelical circles, where this rhetoric and perception of the workings of the world are most vividly expressed. The Church of God in Christ, the fastest-growing Christian denomination in African American communities, says the following concerning the reality of angels and demons:

> The Bible uses the term "angel" (a heavenly body) clearly and primarily to denote messengers or ambassadors of God with such scripture references as Revelations 4:5, which indicates their duty in heaven to praise God (Psalm 103:20), to do God's will (St. Matthew 18:10) and to behold his face. But since heaven must come down to earth, they also have a mission to earth. The Bible indicates that they accompanied God in the Creation, and also that they will accompany Christ in His return in Glory. . . . Demons denote unclean or evil spirits; they are sometimes called devils or demonic beings. They are evil spirits, belonging to the unseen or spiritual realm, embodied in human beings. The Old Testament refers to the prince of demons, sometimes called Satan (Adversary) or Devil, as having power and wisdom, taking the habitation of other forms such as the serpent (Genesis 3:1). The New Testament speaks of the Devil as Tempter (St. Matthew 4:3) and it goes on to tell the works of Satan, The Devil, and Demons as combating righteousness and good in any form, proving to be an adversary to the saints. Their chief power is exercised to destroy the mission of

> Jesus Christ. It can well be said that the Christian Church believes in Demons, Satan, and Devils. We believe in their power and purpose. We believe they can be subdued and conquered as in the commandment to the believer by Jesus. "In my name they shall cast out Satan and the work of the Devil and to resist him and then he will flee (withdraw) from you." (St. Mark 16:17).[1]

Not all historical African American denominations provide such strong statements concerning the reality of unseen forces influencing human existence. Yet, such commentary finds its way into African American Christianity in ways not confined to the formal doctrinal creeds and official theological postures of particular denominations. Paul Tillich's remark holds true in this case: religion is the substance of culture; and culture is the language of religion. Regarding this, one is just as likely to find discussion of these invisible forces battling for influence in human history expressed in both oft-called "sacred" and "secular" songs as in formal theology.

SPIRITUALS AND THE WORLDS AT WAR

Scholars such as John Lovell Jr., have argued for the existence of spirituals long before the formation of independent African American churches in the nineteenth century, and it is through these haunting musical tunes that enslaved Africans articulated their rudimentary religious sensibilities and theological assumptions.[2] These songs speak of the enslaved's sense of a God present in the world, poised to bring about the redemption of the enslaved and the "righting" of the

---

1. "What We Believe," Church of God in Christ, http://www.cogic.org/dctrn.htm.

2. John Lovell Jr., *Black Song: The Forge and the Flame: The Story of How the Afro-American Spiritual Was Hammered Out* (repr.; New York: Paragon House Publishers, 1986).

world. This God is understood to be loving, kind, just, and author of history understood as teleological in nature, both during the time of the biblical stories and the historical moment in which the enslaved found themselves. In the words of one song, "Didn't my Lord deliver Daniel, deliver, Daniel, deliver Daniel? And why not everyone?" Or,

> God is a God!
> God don't never change!
> God is a God
> An' He always will be God.[3]

God's plan for the fulfillment of human history, complete with its reframing of African American life, is accomplished through the perfect blend of divinity and humanity in the form of the Christ event. Drawing from stories of the activities and attitudes of Christ, along with a deep sensitivity to Christ's humble family context, enslaved Africans embraced him and drew bold existential and ontological links between themselves and this representative of God on earth. They found in the material poverty surrounding his biblically rehearsed birth, and in the suffering that informed his raison d'être, epistemological links and similarities to themselves: enslaved Africans faced hardship and undeserved pain and, more to the point, their plight would be rectified through the workings of God in human history.

> Children, we shall be free
> When the Lord shall appear.
> Give ease to the sick, give sight to the blind,
> Enable the cripple to walk;
> He'll raise the dead from under the earth,
> And give them permission to talk.[4]

---

3. James H. Cone, *The Spirituals and the Blues* (Maryknoll, NY: Orbis Books, 1972), 35.

4. Cone, *Spirituals and the Blues*, 34.

The uniqueness of Christ is the perfect balance between transcendent forces or realities and physical presence represented through the God/man, Christ.

The absurdity of the slave system, with its Christian tendencies, gave rise to a cartography of struggle bringing into play a host of forces, only some of them physical but all of them deeply important and felt. The Christ event confronts the evil found in the world guided by the workings of Satan and Satan's dominion. In the spirituals, enslaved Christians spoke of the battle between good and evil, and noted their souls and their existential condition as the prize and the battlefield respectively. In the words of one song,

Kneel and pray, so the devil won't harm me
Try my best for to serve the lord
Kneel and pray, so the devil won't harm me
Hallelujah[5]

Juxtaposed to the work of demonic forces, spirituals speak of the company of angels as a life affirming and heaven-assuring event:

O, I'm going to march with the tallest angel
O, yes, march with the tallest angel
O, yes, march with the tallest angel
When my work is done[6]

Within the spirituals, proper human activity involves a push against demonic forces and an embrace of angelic forces—the assumption

5. "All I Do, the Church Keep A-Grumbling," Negrospirituals.com, https://www.negrospirituals.com/songs/all_i_do_the_chunrch_keep_a_grumbling.htm.

6. "Members Don't Get Weary," Negrospirituals.com, https://www.negrospirituals.com/songs/members_don_t_get_weary.htm.

being the ultimate welfare of humanity is tied to the triumph of good over evil—the kingdom of God over Satan.

BLUES AND DEALS WITH THE DEVIL

In the blues such a distinction is not assumed. What is best for the individual (only limited attention is given to community) as outlined in the blues might entail a relationship with demonic forces over against the Christian God. Such a willingness to entertain demonic forces might suggest one rationale for calling the blues the "devil's music" in that the music was conversant with Christian principles, grammar, and vocabulary, but showed a willingness to entertain forces that Christians fear and fight.

Some strains of the blues, perhaps to signify Christian assumptions within African American communities or as a genuine acknowledgement of a spiritual realm, speak to the workings of spiritual forces often presented in physical form.

> Devil's gonna git you,
> Devil's gonna git you,
> Oh, the devil's gonna git you,
> The way you're carryin' on.[7]

In this way, blues artists acknowledged the manner in which we move through the world accompanied and influenced by unseen forces:

> Black ghost, black ghost, please stay away from my door
> Black ghost, black ghost, will you please stay away from my door
> Yeah you know you worry po' Lightnin' so now, I just can't sleep
> no more.[8]

---

7. Bessie Smith, "Devil's Gonna Git You," https://genius.com/Bessie-smith-devils-gonna-get-you-lyrics.

8. Lightin' Hopkins, "Black Ghost Blues," https://genius.com/Lightnin-hopkins-black-ghost-blues-lyrics.

Whereas the boundaries between these forces and their effectiveness in human life are clear and based on the Christian faith for those singing the spirituals, for those motivated by the blues there is a more utilitarian approach—one that allows for flirtation with both angelic and demonic forces depending on which might offer the most efficient assistance. The blues lack the certainty of a teleological arrangement of history that gives the Christian comfort; instead, the blues romance a comfort with paradox, or with a blending of opposites, manipulated and celebrated by the cleaver. Blues chronicler Robert Palmer captures this epistemological complexity when saying,

> Blues lyrics could be light, mocking, risqué, or could deal forthrightly with the most highly charged subject matter—intimate details of love, sex, and desire; a fascination with travel for its own sake that was rooted in the years of black captivity; the hypocrisies and foibles of preachers and other upstanding folks; the fantastic and often disturbing imagery of dreams; the practice and tools of magic and conjury; aggressive impulses that had to be severely repressed in everyday life; and in some blues, particularly the Delta Blues of Robert Johnson, an unabashed identification with the leader of the world's dark forces, the ultimate other.[9]

The blues speak casually of life circumstances, the play and interaction of contrary forces—both visible and invisible—in ways of great discomfort to those singing the spirituals. There is, in the blues, no great fear of "hell," nor great yearning for "heaven" in that the former can't be any worse than the oppression they currently encountered. The latter takes a back seat to the significance and "feel" of life's earthbound pleasures and desires. The sense of commonality found in the blues is premised on the desire for advancement, for goods, for good feelings, for the good stuff of life. "Powers and principalities" offering

9. Robert Palmer, *Deep Blues: A Musical and Cultural History, from the Mississippi Delta to Chicago's South Side to the World* (New York: Penguin Books, 1982), 18.

excess to the riches of life, regardless of their nature or disposition, are approached. In most cases loyalty is first to the individual, based on the interests and desires of the individual, and codified by any force capable making those desires real. Perhaps flirting with this understanding suggests one of the reasons for Pettie Wheatstraw's labeling as the "Devil's Son-in-Law and the High Sheriff from Hell."[10]

I take no moral stance here, and I make no effort to judge the rhetoric and imagery of demonic forces in partnership or as foe. Rather, my concern is to suggest the rich and robust sense of operative forces pervading and influencing human existence found within the blues.[11] I am aware of musicologist Jon Michael Spencer's critique of blues scholarship that uncritically assumes the blues to have evil intentions, a certain reading of blues as "devil music" in ways that simply reinforce stereotypical depictions of African Americans, and suggest a rather flat and reified notion of the nature and meaning of evil. I would agree with Spencer that the blues are not "evil" per se. That is to say, there is nothing about the blues suggesting it is intrinsically flawed; rather, the tension regarding the non-"godly" dimension of the blues seems an imposed paradoxical arrangement as opposed to being generated internally. In other words, the dilemma of commitments regarding blues and evil stems from a dominant Christian worldview projected onto the blues. Yet, even in saying this, I would not go so far as to suggest there is no interaction (if not in actuality at least in rhetoric) with forces considered evil by blues artists.

I want to suspend Spencer's assumptions concerning the normative state of Christianity as the religious orientation of African Americans, and thereby avoid his rather flat depiction of evil's function in American religion and life. Applying this to musical talent in African

10. Palmer, *Deep Blues*, 115.

11. See Jon Michael Spencer, *Blues and Evil* (Knoxville: The University of Tennessee Press, 1993).

American communities, I argue while some gave thanks to God for their abilities—assuming God favored them with great talent as a gift—others spoke of a bargain with demonic forces as the source of their musical (and social) prowess. None represent this arrangement better than Robert Johnson.

Born in Mississippi, Robert Johnson is perhaps the blues artists most closely linked, as folktales would suggest, to demonic forces. The hardships of his early life—relocations, family disruptions—may have had something to do with his early interest in the blues, which was nurtured through the mentoring of Willie Brown, Charley Patton, and Son House in Robinsonville, Mississippi. During these early years, legend has it that Johnson's musical ability was of limited appeal, pale in comparison to the other musicians making their way through the Delta. However, this changed after Johnson left the area for an uncertain period of time and returned with staggering musical abilities. Accounts by scholars suggest he worked under the tutelage of another musician, practicing his craft, and only returned when his abilities were at a high level.

For others, the account more explicitly involves demonic forces in the service of humans—for a price. By accounts provided by family members and others, Johnson's new abilities resulted from him selling his soul to the devil in exchange for unparalleled talent. Certain of his songs are pointed out as testimony to this exchange.[12] While some artists give visual depictions of the demonic—often portrayed consistent with negative color symbolism as a large black figure—Johnson gave no such attention to the appearance of the demonic. Rather, his concern revolved simply around the ability of such forces to impinge upon human existence. Johnson recognizes the presence of such forces impinging on his life:

12. Palmer, *Deep Blues*, 111–31.

I got to keep moving, I got to keep moving
Blues falling down like hail, blues falling down like hail
Mmm, blues falling down like hail, blues falling down like hail
And the day keeps on remindin' me, there's a hellhound on
my trail
Hellhound on my trail, hellhound on my trail.[13]

Or, the connection between Johnson and the devil as one of exchange is also present in shaded ways in the following lines:

Early this mornin'
when you knocked upon my door
Early this mornin', ooh
when you knocked upon my door
And I said, "Hello, Satan,
I believe it's time to go."[14]

Johnson alludes to the consequences of securing musical abilities from the devil: one must surrender one's soul, oneself to forces beyond one's control. Hence, even this deal with invisible forces is only a temporary correction to fulfilling desires and wants in that after a period of time comes damnation. And, much of the time prior to that is spent anticipating the inevitable, feeling the pursuit by "hell hounds." The alternative for Johnson appears to be movement, unpredictable and constant movement:

I got ramblin', I got ramblin' on my mind.
I got ramblin', I got ramblin' all on my mind.[15]

---

13. Robert Johnson, "Hell Hound on My Trail," https://genius.com/Robert-johnson-hellhound-on-my-trail-lyrics.

14. Robert Johnson, "Me and the Devil Blues," http://www.everydaycompanion.com/lyrics/songs/me_and_the_devil_blues.asp.

15. Robert Johnson, "Ramblin' on My Mind," https://genius.com/Robert-johnson-ramblin-on-my-mind-take-2-lyrics.

Had Johnson simply worked hard, under the guidance of formidable musicians, absorbing lessons without distraction, nor competition; or, had he made a deal with evil forces? Even if the answer to the latter is no, Johnson recognized the significance of such imagery for projecting a reputation as a "bad man," a formidable figure whose activities and music produced a deep gut reaction that both repelled and attracted listeners. Death for blues performers familiar with the world of diverse forces did not necessarily entail an end to all events. Rather it marked a transition, a movement to a new venue for activity; but one arranged in exchange for a liminal period of prowess. There is a sense of the tragic in this move in that life often remained difficult—marked by recognition, but not without its downside. They lived "hard" and died "hard."

In certain ways, even a deal with the devil involved a signifying of such demonic forces in that at times bad men "ruled" hell through the maintenance of their self-centered and destructive ways. Or, in other cases, they joined the ranks of unseen forces and continued to move through human time and space—the "deal" with demonic forces and its aftermath both shrouded in mystery. Perhaps such awareness accounts for Robert Johnson's request for burial near the highway so that his evil spirit might continue to travel vis-à-vis the bus line. The need to hit the road, to traverse time and space, is not dampened by death:

> You may bury my body, ooh
> down by the highway side
> So my old evil spirit can catch a Greyhound bus and ride.[16]

Such deals with feared forces could only enhance his reputation in that Johnson understood lyrics alone (many of which he borrowed

16. Robert Johnson, "Me and the Devil Blues," https://genius.com/Robert-johnson-me-and-the-devil-blues-take-2-lyrics.

from other artists) could not cement his success and musical legacy. Rather, the personae of the artists, the overall ethos of *being* surrounding him needed to entail the wiles of the trickster and the dealings of the "bad man." In short, association, real or imagined, with demonic forces served the purpose.

Even this affiliation, this connection to the demonic, served as a modality of resistance to staid and reified notions of morality and ethics tied to what these blues men considered the hypocrisy of the Christian faith. They, in dealing with the devil, signified the claims of the Christian faith (its doctrine, theology—particularly its theodicies) to the sources of the good life in ways that centered on the validity of the desires and wants Christianity condemned roundly—erotic desires, material goods, and revenge. In this way, Johnson and other blues figures like him were involved in an inverted spiritual arrangement—whereby the needs and wants of the body were given priority over what Christians considered the proper welfare of the soul.

Despised black bodies sought assistance from despised "dark" forces. By so doing, it is possible artists sought to use metaphysical evil to battle the damage done by the sociopolitical and economic fallout of racism as demonic force: evil negates evil. Put another way, novelist James Baldwin in reflecting on his years as a young minister in a black evangelical church argued that, in his neighborhood, everyone belonged to someone: this was the nature of survival in a predator world. Belong provided a "space" and sociocultural arrangements, the nurturing of talents and abilities. Early on, for Baldwin, belonging meant the development of preaching ability that generated acceptance and appreciation. Musical artists seem committed to a similar philosophy of relationship: they belong to something. For some, the proper modality of belonging was guided by the "rightness" of the Christian faith and its commitment to Christ. Yet, for others, the proper space for development of self and talent involved a relationship with demonic forces.

THE DEMONIC AND RAP MUSIC

The bad man, the rebellious figure, continues his flirtation with demonic realities within the form of certain rappers. Such rap artists share many of the existential commitments and the moral sensibilities of blues performers like Johnson, and this includes a similar stance on synergy between demonic forces and rebellious humans.

While rap tends to avoid a direct appeal to demonic forces for the development of musical abilities and other markers of success in a troubled world, it is not devoid of references to sensitivity to the presence and workings of demonic forces. Yet, rather than joining league with them actively, some rappers simply work in ways that seem influenced by the negative tendencies and character of the demonic, while others step through the world seeing the demonic lodged firmly around them. At the very least, some rap artists note an awareness of a delicate balance between life influenced by the divine and by the demonic, and press it into a macabre worldview. Such a tortured existence, one hanging between an absurd world and the workings of invisible forces impinging upon human existence, marks, for example, lyrics by Scarface.

Born Jordan Bradley, November 9, 1970, in Houston, Texas, Scarface made his early fame (or position as infamous) through the rap group The Geto Boys, whose lyrics spoke without remorse of the "dark" side of ghetto existence. This group presented itself as predatory and determined to exercise its wants and desires without attention to moral and ethical consequences.

Since the early 1990s, Scarface has produced solo projects that continue along the same path of existential angst but with a glimpse here and there into the world of "powers and principalities" that influences but is not synonymous with the arrangements of human history.[17] As blues artists note the manner in which evil can follow "bad men," from birth, Scarface presents himself as dogged by the demonic even before he is able to consciously choice sides. He notes,

> I don't remember much about being born
> But I do remember this: I was conceived on February 10th
> Complications detected in my early months of ballin'
> Around my sonogram you could see the evil was swarmin'.[18]

Furthermore, death is ever present and, in some instances, Scarface dissects the details of life's surrender to death: "You start your journey into outer space. You see yourself in the light but you're still feeling outta place."[19] Scarface, like so many other rappers, makes an appeal to relationship with the divine as the best last outreach of humanity; but he also recognizes the tensions between the forces of "good" pushing for this sort of relationship and the demonic that influences humans to behave in less than ethically robust ways. From his perspective, the existence of these two competing forces is real, oozing from every aspect of human existence in the 'hood. Death lurks around the corner, and the life of a "G" requires recognition of this and a willingness to accept the negatively serendipitous nature of such a life. Think in terms of the lyrics to "Make Your Peace" in which Scarface frames

---

17. Whether or not Scarface converted to Islam does not negatively affect this analysis in that the lyrics to the referenced tracks do not clearly indicates an Islamic orientation vs. a Christianity orientation. To the contrary, the imagery and theological language embedded tends to shadow the Christian faith, and the awareness of demons and divine forces appears drawn from the Christian faith.

18. Scarface, "Last of a Dying Breed," on *Last of a Dying Breed*, Rap-A-Lot, 2000.

19. Scarface, "I Seen a Man Die," on *The Diary*, Rap-A-Lot, 2004.

the demonic in terms of an alternate world invisible to human eyes, but nonetheless real:

I had a dream and seen a double sun,
a different world was in the makin'
The rule of this new world was Satan.[20]

Deals with demonic forces do not appear as commonplace in rap, although 2Pac's verse to "Smile," on Scarface's *Untouchable*, directly addresses this arrangement through which goods and prowess are secured:

No fairy tales for this young black male
Some see me stranded in this land of hell, jail, and crack sales
Hustlin' and heart be a nigga culture
Or the repercussions while bustin' on backstabbin' vultures
Sellin' my soul for materials wishes, fast cars and bitches
Wishin' I live my life a legend, immortalized in pictures.[21]

In spite of the above, on the whole, rap artists do not generally suggest that one try to bargain with and outmaneuver these demonic forces. On the other hand, one should simply recognize their presence and their impact on life in that such forces are everywhere, identifiable in the activities of neighbors and friends by the observant. In Scarface's words, "Who the fuck is you gonna trust when your road dog is scheming? And every other corner, you're passin' a different demon."[22] The world involves an absurd arrangement of forces that one cannot completely control, but that one can embrace or signify. It is this perspective that artists such as Scarface accept and articulate in their music,

20. Scarface, "Make Your Peace," on *Balls and My Word*, Rap-A-Lot, 2003.
21. 2Pac on Scarface, "Smile," on *Untouchable*, Rap-A-Lot, 1997.
22. Scarface, "Heaven," on *The Fix*, Def Jam South, 2002.

absorbing the paradox of life with a rather knowing way and with a somewhat defiant posture.

The difficulty of moving through a world haunted by such forces is not limited to Scarface and his existential angst and metaphysical uncertainties; artists such as Snoop Dogg also wrestle with the various forces present in the world. Born October 20, 1971 in Long Beach, California, to Beverly Broadus and Vernall Varnado, the life of Snoop Dogg (aka Calvin Broadus) was marked by the deep concern and religious orientation of his mother and the absence of his father. One of the few things given to him by his father, Snoop Dogg remarks, was a love for music. This love, combined with talent and skills given by God, mark the emergence of a rap career. In short, he notes, "In every rap I ever recorded, in the mad flow of every street-corner freestyle I ever represented, there was only one thing I wanted to get across: the way it is. Not the way I might want it to be. Not the way I think *you* might want it to be. But the way it *really* is, on the streets of the 'hoods of America, where life is lived out one day at a time, up against it, with no guarantees. . . . My raps describe what it's like to be a young black man in America today."[23]

Snoop Dogg's rap shares with the blues a deep sensitivity to the nature and "flow" of life, the manner in which human relationships of all sorts shift and change in a variety of ways. He, like blues artists before him, recognize the "dark" corners of life, noting both the promise and struggle associated with human existence. His is an existentially driven reality, but one that is also sensitive to the presence of realities uncontrolled by human intention. And, the bad man is best equipped to maneuver through this troubled terrain. That is to say, "there was a whole new class of hero coming up—the pimp and the

23. Snoop Dogg, with Davin Seay, *The Dogg Father: The Times, Trials, and Hardcore Truths of Snoop Dogg* (New York: William Morrow and Company, Inc., 1999), 2–3.

outlaw, the thug and the gangster—and if you wanted to stay alive on the streets of Long Beach or Watts or Compton or anywhere else where the American Dream was falling apart and fading away, you better get with their program. It was the only game in town."[24] Like the bad men of the century before him, Snopp Dogg is not troubled by this philosophy of connection; rather, he sees it as being a matter of fact and he embraces the paradox that is life: Stagger Lee reincarnated as a late-twentieth-century gangbanger.

While the often ethically questionable nature of some of his lyrics might suggest a paradox, Snoop Dogg views his musical history as teleological in nature, a purpose-driven development framed and orchestrated by a God who has provided him with talent and opportunity. That is to say, "Just when you think you've got Him figured out, some blindside twist of fate makes you understand that you *can't* figure Him out. That's why He's God and you're whoever the hell you are. He calls the shots, makes the moves, and keeps it all in check."[25] He views his rap lyrics and music, as described above, as a matter of ministry, a way of transforming life and regenerating relationships. From his perspective all of life (and death) are controlled by forces unseen but felt: "Most of the time, most of us don't sit around thinking on how God can snap our string any time He gets mad or bored or needs another angel in heaven or another demon in hell. Most of the time, if we're honest, we don't give a thought to any of that metaphysical shit."[26]

Increased sensitivity to the fragile nature, the complex arrangements, of life came to Snoop Dogg, he recounts, when faced with the possibility of life behind bars without the possibility of parole. It was with the threat of freedom removed, of space reified and time

---

24. Snoop Dogg, *The Dogg Father*, 41.
25. Snoop Dogg, *The Dogg Father*, 149.
26. Snoop Dogg, *The Dogg Father*, 25–26.

controlled by others, that Snoop Dogg's interest in metaphysical questions and concerns was sharpened. He writes,

> My guess is, we all wonder about the time we've got set out for us on the planet and what we're going to do with it before the clock stops ticking and they put us in the ground. . . . And that might be because, for those few, the reality of their life coming to a stone-cold stop is more than just some what-if trick their minds play on them. Every once in a while, a human being, no different from you or me, really does face down those odds, and when that happens, nothing is ever the same again.[27]

Unlike Robert Johnson and numerous other blues performers, there is no hint of conjuration, of folk practices, at work in Snoop Dogg's tale; but the existence of "powers and principalities" seems just as felt, just as compelling. There's a rhetoric of responsibility and accountability in the autobiographical voice of Snoop Dogg that one does not find in blues artists like Robert Johnson; yet, there is a paradox to life that resembles the depiction of life offered within so many blues tunes. Perhaps this paradox is even heightened in Snoop Dogg's story in that the battle between the demonic and the divine is made much more vivid.

On August 23, 1993, a man lay dead on the street, and Snoop Dogg and two others would be implicated in his murder. It is this tragic event, from which he was found innocent, that sparked his theological and existential reflection on and wrestling over deals with unseen forces as a framework for navigating the uncertainties of human (non) existence. As Robert Johnson hauntingly portrayed such a deal for talent in several blues tunes, Snoop graphically suggests a deal in exchange for continued life and prowess in "Murder Was the Case,"

27. Snoop Dogg, *The Dogg Father*, 188.

a project spearheaded by Dr. Dre (with Snoop Dogg receiving one of several writers' credits for the title track). According to some, the title track was loosely "tied" to the murder charge Snoop Dogg faced at the time of its release. In his autobiography, however, Snoop Dogg is less than enthusiastic about that project, seeing it as potentially distracting from his solo project, *Doggystyle*. ("Murder Was the Case" is also a track on *Doggystyle*.)

While arguing the murder charge brought him closer to prayer and God, thereby recognizing the inability of humans to ultimately shape history and control visible and invisible forces, the lyrics suggest a world of forces at work. More important than an autobiographical authenticity to the lyrics—or the validity of seeing the piece as commentary on the trial—is the reflection on demonic versus divine influence open to human use. Shot, one assumes, due to jealousy over his success, Snoop encounters the various forces marking the geography of human existence—all attempting to gain control of his soul:

> My body temperature falls
> I'm shakin and they breakin tryin to save the Dogg
> Pumpin on my chest and I'm screamin
> I stop breathin, damn I see demons
> Dear God, I wonder can ya save me.[28]

Based on Snoop Dogg's personal narrative of relationship to God, one would assume the deal struck in the track is with the divine. However, the storyline is not so clear and the ethical system in large part leaves room to wonder. Is the voice he hears after praying that of God, or one of the demons he sees?

---

28. Snoop Dogg, "Murder Was the Case," on *Doggystyle*, Death Row/Interscope, 1996.

I think it's too late for prayin, hold up
A voice spoke to me and it slowly started sayin
"Bring your lifestyle to me I'll make it better"
How long will I live?
"Eternal life and forever"
And will I be the G that I was?
"I'll make your life better than you can imagine or even
dreamed of."[29]

The life Snoop secures as a result of the deal with the unnamed force entails the material goods and control that might make Robert Johnson proud. Yet, it is one that does not mirror the more narrow and rigid moral and ethical outlooks generally associated with surrender to Christ, at least as typically presented by African American churches. The theological and ethical message is muddied in that the character's behavior results in a prison sentence. Is this punishment for not practicing more conservative Christian values, or is it simply the uncertain, perhaps double-crossing, arrangements of a deal with the devil? Is it a divine punishment, or the end of one's "run" through life—similar to Robert Johnson's deal with the devil not preventing what legend calls a painful death? Only Snoop knows; we are left to wonder with only a few certainties—one being the presence of both "good" and "evil" forces shaping and shifting the nature and substance of human existence.

A NOT-SO-FINAL WORD . . .

A sensitivity to a world packed with both visible and invisible forces marks the lyrical content of African American forms of music such as the blues and rap. In both cases, the more ethically and morally

29. Snoop Dogg, "Murder Was the Case."

aggressive artists flirt with such forces, signifying them or partnering with them based on a deep sense of individualized need and desire. The lyrical content offered by these artists, whether blues figures such as Robert Johnson or rappers such as Scarface and Snoop Dogg, suggest a theological articulation of life premised on the reality of the biblical notion of powers and principalities. While they might not approach such forces as did New Testament writers or as contemporary Christians might hope, they nonetheless move through the world sensitive to the host of forces and realities impinging on life, shaping and transforming it—all the while, in an ironic way, also enriching it. This is certainly one way to read Johnson's deal with the devil, or Snoop Dogg's dream of an arrangement that provides wealth and power, while delaying death. In either case, there's a haunting and eerie narrative of the battle for human's soul, one firmly lodged in the lyrics of African American music.

9 | TUPAC SHAKUR'S LIFE AND DEATH IN MUSIC

God has a plan and the Bible unfolds this wonderful plan through the message of prophecy. God sent Jesus into this world to be our Savior and that Christ is returning someday soon to unfold the wonderful plan of eternity for my life and your life.

This chapter continues the exploration of life and death—"good" and "evil"—found in several other chapters. However, here that exploration is limited to the ways in which Tupac Shakur's death has been presented and explored in his music and by his fans. Is he dead, or is he alive?[1]

The above lines open Tupac Shakur's "Blasphemy," a haunting track on *Makaveli: The Don Killuminati: The 7 Day Theory*.[2] From the cover art, depicting Tupac on a cross, to the lyrics and the urban legend surrounding the meaning of the seven-day theory, this album has fed conversation and much debate concerning the nature and meaning of Tupac Shakur as rap artist and perhaps prophet, or savior.

1. As indicated in the acknowledgements, this chapter was first published as a coauthored piece written with Paul Easterling—hence, the use of "we" rather than "I" when making claims.

2. Tupac Shakur, *Makaveli The Don Killuminati: The 7 Day Theory*, Death Row/ lnterscope, 1996.

Some fans assert that Tupac did not die in Las Vegas when shot some years ago, but rather he is still alive. Some argue he is preparing for his "second coming," a return that will have deep consequences.[3] Such a discussion, while typically restricted to the internet and "insider" exchanges, has consequences for an academic understanding of the religious significance of rap music in particular, and hip hop in general.

Scholars have given limited attention to this dimension of rap music; however, within this chapter, as a corrective, we give repeated attention to the tone and implications of Tupac Shakur's work, and the legends surrounding his life/death and assumed, by some, return. In short, we explore the manner in which both Tupac Shakur and his fans theologically link him to a larger Christian discussion of the Christ figure and eschatology.

From the spirituals onward, African Americans have expressed a deep sensitivity to the inevitable end of human history and have played out the workings of their eschatology explicitly and implicitly in various forms of their cultural production and religious outlook.[4] These songs, developed early during the presence of enslaved Africans in the Americas, expressed a certainty concerning the second coming of Christ and the judgment that would follow:

Got to go to judgment stand your trial,
Got to go to judgment stand your trial,
Got to go to judgment stand your trial,
Can't stay away.

---

3. See Beca Grimm, "Flashback: Tupac Shakur Doesn't Come Back from the Dead on 7/7/07," *Rolling Stone*, July 7, 2017: https://www.rollingstone.com/culture/culture-news/flashback-tupac-shakur-doesnt-come-back-from-the-dead-on-7-7-07-200273/.

4. James H. Cone, *The Spiritual and the Blues* (Maryknoll, NY: Orbis Books, 1991 [1972]), 94.

A general interest in the religious world of African Americans has been presented forcefully in the scholarly attention that has been directed at the spirituals such as the one above. This musical form, what has been called the first American music, provides an initial glimpse into African American culture vis-à-vis musical production. It also provides insight into the articulation of eschatological sensibilities surrounding the life/death/life of Jesus the Christ. While a certain suspicion concerning human history and its conclusion lurks under the surface of various musical genres within African American culture, musical expression of such concerns (if not wishes) comes to a head, we believe, in the more recently developed music genre popularly known as rap. This can be seen in terms of where rap takes root within an environment of aesthetic rebellion and sociopolitical pessimism expressed through modalities of linguistic creativity. One of the more significant examples of this posture toward the world is perhaps that of Tupac Shakur.

KNOWING TUPAC

Tupac's story begins with the indictment of twenty-one members of the Black Panther Party ("Panther 21") on April 2, 1969. They were charged with conspiracy to destroy the New York Botanical Gardens and other locations within the city. One member of this group, Alice Faye Williams, later renamed Afeni Shakur, was indicted in 1970 for allegedly withholding information concerning the so-called Panther conspiracy and for allegedly planting bombs in public places. Afeni Shakur, pregnant at the time, was held in jail until May 13, 1971, when the charges were dropped. Tupac Shakur was born on June 16, 1971 in New York, one month after his mother was released from the women's correctional facility in Greenwich Village.[5]

5. Armond White, *Rebel for the Hell of It: The Life of Tupac Shakur* (New York: Thunder's Life Press, 1997), 15–16.

While growing up, Tupac moved frequently with his mother and sister between New York, Baltimore, and Oakland in a futile attempt to escape the ravages of poverty. While in the grip of periodic struggle with endemic poverty, he witnessed also the hardship of his mother's struggle with an addiction to crack cocaine. In Baltimore he attended the Baltimore School of Arts, where he was exposed to the performing arts and humanities that expanded his thinking beyond the tensions and traumas of his socioeconomic surroundings. Yet, he never lost sight of the absurd nature of life within impoverished communities, and he expressed this realization through his activism. For example, in 1989, at the age of twenty, he became chairman of the "New African Panthers," an organization reflecting the goals and aims of the original Black Panther Party.[6] In addition, and of greater import for this discussion, Tupac addressed these socioeconomic and political concerns through music.

His involvement with the group Digital Underground led by Shock G eventually resulted in the production of solo efforts such as his debut album *2Pacalyse Now* (1991). Subsequent albums highlighted the ongoing tensions of life for a young Black male in the United States. The rough and raw nature of Tupac's lyrics was matched by a rugged lifestyle, one that held extreme consequences, including charges resulting in jail time. In 1995, for instance, Tupac was sentenced to eighteen months to four and a half years on sexual abuse charges. He served eight months and was released on bond posted by Marion "Suge" Knight, chairman of Death Row Records.

Tupac continued to produce at a staggering pace and continued to live the life of the "thug" as chronicled in his lyrics. However, this life took a major toll: Tupac was shot and killed in Las Vegas, on September 13, 1996. Some asked, "Is he dead?" Had the undertones of

6. White, *Rebel for the Hell of It*, 38.

his lyrics provided clues to events that would come? Had Tupac been accurate in arguing for the prophetic nature of his lyrics and the complex nature of his existence? Should his followers await his return as Christians await the return of Jesus the Christ? Did Tupac confound his enemies and elude death, with the craftiness of the trickster?

TUPAC BETWEEN WORLDS

Although this phenomenon is found in the cultural production of Native Americans and other cultures across the world, here we will focus on the trickster's presence in African/African American cultural forms where she or he is a smart, versatile, and wily character who not only outwits his or her enemies but also beats the ultimate adversary—death. According to Henry Louis Gates, author of *The Signifying Monkey: A Theory of Afro-American Literary Criticism*, the trickster figure that appears in African American oral and written traditions is directly linked to the trickster figures of Yoruba mythology. He states, "This curious figure is called *Esu Elegbara* in Nigeria and *Legba* among the *Fon* in Benin. His New World figurations include *Exu* in Brazil, *Eshu-Elegua* in Cuba, Papa *Legba* (pronounced *La-Bas)* in the pantheon of the *loa of Vodou* of Haiti, and *Pap La-Bas* in the *loa* of Hoodoo in the United States."[7]

These figures are messengers of the gods; they are mediators between humans and the divine and they speak with two tongues.[8] Moreover, the trickster is the master of all languages who manipulates and redefines language to transform reality as we know it. The qualities of this character are mastery over style, and mystery because he guards the crossroads between life and death, good and evil, white and

7. Henry Louis Gates Jr., *The Signifying Monkey: A Theory of Afro-American Literary Criticism* (New York: Oxford University Press, 1988), 6.

8. Gates , *The Signifying Monkey*, 6.

Black, east and west. The trickster is the master of binaries. He is the one who masters the balance of the universe. Other qualities include "individuality, satire, parody, irony, magic, indeterminacy, open-endedness, ambiguity, sexuality, chance, uncertainty, disruption and reconciliation, betrayal and loyalty, closure and disclosure, encasement and rupture."[9]

This trickster persona found, according to Gates, in African American literature is also found in hip hop. For instance, within rap music there are several characters who exemplify the qualities of a trickster: Shock G/Humpty Hump of Digital Underground, Flava Flav of Public Enemy, Ol' Dirty Bastard of the Wu Tang Clan, and Madlib/Quasimoto of Stone's Throw Entertainment. These artists use hip hop to tell stories, to deliver coded messages to the community, as well as redefine the world (or at least the hip hop world). For instance, Gregory E. Jacobs, also known as Shock G, created the character Humpty Hump as a more playful and oversexualized alter ego, which balanced Jacobs's more serious persona as Shock G. These two personalities formed a character who celebrates the multiplicity of human personality or the contradictory nature of human personality as some might interpret it. Further, this character is a trickster because it allows Jacobs to balance himself on the crossroads of seemingly contradicting human traits, in a sense scoffing at those who are simple enough to imply that all humans must see and interpret life the same way.

The character created by William Jonathan Drayton Jr. is perhaps hip hop's most popular and significant trickster—Flava Flav. Flava Flav's mere presence as a member of one of hip hop's most serious and militant groups is of significance in that he appears to seemingly contradict everything for which Public Enemy stands. As Chuck D, Professor Griff, and the Security of the First World march through the streets of Brooklyn as demonstrated in the video "Fight the Power,"

9. Gates, *The Signifying Monkey*, 6.

Flava Flav is dancing, gyrating, and playing to the crowd. As trickster he was the "hype man" for Chuck D, adding emphasis to all of his lyrics with his trademark battle cry "Yeaaaaaa Boooyyyyyy!!!" He also gets his own shots in against the system with songs such as "911's a Joke," which poked fun at the 911 emergency system that treats Black lives as less important than others. In addition, to solidify his position as chief Lao of Public Enemy, Flav always wears an oversized clock around his neck, which signifies his mastery of the crossroads of existence: over life and death as well as good and evil. Similarly, Russell Jones of the Wu Tang Clan provides a trickster element to the group through his persona as Ol' Dirty Bastard—also known as Big Baby Jesus, Osiris, and Dirt McGirt. This character has an awkward lyrical delivery, littered with metaphors drawn from Nation of Gods and Earths philosophy. Finally, Otis Jackson Jr., better known as Madlib (Mind Altering Demented Lessons In Beats) brings back the genius of dual personalities in hip hop with his alter ego, Quasimoto or Lord Quas. Created in part because Jackson did not like the sound of his voice on record, Quas is often heard with his high-pitch delivery lyrically battling Madlib as if they were rival emcees.

Yet, in the world of hip hop, perhaps Tupac (through his persona as Makaveli) is the ultimate trickster not only because he was able to signify reality through his lyrics but because he is said to have conquered death. The others play with language and shape the world through manipulation, but Tupac, as trickster, changes the nature and meaning of life and, through the thought and practices of his fans, becomes immortal. Tupac left clues within his lyrics. For instance, in the song "Heartz of Men" on the album *All Eyez on Me*, three minutes and thirteen seconds (3 + 1 + 3 = 7) into the song, Tupac says, "I died and came back."[10] Would he return after the proverbial dust had

10. 2Pac, "Heartz of Men," https://www.youtube.com/watch?v=pXOuIqy0voQ.

settled to reign victorious over his enemies? Or is it a publicity stunt that guarantees many of his faithful fans would continue to purchase his posthumous albums in a desperate attempt to find more clues that their thug savior would one day return to them?

His language and grammar as well as the theories presented by his fans suggest a Christ-like persona: one who defies historical arrangements while also being their architect. One gets some sense of this in the words of Michael Dyson:

> Tupac had stopped being a star and had become a grammar: His moves, gestures, and performances were a startlingly faithful articulation of their conflicted, confused inner lives. Much of his art insisted that their bodies were his. It was if he were saying, "I will be your sacrificial lamb. I will suffer for your sake, in your place."[11]

Furthermore, as one fan noted online,

> One afternoon, I had managed to borrow a cassette from my neighbor. That's when I heard my first song by Tupac, Only God Can Judge me. That song forever changed my life in which ways that one would never imagine. Tupac, has been my anti-drug, anti-gang, my anti-violence; and more importantly, a type of father figure in a home which consisted of my lonely self. I became a fanatic soon after that. I read all the books I heard Tupac read, I vibed to every song that he ever created. He was my best friend in a time of desperate need. He showed me Words of Wisdom in a trapped society, and for this, I am truly grateful.[12]

This recognition of Tupac's ability to guide life and frame proper moral and ethical postures toward the world certainly resembles in

11. Michael Dyson, *Holler If You Hear Me: Searching for Tupac Shakur* (New York: Basic Civitas Books, 2001), 233–34.

12. http://www.hitemup.com/tupadtestimonials.html [Link no longer available].

tone and texture the testimonial statements of Christians who speak of Jesus the Christ as "a way maker," "as a father to the fatherless," and so on.

The aesthetic of Tupac's body speaks to his visibility, his positioning between worlds—between the American capitalist and the outlaw, the social icon and the despised Black body. Furthermore, the vocabulary and grammar of Tupac's stance toward the world, like that of Christ, are expressed in a text. But, unlike Christian Scripture, Tupac provides a "sacred" word carved into the despised Black body, in this way highlighting the centrality and significance of the body vis-à-vis tattoos. Central to this presentation of the word in flesh is "thug life," written across his abdomen, the fundamental framework of the life stance he promotes. This is the underlying philosophical and theological mantra—that is, the system of ethics marking allegiance to the "Black Jesuz." The tattoo connotes both sign and suffering in that the pain of securing the tattoo speaks to a commitment to a particular life stance, a recognition of and celebration of a way of life. The process of marking the body in this manner also speaks to the gaining of insight, of knowledge, and surrender to a certain way of existence. The completed design motivates and guides his followers, those committed to "Black Jesuz." One might even say that those devoted to Tupac, who mark their bodies with signs and symbols related to their devotion, experience stigmata—in other words, they are participating in the pain and pleasure "preached" by Tupac through markings of Tupac's realness, even in his absence.

THE (IN)VISIBLE

Lindon Barrett raises an interesting point concerning the nature of the deceased Black body. Recognizing the manner in which Black bodies both appeal and repel within the context of white supremacy, Barrett proposes, "In effect, the dead Black body may be an ultimate figure of regulation, unruly desire and its risks fully mastered."[13] Such a theorizing of death and the rigid and reified dead (Black) body is significant here in that it points to the psychosocial, perhaps even religious, significance of his return. Tupac hints at such possibilities, displaying his body (e.g., on a crucifix) in ways suggesting both death and life; and his fans give this in-between space of existence more authority through explicit attention to a second coming. In this way, talk of a second coming serves to reconstitute the body as looming, as present, as a continuing threat to the mechanisms of life within a white supremacist nation. According to one fan,

> I wanted to be just like him brave and fearless he inspired me to be who I am, speak my mind, do what I want, not care what other's think, and not feel restricted to say something others might not like lastly I feel like he was the most influential artist of the 90's who changed the face of rap, broke barriers and had the whole world watching in suspense like he said "All eyez on me" he introduced the world to "THUG LIFE" and like most of history's guineas [sic] he was misunderstood and lived a short life and like most he was murdered. But I kept the faith thru his struggle for life but I believe he's coming back call me crazy but we'll see on 2003![14]

Tupac Shakur pushes beyond the ability of white supremacy to create and control Black bodies by refusing to be named or captured, to be confined to time and space in particular ways.

Symbolized in Tupac and given, to some extent, iconic importance, the Black male body is afforded a certain power over the traditional framing of life, the stereotypical arrangement of Blackness

13. Lindon Barrett, "Dead Men Printed: Tupac Shakur, Biggie Small, and Hip-Hop Eulogy," *Callaloo* 22, no. 2 (1999): 306.

14. http://www.hitemup.com/tupadtestimonials3.html [Link no longer available].

that shrouds certain bodies. Suggested by the stories of Tupac's return is the signifying power of visible invisibility. That is to say, discussion of Tupac's return points to the ability of a Black body to haunt popular imagination in ways that impact perception and activity as the present/unpresent. Tupac is said to be preparing for a second coming—a reemergence that will bring a new worldview, a new set of life arrangements.

The meaning of the discourse of a second coming is one that, in this instance, extends well beyond a simple manipulation of christological images and orientations. In fact, African American religious thought is reoriented not away from the body as the awkward conduit for divinity, but rather, toward an appeal to the "thuggish" dimensions of life. Hence, christological considerations are brought into the service of Blackness in ways extending beyond Black theology's appeal to an ontological similarity to the divine qua Blackness. Such bodies, like the in(visible) body of Tupac Shakur, house a certain power in that they are able to short-circuit the attempts to refer and control and determine the power place and space for Blackened bodies. Present here is the ultimate triumph over social regulations and rigid modalities of existence. Is he dead?

> Y'all can't kill me!
> Y'all can't kill me![15]

Or,

> I'm certified crazy, so sick the world made me
> Now diggy-die, everytime I ride it's for reasons
> Hard to kill a nigga cause I'm comin back like Jesus.[16]

---

15. Tupac Shakur, "Redemption," on *RU Still Down? (Remember Me)*, Aramu Entertainment, 1997.

16. Tupac Shakur, "Killuminati," on *Still I Rise*, Interscope Records, 1999.

Alice Campbell, in a student paper, provides popular commentary on the suspicion surrounding this question:

> Some things still don't add up, such as Shakur's autopsy photo. According to tupacnet.org, the photo was featured in the book *The Killing of Tupac Shakur*, by Cathy Scott. The picture is hard to validate since only a profile of Shakur's body is seen and there is no evidence of the prominent "Thug Life" tattoo that is on Shakur's stomach. The Black and White picture's very poor quality makes it difficult to tell whether or not it really is Shakur . . . But looking at the facts, the strange coincidences and the mysterious messages in Shakur's music, one could easily conclude that Shakur faked his death.[17]

This statement summarizes much of what constitutes the "seven-day theory" of Tupac's death/life. Much of the debate and speculation concerning this theory is found on the internet and involves an elaborate arrangement of speculation premised on misdirection and blurred clues such as this: "Shakur's last album before his death was *The Don Killuminati: The Seven Day Theory*. Its cover eerily depicted him crucified and was recorded under the pseudonym 'Makaveli', an allusion to Niccolo Machiavelli of old, who suggested faking one's death to fool enemies. The executive producer was mysteriously listed as 'Simon' instead of Suge Knight."[18]

Almost immediately, rumors began to circulate based on what many considered suspicious numerically centered developments, such as the number seven: *Makaveli—The Don Killuminati: The 7 Day Theory.* Again, some claimed Machiavelli's (in this case "Makaveli")

---

17. Alice P. Campbell, "Notorious Rapper's Supposed Death Surrounded by Speculation," *luterco111* (College of the Mainland, December 2003).

18. "2Pac," http://www.rapdict.oqy'2Pac. Also, "Tupac Shakur," Answers.com. [Link no longer available].

notion of faking death to fool enemies was utilized by Tupac.[19] Furthermore, Tupac called himself the *Don*, a title that signified that he was the godfather of the Outlawz; and the last name, *Killuminati*, plays on the rumored doomsday organization, *The Illuminati*, founded in seventeenth-century Germany and said to be secretly controlling the world. All this contributed to the mystery of his death. Theories abound concerning the significance of the number seven for Tupac, particularly the manner in which the use of the number—the number of "perfection"—speaks in code to the mission and "afterdeath" work of Tupac. For example, it is said that it only took Tupac seven days to complete *Makaveli—The Don Killuminati: The 7 Day Theory.*[20] In the first song "Bomb First (My Second Reply)," Tupac fires seven gunshots throughout the song.[21] Also in the video for "Toss It Up," Tupac smashes a mirror with a sledge hammer to signify seven years of bad luck for all those who are superstitious.[22] Moreover, one of his last videos, "I Ain't Mad at 'Cha," begins with an eerie dramatization of Tupac's death that is remarkably similar to how he actually died. This premonition coupled with the ominous reoccurrences of the number seven provided the fuel for the seven-day theory. Next, Tupac was only twenty-five when he was supposedly murdered: 2 + 5 = 7.[23] Furthermore, he died on Friday, September 13, 1996 at 4:03 pm

19. Mark Steyn, "Machiavellian: Was 2Pac Shakur's Murder Just a Publicity Stunt?" https://slate.com/news-and-politics/1996/12/machiavellian.html.

20. John Gotty, "Why Tupac's 'Don Killuminati: The '7 Day Theory' Still Stands as His Most Complete Album," https://stillcrew.com/tupac-makaevli-the-don-killuminati-the-7-day-theory-most-complete-album-387a26baf12e.

21. 2Pac, "Bomb First (My Second Reply)," https://www.youtube.com/watch?v=kFw72yhzWX8.

22. 2Pac, "Toss It Up," https://www.youtube.com/watch?v=AUf5kXTA8MM.

23. 2Pac ft. Danny Boy, "I Ain't Mad at Cha," PaperChaserDotCom, https://www.youtube.com/watch?v=oXkKURgzYVY.

(4 + 0 + 3 = 7), which was exactly seven months after the release of his double album *All Eyez on Me.* Other interesting possibilities concerning the significance of the number seven include certain phenomena in Tupac's movies. For instance, Tupac's badge number for the character he played alongside Jim Belushi in *Gang Related* was 115 (1 + 1 + 5 = 7). And, inverted sevens can be seen on a menu in the diner scene of Tupac's movie *Gridlock'd* costarring Tim Roth.

These indicators mean more than just coincidence for many of Tupac's loyal fans. This deluge of data leads to predictions of the date of Tupac's return, such as seven years after his death, which would have been September 13, 2003. As indicated on one website, "Saturday marks the seventh anniversary of the death of rap star Tupac Shakur. Although a lot of folks won't admit it publicly, trust me, some will be looking for him to return from the dead. Yes, I know it sounds crazy. But if the rumors about him faking his death, which emerged shortly after the November 1996 posthumous release of his Makaveli album 'The Don Killuminati: The 7 Day Theory,' are true, then Tupac should surface this weekend."[24] When September 13, 2003 did not bring the return of Tupac, some maintained their expectations and argued he will reappear on another date that corresponds to the number seven.[25]Tupac invites speculation as one would expect of the trickster—signifying assumptions concerning the nature of his importance, the power of his lyrics and the nature of his existence. For example, he says,

Even if I die, I'm gon' be a fuckin' problem.
Do you believe in ghosts, motherfucker?
Real live Black . . . ghosts.
Feel me?[26]

24. http://tupac-online.com/News/0-257119-00.html [Link no longer available].
25. http://past2003butstillhopc.tripod.com/ [Link no longer available].
26. Tupac Shakur, "Ghost," on *Resurrection*, Amaru/Interscope, 2003.

Furthermore, what one also finds in popular debate over Tupac Shakur involves a blurring of the line between life and death. Regarding this, what Nick De Genova says concerning Richard Wright is true of Tupac. In fact, we would argue the existential sensibilities and their religious ramifications expressed in the prose of Richard Wright are found in the lyrical flow of Tupac. Hence, the existential and religio-theological links to the following words regarding Wright:

> Indeed, for Wright, there was no way to disentangle life from the constitutive violence of a social order founded upon racial subordination and effected in outright terror. When terror is a way of life, "life" itself entails complicity with that terror; the challenge of self-preservation is itself inseparable from the conservative impulse to cut a pact with the devil, a series of compromises which reduce life in some sense to a protracted way of death.[27]

As De Genova rightly notes, death has various meanings within the modalities of African American cultural expression and thought. Talk of Tupac's return, however, like Wright's wrestling with meaning vis-à-vis death, presents us with one of the more troubling takes—one that sees in violence both demise and return, dilemma and promise. It is also possible, highly probable, that Tupac Shakur's remarks from prison speak to a death and resurrection, a movement from "old" ethical patterns to an alternate worldview; or, what Christians might refer to as the death of the old human nature, and the emergence of an individual more in line with the will of God. When referring to comments made prior to his incarceration that prison would mean death, he remarks, "The addict in Tupac is dead. The excuse maker in Tupac is dead. The vengeful Tupac is dead."[28]

---

27. Nick De Genova, "Gangster Rap and Nihilism in Black America: Some Questions of Life and Death," *Social Text* 43 (Autumn 1995): 91.

28. Kevin Powell, "2Pac Shakur," *Vibe Magazine*, April 1995, 52.

Talk of Tupac's return signifies traditional African American Christians' perceptions of the second coming by dissociating it from a rather static arrangement of moral and ethical sensibilities, breaking the back of normative theological structures of an existential purge.

In times of war we need somebody raw, rally the troops
Like a Saint that we can trust to help to carry us through Black
Jesus.[29]

As such it does not involve a corrective of existential circumstances and the "thugness" generated; rather, talk of Tupac's return points to the pragmatic importance of the thug's existence as affirmation of struggle even when this seems bleak. This realization, however, is not limited to traditional physical encounter:

To my homeboys in Clinton Max, doin' they bid,
Raise hell to this real shit and feel this.
When they turn out the lights I'll be down in the dark
Thuggin' eternal through my heart.[30]

This notion is not an aberrant religio-theologically perspective in that it seems to merely keep focus on the tragic, the rather grotesque nature of the death event when it spurs a certain modality of a hoped-for existence. It could be argued that this seems to speak to what James Cone has in mind when discussing the ramifications of the crucified Christ: "Like a Black naked body swinging on a lynching tree, the cross of Christ was 'an utterly offensive affair,' 'obscene in the original sense of the world,' 'subjecting the victim to the utmost indignity.'"[31] In this way, those seeking and assuming the return of Tupac speak of

29. Tupac Shakur, "Black Jesus," on *Still I Rise*, Interscope Records, 1999.

30. Tupac Shakur, "Hail Mary," on *The Don Killuminati*, Death Row, 1996.

31. James H. Cone, "Strange Fruit: The Cross and the Lynching Tree," *Harvard Divinity Bulletin* 35, no. 1 (Winter 2007): 54.

his existential circumstances and ontological significance in ways that mirror the despised Christ. As one fan put it,

> I look at 2pac like a black jesus. I worship pac like jesus Christ . . . 2pac was crucified by haters on earth just like jesus christ was. 2pac's spirit rose from the cross just like the spirit of jesus christ did. Pac's spirit guides me through life . . . I love you pac. Thank you for blessing the world with your music and wisdom . . . In 2pac's name I pray . . . Amen.[32]

Or, as artist Nas remarked, "Tupac was Jesus Christ. . . . He was a part of us."[33] In either case, the traditional framework for connection to the divine is signified, allowing for slippage between two realms of existence. Yet, even this points to a specialness grounded in an earthy existence. In Tupac's words,

> I got shot five times and I got crucified in the media. And I walked through with the thorns on, and I had shit thrown on me, and I had the word thief at the top; I told that nigga, "I'll be back for you. Trust me, it's not supposed to be going down, I'll be back."

And here's the vital connection:

> I'm not saying I'm Jesus, but I'm saying we go through that type of thing every day. We don't part the Red Sea, but we walk through the 'hood without getting shot. We don't turn water to wine, but we turn dope fiends and dope heads into productive citizens of society. We turn words into money—what greater gift can there be?[34]

---

32. http://www.nobodysmiling.com/hiphop/ncws/86232.php [Link no longer available].

33. Quoted in Allen Callahan, *The Talking Book: African Americans and the Bible* (New Haven, CT: Yale University Press, 2006), 230.

34. "Inside the Mind of Shakur," in *Tupac Shakur*, by the editors of *Vibe* (New York: Crown Publishers, 1997), 98.

Yet, suggestions are multidirectional in nature and there are hints of such a perspective toyed within in his lyrics:

Tell me I ain't God son Nigga, my mom a virgin.[35]

There is not a sense of existential hopelessness maintained in this call for Tupac's return. Instead, it is recognition that destruction is part of a process, the mechanism often through which a promise is fulfilled, and through which life is regenerated. There is a tragedy here, but one that resembles that of the cross. Perhaps even the cross of the Christian's divine/human, whereby the workings of the despised one offer the unlikely alternative arrangements? What De Genova says concerning Richard Wright's character Bigger Thomas is true of the crucifixion, so to speak, of Tupac, from the perspective of those who seek his return: "Although he acts very much alone and tests fate as an individual, his nihilistic posture is a source of deep pride for the other Black people who bear witness."[36] Bearing witness, however, the followers of Tupac do not doubt their devotion and the praxis it entails; rather, they look at those who reject the workings of the Black Jesuz with a mixture of pity and animosity. What he will bring is uncertain; but that his return is desired by some, is firm. Like the trickster, Tupac slips between worlds. A physical resurrection return is not the central concern here. Talk of Tupac's return, his continuing life, provides a critique of or signifies attempts to capture and control Black bodies—a marker of discrimination in the United States. Whereas lynching trees offered a ritual of reference meant to delimit the possibilities and placements of Black bodies through their destruction; both physically and ontologically, Tupac's "playful" depiction of himself on a cross, followed by his continued existence after the event, speaks to the vital nature of Black bodies. This is

35. Tupac Shakur, "Blasphemy," on *The Don Killuminati*.

36. De Genova, "Gangster Rap and Nihilism in Black America," 100.

the ability of said bodies to fight against restrictive forces. His invisibility for the moment is chosen not enforced, and it does not negate his significance, but rather intensifies it. This is particularly the case when one remembers that his body is invisible, but his voice is very much present through the numerous albums released after his death or disappearance.

Perhaps Tupac Shakur's fans who speak of a return or an enduring presence are pointing to something prophetic about his lyrics, and thereby speak to the enduring challenge of his life and words. As Michael Dyson notes, "In Tupac's case the crush of rumors that circulated in the aftermath of his demise suggests a huge investment in the denial of death. Many youth simply could not abide the destruction of a beloved icon. Rumor is the attempt to shape the consequence of death since its circumstances are well beyond control."[37] Dyson is correct in that Tupac is a saint of sorts—a "ghetto saint"—and saints linger with us, in one way or another. If nothing else, their reflection in thought and practice on the religious provides a presence, a paradigmatic presence that calls for further reflection. In a word, "we must not forget that unpopular and unacceptable views are sometimes later regarded as prophetic. It is a central moral contention of Christianity that God may be disguised in the clothing-and maybe even the rap-of society's most despised members."[38] And, what is more, "they view his risen, disappeared body as the absent evidence of his eternal ascension. Tupac has joined those Black saints who tarry with the ancestors to watch over our blighted Black babies."[39]

Such talk of Tupac offers an alternate theological orientation, one filtered through a complicated relationship between the trickster and

37. Dyson, *Holler If You Hear Me*, 251.

38. Dyson, *Holler If You Hear Me*, 209.

39. Dyson, *Holler If You Hear Me*, 268.

the gangster. Talk of his return, to the extent such talk occurs, suggests the continuing and somewhat delicate balance between Black bodies as both despised and ever-present. The marked, Black body becomes a text outlining the somewhat bleak and troubled nature of life in the United States, but couches this condition within the larger possibilities of transformation.

10 THE DIVINE STATUS IN HIP HOP

The poetic quality of music and the imaginative style of lyrical expression have given African Americans ways to describe and critique life arrangements within a society always on guard against challenges to the status quo. Over the course of my fifty years, I've grown into this truth.

The previous chapter highlighted an iconic figure in hip hop culture—Tupac—and explored the theological significance of his self-understanding and how fans dealt with his death. As this and the next chapter note, one might say there is a "gospel of Tupac," or the teachings of "Black Jesuz." Furthermore, this chapter continues the reinterpretation of religious signs and symbols by discussing ways in which artists like Jay-Z and Kanye West, brought up elsewhere in this volume, signify religious authority through critique and, ultimately, claim divine status—imposing an alternate "good word."

As the introduction to this volume makes clear, it was first within the context of church work that I came to know and appreciate the manner in which music often challenged the sermon as the dominant modality of theologizing. Music marked out the various phases of Sunday worship, leading parishioners through the order of service from the procession to the benediction. It often anticipated and addressed their thinking regarding particular concerns. The rest of the week, once the worship buzz ended, music—as the epigraph suggests—marked the rhythm of life, with its messages becoming magical mantras for church folk "in the world but not of it."

MESSAGE IN THE MUSIC

Despite the spiritual aura, musical articulations of the gospel message flirted with secular modes of expression. Sometimes, the result—as in the case of traditional and contemporary gospel—was the Christian faith with a new rhythm. But as so many in churches feared, this flirtation with secular musical aesthetics could easily draw the unsuspecting Christian into a full embrace of godlessness. For example, contemporary gospel too easily softened believers to the allure of R&B and pop. But for young people like me, warnings against this danger meant nothing. We were determined to like what we liked, play the music we enjoyed playing, and still show up for Sunday service—singing, "This little light of mine . . . I'm going to let it shine!"

After all, like our parents (to the extent they'd admit it) before us, we found something of ourselves—an epistemological recognition and existential comfort—in the "questionable" musical forms that kept us tuned in. And, as I was growing up, no musical genre expressed this better than rap music—that lyrical dimension of the larger cultural world of hip hop.

What I noted in the introduction, I'll restate here: rap artists spoke so creatively and compellingly that resisting their stories was a futile act. Their language—grammar and vocabulary—was organic and captured so much of what I knew and felt about the world, regardless of my Christian filter. They recognized an ontological "truth" that brought into focus both the promise and the pitfalls of life in the United States as—in my case—a young black male. This appreciation, to be sure, wasn't without its tensions.

For instance, I was a Christian, but I was moving to the rhythm of rap artists whose ethics and moral codes were creative, organic, but not always in line with what I had been trained to privilege as proper conduct. In hindsight, this tension—at least in part—revolved around hip hop culture's reframing of religious authority, done through a signifying of theistic structuring(s) of meaning.

But should I have expected anything less than this signification of theological themes and assumption from rap, the child of the blues? That is to say, hip hop culture in the form of rap music was simply the most recent incarnation of philosophical-theological counterpoint—or, the marginalized manifestation of poetic protest.

CHURCH AND PLAYIN' WITH "GOD"

Rap music had me, and I didn't mind or fight its grip on my imagination. This is despite the fact that I first encountered it while training to be a minister within the African Methodist Episcopal Church.

I was both insider and outsider—the young black male of concern within so many rap lyrics, as well as a minister type who represented a particular hustle infesting black life. Put a different way, many artists were speaking to me *and* about me. This made for a particularly stubborn epistemological dissonance. I walked the border between two worlds—hip hop culture and the church—finding in both something that appealed to my self-understanding and my relationship to human history.

Perhaps this was all a consequence of the world being a place of contradictions, of desires for meaning within a context best prepared to leave us frustrated and unfulfilled? My church life acknowledged this predicament but quickly turned to metaphysical claims. On the flipside, some rap artists brought into question many of my religious assumptions and shot holes in the narrative of ministerial excellence: the minister is the man (usually a man) closest to the will of God and best able to hear the voice of the Lord. No, rap artists exposed, in verse, the frailties of ministers and their abuses of resource and people.

Lyrics, often without mercy, exposed ministers as pimps, frauds and other questionable figures; the holiness was exposed as hollow.

In a word, the preacher wasn't the only one who could weave a story, or frame moral and ethical obligation over against the cartography of life. The preacher might "whoop" but the MC spit fire, and that fire burned my mind long after the sermon (even my sermons) were over. Rap vibrated through my mind long after the echo of scripture had subsided.

Even after I left the church and rejected Christian ministry, I remained intrigued by rap music's ability to maneuver between worlds and in the process deconstruct and reconstruct religious sensibilities, responsibilities, and notions of authority. For instance, UGK argued that "the game belongs to me," and this allowed for a capturing of human agency or lucidity—and thereby an ability to work the systems of "production" to one's benefit.[1]

On top of this, UGK chronicled the structuring of life available to young people in the urban, southern context that spoke to the struggles for life meaning in ways that can't be captured adequately by the somewhat sterile and disembodied framings of life offered by many churches. Artists like the Geto Boys and then the solo artist Scarface chronicled in lyrics a life less certain. There is a roughness and grittiness to life within, for instance, "Mind Playin' Tricks on Me" and "Mind Playin' Tricks 1994" that speaks to the absurdity of our encounter with a harsh and unresponsive world.[2] This harsh and unflinching take on life works over against the dreamlike state of the church's response to the challenges of human existence—"Just

1. UGK, "Game Belong to Me," on *UGK (Underground Kingz)*, Jive Records, 2007.

2. Geto Boys, "Mind Playin' Tricks on Me," on *We Can't Be Stopped*, Rap-A-Lot Records/Priority, 1991; Scarface, "Mind Playin' Tricks 1994," on *The Diary*, Rap-A-Lot Records, 1994.

a little talk with Jesus makes it right" seems underwhelming in comparison.

Still, other artists pushed for the reconstitution of metaphysics to render theological themes highly unrecognizable to religious traditionalists. While examples of this abound, I think one of the more compelling would have to be Tupac's transfiguration of Christ in the form of "Black Jesuz," who is the patron saint of thugs. Black Jesuz's moral code runs contrary to the stuff of a standard Christianization of life; but, what would one expect when this new figure of authority proclaims a genealogy composed of thugs and killers? Rather than the biblical text, one could argue that Tupac—as Black Jesuz at times—provides a sacred text written on his body, the ink of his tattoos over against the ink of the King James Bible, and this is coupled with the "10 rules of the game" over against the biblical Ten Commandments.

THE NEW DIVINITY

For some time now I have listened repeatedly to three tracks. The first is "No Church in the Wild" by Jay Z and Kanye West; the second is "Crown" by Jay Z; and the third is "I Am a God," by West.[3] The first dismantles authority by cutting to the core of the modern West—its traditions and epistemological safeguards. Jay Z challenges the framing of knowledge as associated with the Greeks by exposing the inherent bias in the crafting of knowledge; he dismantles the ethics of the Christian faith (the church), and challenges constructions of being that don't stem from a materialistic base—a hip hop twist on Sartre's proclamation that existence precedes essence.

---

3. Jay Z and Kanye West, "No Church in the Wild," on *Watch the Throne*, Roc-A-Fella/Def Jam, 2011; Jay Z, "Crown," on *Magna Carta Holy Grail*, Roc-A-Fella/Universal, 2013; Kanye West, "I Am a God," on *Yeezus*, Roc-A-Fella /Def Jam, 2013.

What Jay Z and West offer in "No Church in the Wild" is a modality of the religious that reclaims its core meaning—to bind together. The authority of the metaphysical other—through religious leadership for instance—can be dismantled because it can be challenged. In its place they establish a new religion framed by mutuality and, of course, lucidity—over against the violence, deception, and epistemological manipulation Jay Z exposes in the first verse.

West adds to this a new framing of ethics by maintaining the authoritative significance of the individual in connection to others. He does this by privileging exchange and consent as the bases of relationship. The chorus sums it up:

Human beings in a mob
what's a mob to a king
what's a king to a god
what's a god to a nonbeliever
who don't believe in anything?[4]

This chorus exposes religious authority as premised on the crafting of stories and codes demanding and sanctioning compliance, and all this revolves around a privileging of obedience over will. Recognition of this situation, as West notes, as a point of theological insight, "is something that the pastor don't preach, something that a teacher can't teach."[5] It cuts against the authority of their pedagogy and flies in the face of their circumscribed and truncated ethics.

What Jay Z and West offer is not a mapping of life vis-à-vis negation—"thou shalt not . . ."—but rather it is premised on an affirmation: do as you like by means of consent and through recognition of mutuality present even in the context of a troubled world.

4. Jay Z and Kanye West, "No Church in the Wild."

5. Jay Z and Kanye West, "No Church in the Wild."

It is this reconstituted life (called a religion in the song) that makes possible the proclamation of divinity one finds in "Crown"—"you in the presence of a king, scratch that, you in the presence of a god." The miracles associated with divinity are distilled in this track and lodged in the workings of urban life, thereby marking out material desires. Jay Z (aka Hova), as a god, pushes against restrictions, refusing to be "wiped out of history," but instead imbuing said history with the narrative of urban miracles—"put in the belly of the beast [New York's public housing] I escaped / but a nigga never had a job."[6]

He offers the American dream metanarrative turned on its head through an alternate epistemology of success, or salvation. "If it wasn't for the bread," he notes, "probably be dead."[7] The narrative of making it as a consequence of docility in the presence of the Christian God—who might give you a beat down, like Job received, but will finish the process by granting more stuff—is flipped and subdued by the metaphysics of a new savior, aka the streetwise Jay Z and his communicative skills. Like Black Jesuz, Jay Z-as-a-god welcomes agency as a marker of having "game." It is an authority premised on consistency rather than traditional markers of obedience—not following what others say, but doing what one does—in other words, "do you." Divinity in this instance isn't marked by superhuman capacities to judge and punish; instead, it is based on lucidity—awareness grounded in the material world and marked off by a measured realism embracing the workings of the world.

In "I Am a God," also discussed in an earlier chapter, West, having something of a split (divine) personality, constitutes Yeezus as a morphing of the christological event and personality so as to highlight the roughness of Christ's encounter with the world—not the garden and prayer, but hanging with the despised; not virginal qualities

6. Jay Z, "Crown."
7. Jay Z, "Crown."

(tempted but without sin as Scripture suggests) but rather thoughts of Jesus with/in Mary. West, with a much more metallic and harsh tone, speaks his divinity by pronouncing a new relationship to the empirical quality of life.

Unlike Jay Z, as I've noted elsewhere in this volume (e.g., chapter 4), West's divinity is not the "most high," simply close to the ultimate source of truth, or the resurrection of hip hop as the epistemology of life. By controlling the life of hip hop, he controls ontology, epistemology, and the details of existential happenings. Again, lucidity—deep awareness of life—marks an intimacy with the dark corners of life acted out.

Whatever one decides to make of these claims to religion, or to divinity, the challenge to traditional modalities and framings of authority—religious authority—is clear and compelling. Chuuch!

11 ARTISTS DEIFIED

The last two chapters presented examples of how artists become deified and what that means for our understanding of hip hop's relationship to and critique of religion. This chapter takes a step back and re-engages some of this book's earlier concern with the content of our humanity. In particular, it extends explicit attention to the potential bond between humanism and musical production. And, it does this in terms of what this connection might tell us about the nature and meaning of death outside of traditionally theistic narratives.

My book *The End of God-Talk* represents the first African American humanist theology. Building on the pioneering work of the late William R. Jones, I outlined in that volume several of the major categories underpinning a godless theology, from a black perspective.[1] The

1. See William R. Jones, *Is God a White Racist? A Preamble to Black Theology* (Boston: Beacon Press, 1999). My humanist theology is indebted to Jones. However, it also extends my work in *Varieties of African American Religious Experience* (Minneapolis: Fortress Press, 1998). While that book is a bit misnamed, it is actually an effort to ground theology in something other than the assumptions of the Christian faith. Hence, it was meant as a prolegomenon, a critical analysis meant to introduce theology as a methodology capable of cutting across traditions including humanism. Most have failed to note this particular function of the text, although it is clearly stated in the introduction and the final chapter of the book.

text moves from sources that highlight the deep value of nonwritten "texts" (e.g., the body), to "community" as an alternative to god, to an evolution-based theological anthropology, to the value of symmetry as a humanist corrective to theories of salvation, to a perspective on ethics highlighting Harriet Tubman, Henry David Thoreau and Frederick Douglass, and concludes with a strategy for ritualizing ordinary life that anticipates current humanist community and secular "church" activities. That book marks the beginning of my more focused attention to humanist theological sensibilities as a proper method for investigation of a range of subjects. What I discuss in this chapter, tied to some of my related thinking in chapter 4, is an important conceptual paradigm mentioned in passing in that volume, one with great impact on a historically bound sense of life—that is, death.

My approach to death in the *End of God-Talk* is more a critique of notions of transcendence that lurk in the corners of typical liberation theologies than the outlining of a full humanist theological perspective on death. Elsewhere (e.g., chapter 4) I discuss death as a matter of ontological and epistemological meaninglessness, but here I simply mean death in connection to bio-chemical functions. In the case of chapter 4, I argue for a link between life and death that is epistemological and ontological in that it explains a particular relationship to meaning; and this is done without any intentional presentation of a humanistic sensibility. In these pages, I use rap music filtered through my sense of humanism and—once again—the thought of Albert Camus to outline a perspective that counters theistic takes on the topic of death and, in this way, it suggests (as a type of heuristic) the nature and meaning of death consistent with an African American humanist theological perspective. The purpose is to expose longstanding effort to render death abnormal to the extent it is perceived to push against what is right and acceptable about being human. In place of this thinking, I suggest physical death should lose its distinctiveness and become less easily distinguished from what we call life. In this regard, one might think in terms of material, physical life/death as opposed to a much clearer distinction such as death as entrance to the *after*life. And, conceptually framing and methodologically guiding this shift is a simple idea: To some extent theology is anthropology, and therefore it must entail a type of thanatology.[2] Unlike chapter 4, the aim isn't to use music to make a claim concerning being, but rather to point out the way in which the experience of "blackness" is unified and not easily distinguished by a difference in materiality intended by life over against death. Black bodies, in a word, have the same place in US history whether animated or not. Life, in a sense, then, is tied to a question that says something about race and other markers of difference: How and why did one physically die?

A FEW WORDS ON CONTEXT

Death is a constant that impinges upon all modalities of existence and through which we believe we ultimately bow to the limits of knowledge and being. That is to say, it speaks a popular idea: human life is within limits and those restrictions can be acknowledged and through technological advances pushed, but they cannot be denied nor exceeded.

I spent a good number of years in Christian ministry, with one of my professional obligations being the ritualizaton of death—giving eulogies, burials, comforting the living, and so on—all meant to address this fundamental point regarding death. Beyond the scope of the pulpit and the discourse extending from that source of authority, African American expressive culture in general points to black bodies as subject to death. From the early spirituals and folk

2. This chapter is one of several on death in this volume. All draw, to differing degrees, from Albert Camus and rap music; but they address different dimensions of the question of death.

narratives during the period of slavery forward, African Americans have used systems of expressive culture to do a different type of work—an aesthetically contrived rebellion. W. E. B. Du Bois argued that artistic production had to serve a larger purpose, had to speak to the human struggle for advancement (in his case racial justice). Yet, Du Bois—and he isn't alone in this—addressed personal confrontation with death through artistic production that didn't necessarily produce racial equality (i.e., public protest), but it did speak to the nature of death. His literary reflection on the death of his son in *The Souls of Black Folk* says something about an epistemology of meaning that confronts death not as something dehumanizing, but rather as a marker of our human connection—the integrity and weight of human relationship.[3]

Beyond what Du Bois offers, attention to death, of course, includes the example of brutal and reasonless death justified simply by the fact that African Americans *are* and are available as objects manipulated so as to support the sociopolitical status quo. One need only think in terms of death hauntingly chronicled in songs such as Billie Holiday's "Strange Fruit."[4] This song and less graphic modalities as well map how African American expressive culture describes black bodies as always exposed to death. In expressive culture, the fragility of the embodied body as bio-chemical reality that is born, lives, and dies isn't denied as such. Even deals with cosmic forces—as is alleged to have taken place with blues artist Robert Johnson—don't deny death but rather give life within its parameters a particular robustness or

3. W. E. B. Du Bois, "On the Passing of the First-Born," *The Souls of Black Folk* (Mineola, NY: Dover Publications, 1994).

4. See for instance: Billie Holiday, "Strange Fruit (Live 1959)," phalenopsis1, https://www.youtube.com/watch?v=YbcZstt8ACY. For a history of the song, readers should consider David Margolick's *Strange Fruit: The Biography of a Song* (New York: Harper Perennial, 2001).

charge.[5] Death still comes and conversation about this coming isn't "sequestered."[6] In this regard, death—however it manifests—pushes into the public workings of the nation and pesters the private arrangements of life.

DEATH OVER AGAINST LIFE

The nature and meaning of death have changed over time. The locations for death and the framing of death have altered in light of a variety of socioeconomic, political, and cultural shifts in collective life over the centuries. Yet, something related to the awareness of death remains in place and undergirds reflective awareness of life's vulnerability. We live with the understanding and presence of an assumed end to physical existence.[7] There have been efforts, of course, to control, monitor, and ritualize material death (the end of vital biological functions)—in some ways to privatize it so as to make it manageable, to make it easy as understood within a particular sociocultural understanding, and to render it over against life.

Death experienced in this form gives the person time, resource, and opportunity to work out "arrangements" in a way consistent with individual need/want and in light of communal assumptions and priorities. It might involve arrangement of resources, nurturing relationships, and so on. This is an economy of death that is manageable and

---

5. Interesting work on Robert Johnson includes Peter Guralnick's *Searching for Robert Johnson: The Life and Legend of the "King of the Delta Blues Singers"* (New York: Plume, 1998).

6. Philip A. Mellor, "Death in High Modernity: The Contemporary Presence and Absence of Death," in *The Sociology of Death*, ed. David Clark (Cambridge, MA: Blackwell Publishers, 1993), 11–12.

7. Allan Kellehear, *A Social History of Dying* (London: Cambridge University Press, 2007), 47.

to some extent "owned" by humans. The opposite of this, the type of death avoided, involves a hard death, entailing death that is untimely (outside the socially assumed chronological frame for human life), death that is violent or in some other way outside the pattern of life/death desired by the person, or death that for any other reason is outside the dominant narrative of life leading to a peaceful demise—which is to say death *not* as the conclusion of a productive and fulfilling life.

This framing offers death as disruptive of sociocultural arrangements that mark out life or physical being within a given community. In this way, physical death produces *dis*-ease and fosters a certain type of anxiety within individuals. Even in theistic traditions, such as Christianity, that often pose death as transition to new life, death remains a problem of sorts in that it is a sign of human flaw—the conclusion to human shortcomings. Would humans experience death as we know it if not for humanity straying away from God?

While we may experience a form of "transcendence" (a difficult word for me to use) as we live in the memories of those left behind, physical confrontation with the world (i.e., "life") comes to an end. If expressed as a written text, it might appear something like this: l/i/f/e. There is a beginning and a clear end—with slippage between clearly identified markers of time and space—after which the meaning of that particular person is only a memory: an unreliable series of ideas arranged with intent and historical purpose. "In the last analysis," as has been written, "human societies are merely men and women banded together in the face of death."[8]

Instead of understanding death as a problem of being—that is, existing in opposition to life—some rap artists suggest it is a matter of proportion—that is, as connected to life. To speak of one is to say something about the other. "Blackness" functions with respect to life and death in similar ways within our social world.

8. David Clark, "Introduction," in Clark, *The Sociology of Death*, 3.

RAP MUSIC ON DEATH: TUPAC IS JESUZ

Like the blues, rap music makes use of the traditional language and grammar associated with mourning of loss, of other modalities of emotional and psychic pain associated with physical death. However, in addition, rap music has altered the tools of discourse by giving terms new epistemological arrangements and concerns. In some instances, this involves not simply a signifying of sociocultural categories of relationality, but also manipulation of religious figures with the aim of having them do a different work. For instance, there is Tupac Shakur's "Black Jesuz" also discussed elsewhere in this volume.

As Albert Camus reminds, talk of mechanisms of transformation, stories of transcendence and change, all lead to the same end, to the same conclusion—the overlap between life and death and the presence of absurdity—either fought or embraced. This is a different knowledge of death. It is not marked by wallowing in fear of death, but instead involves recognition of death as already wrapped in life. A similar recounting, I think, is present in Tupac Shakur's "Blasphemy" and "Hail Mary," two tracks from the same album that speak to a new understanding of death. Similar to the converted missionary in Camus's story "The Renegade, or a Confused Mind"—converted from Christianity to worship of a fetish—these tracks turn religion inside out. Its value and meaning, its expression and goals, are altered so as to reject its certainties of a future lodged in hope in favor of familiarity with the absurdity of death/life. Pain and redemption are merged and rendered indistinguishable. And, listeners (readers for Camus) are confronted with a choice to make: When and how is death? Material death is juxtaposed to a new epistemology of death.[9] With Tupac,

---

9. Albert Camus, "The Renegade, or a Confused Mind," in *Exile and the Kingdom* (New York: Vintage International, 2007); Tupac Shakur, *Makaveli: The Don Killuminati: The 7Day Theory*, Death Row/Interscope 1996; Albert Camus, *The Rebel* (New York: Vintage International, 1991), 297, 300–301.

death is absorbed—not dismissed or feared—but taken in as a part of life. In his words, "This Thug Life will be the death of me."[10] He, as a Christ figure, offers a system of analysis and of engagement that doesn't betray the content of death. Rather than fear or avoidance as the grammar of death as presented in the dominant and guiding logic of death as problem of being, Tupac embraces death as knowledge of life. In at least two cases he accomplishes this by retelling Christian stories of life . . . death. In this retelling God is displaced by another—a new prophet who is in line with the logic of the thug and for whom death is not a condition to be fixed. This process of countertheology begins with a recasting of the Christ event:

> Tell me I ain't God's son, nigga mom a virgin;
> We got addicted had to leave the burbs, back in the ghetto;
> Doin wild shit.[11]

And, this new Christ, this "Black Jesuz," has his own miracles to perform. Moses, Tupac reminds, may have split a sea but he, Black Jesuz, "split the blunt and rolled the fat one. I'm deadly, Babylon beware."[12]

Linked in the song are revenge and desire, the assertion of self as acknowledgement of something valuable within the person—something worthy of protection and safeguarding.[13] This establishes epistemological grounding for the parallels he sets between himself and Jesus the Christ. The latter is pulled from his privileged station and Tupac—the "Black Jesuz"—takes his place alongside God. As Tupac says, "All eyes on me."[14] What is more, Tupac notes that "Only God

10. Tupac Shakur, "Blasphemy," on *The Don Killuminati*.

11. Tupac Shakur, "Blasphemy."

12. Tupac Shakur, "Blasphemy."

13. Camus, *The Rebel*, 55; Tupac Shakur, "Blasphemy."

14. Tupac Shakur, "All Eyez on Me," on *All Eyez on Me*, Death Row/Interscope, 1996.

Can Judge Me," but what does that mean for the god/man? It must be remembered that he exists with God, as the new Christ. Hence, he judges himself because he has dismantled through word and deed the logic under girding perceptions of life and death through the structuring of meaning qua THUG LIFE—a type of glorious, chaotic, march through the world—a defiant gripping balls as Jay Z (the one accused of demonic deals and conspiracies articulated through signs and symbols) might describe the accompanying posture.[15] Tupac's throne is equal to God's but it touches both heaven and earth. While I don't read Tupac as a Christian, he isn't necessarily a humanist or atheist; that is, he reframes (but keeps) the location and function of God.[16] For example, in certain circles, as noted elsewhere in this volume, conversation concerning the life of Tupac Shakur after he is shot and presumed dead continues.[17] In a word, some continue to believe he isn't dead, but is away, preparing for his return. Tupac as the embodiment of life/death?

Both Tupac and Camus recognize such a repositioning as a matter of blasphemy—a certain posture toward rebellion. Adopting this posture, Tupac cautions listeners not to push him or provoke him because "revenge is like the greatest joy next to gettin' pussy."[18] In a certain sense, Tupac qua "Black Jesuz" reincarnates the rebel who brings into question assumptions concerning the basis of knowledge related to death and the accompanying focus of ethics. Put another way, and drawing loosely from Camus's construction, Black Jesuz

15. Thug Life: "The Hate U Give Little Infants Fucks Everybody." Tupac Shakur, "Only God Can Judge Me," on *All Eyez on Me*; Jay Z, "Moment of Clarity," on *The Black Album*, Roc-A-Fella/Def Jam, 2003.

16. Camus, *The Rebel*, 24–25.

17. For example: "Top 20 Reasons Why 2Pac Is Alive," Donmega.com, http://www.donmega.com/20-reasons-why-tupac-is-still-alive.php.

18. Tupac Shakur, "Blasphemy."

recognizes rebellion as needed by all.[19] In a word, it is rebellion on behalf of and for a much larger audience by means of which death is conquered through removal of any assumption that it constitutes a crisis of being—life's end. Death, where is your sting? The answer is written on and through Tupac's body: death, then, is already and always.

Tupac normalizes death in that he claims a connection to God, that is, the ultimate structuring of meaning. That is to say, Tupac makes death a matter of life by taking from it any abstraction. Even his body—marked with tattoos speaking to this new reality—presents an alternate epistemology of meaning. It's a new message, but like those tattoos across his body, it has a certain type of permanency.[20] The ink may fade, but the new message will always call attention to itself, and seeing his body will force a particular epistemological dissonance. He offers his flesh as a new communion into life to death and death to life. The tattoos mark the way.[21]

The success of his effort isn't of concern to me because it is not the measure of importance from my perspective. That is to say, theology is altered through his narrative (as well as others like it) in that historical lucidity trumps "mysticism"—hard living in the "hood" over Gnosticism and esotericism. There are recognized values—such as Tupac's THUG LIFE—but these constitute a particular framing of meaning and ethics that cuts against the structures of reality meant to foster death as a problem of being. Christianity is dismantled and replaced by a new measure of reality.

The first Christ turns the other cheek, accepts offense for the sake of something greater and does so with an eye toward death as a

19. Camus, *The Rebel*, 23.

20. See the photo of Tupac at ThePlace, http://www.theplace2.ru/archive/tupac_shakur/img/12-35.jpg.

21. Tupac Shakur, "Hail Mary," on *The Don Killuminati*.

transitional affair. The Black Jesuz, however, responds to offense and recognizes the importance of attention to an alternate gospel that privileges those very things the dominant society pretends to reject regarding life/death. An epistemology supporting death as the end of reality is replaced by an alternate knowing that gives priority to the weight of human existence as a matter of living into death.[22] What ideology or even theology can be employed to hold together this type of ontological contradiction? Even the question serves to shatter the illusion, to break through efforts to control what really can't be controlled, to banish death and restrict its presence to a select "location" segregated and despised.

RAP MUSIC AND DEATH: NEW AUTHORITY

Tupac challenges the arrangements of death by claiming control over the construction of life/death, whereas Jay Z and Kanye West, in "No Church in the Wild," question the nature of authority with implications for how we are conditioned to understand life and death.[23] The brilliance of this song—besides the intrigue generated in light of the strong opposition to it from certain, predictable quarters—as noted in the previous chapter, is its fundamental challenge to the basis of Western morality and ethics. By dismantling the sources of this authority represented by the mob, the king, and God, all falls to the will of the unbeliever—the one who refuses to sanction the prime Unity used to hold in place modalities of subjugation.[24] Meaning is premised on consent and agreement without the assurance of an overarching guide: "We formed a new religion," raps West, "no sins

22. Camus, *The Rebel*, 55; Tupac Shakur, "Blasphemy."

23. Jay Z and Kanye West, "No Church in the Wild," on *Watch the Throne*, Roc-A-Fella Records, 2011.

24. Ibid.

as long as there's permission."[25] One might even suggest this unbeliever is Camus's rebel, one with lucidity and awareness; or in the words of Jay Z and West, "watch the throne."[26]

If death as problem requires acceptance of authority, a surrender to the logic of dominance, Jay Z and Kanye West push against this structuring of reality, thereby dismantling the prevailing unity of ideas undergirding death as anything other than life/death. Those embracing this sense of death become the marker of the real, the measure of prosperity, control over aesthetics, acquisition of "goods," physical prowess, and so on—important markers of meaning within the United States. In other words, they expose the "real." Other formulations are without authority and are signified by rendering death the marker of life in an absurd world, or the "jungle."

Can death withstand this challenge to its logic, form, and function? A prime marker of this system of reality, the housing for its prime form of authority, the church, has no place within the world constructed by Jay Z and Kanye West, where authority is not surrendered to another but is established in connection to others. That is to say, they urge listeners to live into death—just "ball" until it's over. In crude terms, according to Jay Z, "Ball so hard, this shit crazy; Y'all don't know that don't shit phase me."[27] This is the new framing of life/death—the retaking of authority, the establishment of new ground rules. Maybe even to ritualize death differently? Embedded in this is a call to recognize "greatness" along new lines that blast truncated notions of death.[28]

This is enough to disrupt the nature of death to the extent it troubles the epistemology justifying and the ontology shaping death as a

25. Jay Z and Kanye West, "No Church in the Wild."

26. Jay Z and Kanye West, "Who Gon Stop Me," on *Watch the Throne*.

27. Jay Z and Kanye West, "Niggas in Paris," on *Watch the Throne*.

28. Jay Z and Kanye West, "Who Gon Stop Me"; Jay Z, "F.U.T.W.," on *Magna Carta*, Roc-A-Fello Records, 2013.

problem of being. The forms of authority that sanction and buttress this poor thinking on death as the safeguard for a particularly Camus-rejected understanding of the unity of meaning is disrupted and the sacred nature of this logic challenged. Authority is toppled, and it isn't replaced with anything to offer the same type of unity of meaning. Perhaps this is one way to understand the implications (intended or not) of Jay Z and Kanye West's "No Church in the Wild"?[29] It raises questions, strong questions, concerning the nature of social authority. Hence, it topples the structuring(s) of life by lodging the final process of authority with "nonbelievers" whose stance (e.g., rejection or perhaps rebellion) calls into question all that is dependent on consent to death as separation. Sacred markers and mechanisms of authority are dismantled, and the secular reigns! And, what falls as a result of this shift is the framing of a wrongful death.

LOOKING AT DEATH

Richard Wright speaks to something along these lines (but without the same intent) when in "The Man Who Lived Underground," the protagonist Fred Daniels, who is in the sewer hiding from the police accused of a crime he didn't commit, uses darkness to enter into a movie theater from underground. He is as dismissive of these delusion seekers as he is of the delusional church folks he encountered from below their sanctuary.[30] Yet, he is more like them than he can initially admit. He thinks his presence underground has altered him, made him ghostlike and untouchable as he moves from surface to

29. Jay Z and Kanye West, "No Church in the Wild."

30. Richard Wright, "The Man Who Lived Underground," in *Eight Men* (New York: HarperPerennial, 1996), 30. For more of my analysis of this story, see Anthony Pinn, *The End of God-Talk: An African American Humanist Theology* (New York: Oxford University Press, 2012), chapter 4. Chapter 3 will be of interest as well.

sewer. But there are too many instances when this line of reasoning is broken, when his presence is real, substantive, but not quite human. His isn't a death that constitutes a problem of being—a clear distinction from living. Daniels's final encounter with police officers when he tries to explain his circumstances—as if he is human to them—points to this fact and their action (to shoot him) is meant to confine death as physical control, social regulation (i.e., law and order) and ontological positioning. Readers learn, as Daniels experiences this violence, death bleeds into life and life into death.

What Wright offers is thought-provoking on a variety of levels, yet it is with greater appeal that the cultural worlds produced by certain rap artists subvert bad notions of death by giving explicit attention to death, and by promoting the end of the "end" in ways that trouble or challenge typical religious markers of an "after" death. The grit and misery surrounding death is not given a theological gloss as one finds in the spirituals or slave narratives, sermons and prayers, for instance, but rather is left raw and harsh. One of the early anthems of hip hop—"The Message" by Grand Master Flash and the Furious Five—speaks to the perpetual presence of the smells, sights, sounds, and feel of decay, of decline within the arenas of life. And I say, amen to this perception of life/death.

While helpful for understanding where an African American humanist theology might go with respect to a theory of death, what Tupac, Jay Z and West offer isn't a humanist theology proper. Rather, they offer a graphic and poetic response that crushes theodician responses to death; in fact, they hint at the end of theology and the transformation of anthropology into thanatology. Still, the same could be said of a humanist theology—a maintaining of tension, recognition of the absurd, and an effort to accept the importance of life within a context of death.

12 HIP HOP CULTURE IS GLOBAL

With this chapter, I move from a consideration of hip hop within the United States to its impact on a global setting. This interest in the internationalization of hip hop stems from my work over a good number of years at the Institute for Philosophical Research in Hannover (Germany). The Institute's engagement with Germany-based artists offered opportunity to think beyond my own context. In fact, this chapter is an early set of remarks I gave (and some of which are found dispersed throughout the publication stemming from that gathering) during a citywide hip hop program sponsored by the Institute.[1]

Hip hop culture, in a general sense, is an infusive discursive practice not bound by space or by place and it doesn't seem to respect—nor even recognize—geographic restrictions and barriers, unless they somehow aid in its transition. One could say, in fact, hip hop culture points to a simple reality: movement and life are wrapped together, mutually reinforcing, and, in particular ways, indistinguishable.

One might call this a process of signification by means of which, while in constant motion, hip hop has turned some of the basic assumptions (e.g., inevitability of human progress; optimism concerning

1. Collaborator on experimental book with Juergen Manemann and Eike Brock serving as the two lead authors, *Philosophie Des Hip Ho. Performen, was an der Zeit Ist* (Bielefeld: transcript Verlag, 2018).

human nature; the triumph of reason) of the modern West on their head. And it has done all this while embracing other mainstays of the modern world such as the value of the individual (a type of individualism), the presence of "truth" and the significance of the empirical. It doesn't matter whether this manipulation of modernity has been conscious or not; what is significant is the outcome—hip hop culture's impact across cultures and the socioeconomic and political arrangements of nation-states.

It is a cultural development, an art, a worldview and posture toward the universe that seems to have few limitations, few restrictions of movement and placement. As this culture moved, with respect to local customs, from the Bronx—a segment of New York City—across the United States and into other nations, it has established communities that are both physically arranged—such as crews—but also virtual and known not by physical proximity but through shared values, ideals, postures, and modalities of communication. The mechanics of this culture, its flow and "swagger" serve to transform the culture into some type of rhythmic meme, influencing and informing new hosts or populations.

Based in part on the creators of this cultural meme called hip hop—despised black and brown young people in the economically challenged New York borough of the Bronx—but also because of its aggressive repurposing of earlier musical genres, aesthetics, and language, it was assumed hip hop would not (could not) survive long term. From the perspective of many, it wouldn't make it out of New York City. The creators didn't have the "stuff" necessary to pull that off. Yet, critics failed to recognize these young people, using the resources available to them, rehearsed in their language, actions . . . their general movement through the world, concerns, angst, ideals, possibilities, desires, and sensibilities shared by a host of people across the globe. The initiators needed only to find ways to reach them, to spread their new "gospel."

HIP HOP'S CALL TO ENCOUNTER "SELF" AND THE "OTHER"

Beyond philosophical speculation, truth be told, few actually live this movement; this push beyond the local is difficult at best for a variety of reasons. (Let's be clear regarding that to which I refer: I mean an encounter with hip hop's push beyond a particular nation-state as an embodied encounter over against technological innovation afforded online.) The political and economic conversations regarding hip hop have been somewhat flat or truncated in that they are typically confined to nation-state arrangements. Even when cutting across geographies, the integrity of the various boundaries (e.g., a closed rhetorical strategy and localized customs) constituted by the arrangements of the nation-state are respected somewhat. Of course, these boundaries are also porous to the extent, for instance, a particular language is connected to experience and feeling despite it not being the local mode of communication. For instance, audiences outside English-speaking countries appreciate US artists who perform in English; they feel and understand the "flow" of hip hop's inner meaning despite linguistic limitations. This effort to translate/transition hip hop raises interesting questions concerning the nature of geographic/cultural context (or what we might call "world") and the significance of embodied (and constructed) bodies encountering this "world."

Recently I had an opportunity to think through these issues—the nature of engagement with the world and the embodied body experiencing this contact. What is more, I was given an opportunity to do this beyond my familiar context of the United States and in the context of a dominant language not English.

The Institute for Philosophical Research in Hannover, Germany, through the efforts of Prof. Dr. Jürgen Manemann and Dr. Eike Brock, held an event that brought academics from Germany and the United States into conversation with German hip hop artists, with the goal being an energetic discussion of various tracks performed by these artists.[2] The track was introduced, the artist performed, and then an academic provided commentary followed by an exchange with the artist and the audience. This event (and it was an event!) brought together hundreds of people, across various generations, all intrigued by hip hop and the idea of intellectual engagement with this expansive cultural development.

In what remains of this chapter, I share some of my thoughts concerning the two tracks, or songs, for which I provided commentary. Then and now, I want to explore the conceptual arrangement of "in the world," from two dimensions and in light of the work of two artists. I offer these reflections as case studies of sorts related to the nature of movement in the world, as embodied beings. First, I use Spax's "Cosmopolitan" as a way to explore the nature and meaning of our interactions in and with the world. After that, I give some attention to the embodied body that interacts with the world using Sookee's rather controversial but deeply engaging track titled "If I had a . . ."

Case Study #1: Spax—"Cosmopolitan"

Spax (born Rafael Szulc) lives in Hannover, Germany, but has produced work with international influences such as twentieth century United States groups Public Enemy and the Beastie Boys.[3] Having had numerous collaborations and group work, Spax's international

2. See Forschungsinstitut für Philosphie Hannover, http://www.fiph.de.

3. Interestingly enough, the juxtaposition of the political over against the playful is clear to two expressions: Public Enemy's "Party for Your Right to Fight" (on the 1988 album titled *It Takes a Nation of Millions*, Columbia Records) and Beastie Boys, earlier "(You Gotta) Fight for Your Right (to Party)" from the 1986 album titled *License to Ill*, Mercury Records, 1986. A somewhat synergistic representation of these two sensibilities is represented by Spax's track discussed in this chapter.

connections raise for him questions concerning what it means to live in the world, what it means to engage the world and, ultimately, what it means and how it feels to be at home in the world. What is our rightful space? "Cosmopolitan" is his answer to such questions, all queries that naturally arise within the context of a cultural development defined by movement. In this song, he says, for instance,

> People draw boundaries;
> Boundaries separate people—turn people into strangers;
> I'm searching (to make) friends—like a piece of a puzzle.[4]

But still, we, human animals, are creatures of comfort—who seek the familiar, the likeminded, those with a similar worldview. Mindful of this, one of my favorite novelists, James Baldwin, reflects back on his own life and draws general lessons, among them the idea that we desire to belong to something—belonging is a social necessity.[5] It is in this belonging that one gathers a sense of fundamental comfort, a sense of home. But what of the boundaries that define space, that mark it out and foster our cartography of life? Theorist Benedict Anderson argues these connections, a sense of community as a fundamental marker of belonging, of home so to speak, has little to do with physical proximity—but rather has to do with agreed-upon understandings and practices generated by those understandings.[6] Yet, who can ignore the ways in which, for instance, national boundaries have mattered?

---

4. I am grateful to Dominick Hammer and Eike Brock for providing translation of this track as well as the other engaged in this chapter.

5. James Baldwin, *Go Tell It on the Mountain* (New York: Vintage International, 2013).

6. Benedict Anderson, *Imagined Communities: Reflections on the Origin and Spread of Nationalism*, rev. ed. (London: Verso, 2006).

Texas, the state in which I live, is marked out and in some sense defined in light of a boundary known as the border between Mexico and the US. But, do we live at our best if we confine ourselves to the workings of a particular geography, a particular nation-state? Or, as Spax suggests, maybe we should feel at home in the world, by means of a global identity that recognizes difference not as a problem to solve but an opportunity. There is a shared humanity not properly represented through the sociopolitical arrangements of the nation forged through opposition. Spax suggests an understanding of "home," of "belonging" that reminds me of the philosopher Anthony Appiah's cosmopolitanism—the idea that we are defined by a general humanity that cuts across regions but that this is a sense of commonality that respects difference. For Spax, this fluidity of "belonging" is outlined by a general commitment to the dignity and integrity of all—marked by a certain appreciation for play.[7]

The world is my playground.

But what of the local, the commitment to relationships that are not so globalized but take place within the context of a fixed locale? Perhaps we might think about it this way, we push for a sense of home that appreciates the particularities of our local context, but always means comfort in a more expansive context.

The sky above the city shines peacefully—
On the radio jazz is playing—
I have to turn the volume up—
I want to be like the music—at home everywhere.

And for Spax, what makes this possible—love. Perhaps he might agree with the moralist Albert Camus that absurdity is king, but love

7. Anthony Appiah, *Cosmopolitanism: Ethics in a World of Strangers* (repr.; New York: W. W. Norton & Company, 2007).

saves us from it.[8] I don't know that love, recognizing there is something of a wish in this, is sufficient. Maybe there is something to Rene Girard's assumptions regarding the need for a scapegoat—something or someone upon who can be placed the angst of life.[9] Whether love is sufficient or not, one should—I think—appreciate the appeal to movement, the comfort with difference and complexity marking out a push beyond the familiar.

Spax's approach points in the direction of empathy, the ability to place oneself within the circumstances, the existential arrangements, of the "other" so as to appreciate and more fully respond to the ontological worth and value of the "other." That is, what do we learn about others from the ways others view us?

Case Study #2: Sookee, "If I Had a . . ."

Sookee (born Nora Hantzsch) lives in Berlin but has an international presence and reputation, being labeled by many as one of the most significant "queer" rap artists alive. Drawing on her academic training in feminist and queer studies, Sookee removes our comfort with the given structures of individual and collective life by interrogating the assumed fixed nature of gender and sexuality that shape so much of our assumed identities. Hip hop becomes, when she holds the mic, a tool, a discursive strategy for combating modalities of injustice and violence such as homophobia and gender bias.

---

8. See Albert Camus, *Notebooks: 1935–1951* (New York: Marlowe & Company, 1998), 98. Read in light of Camus, *The Myth of Sisyphus and Other Essays* (New York: Vintage International, 1991); Camus, *The Rebel: An Essay on Man in Revolt* (New York: Vintage International, 1991); Camus, *The Plague* (New York: Vintage International, 1991).

9. Rene Girard, *Violence and the Sacred* (Baltimore: Johns Hopkins University, 1979).

Through Sookee's lyrics and imagery, one way to deconstruct problematic relations and structures that assume, for instance, the male as the proper subject of power is to dismantle fixed notions of identity through the performance of gender as a transferable identity marker. In this way, Sookee raises questions about the self through encounter with the other. But, rather than sympathy, Sookee, in "If I had a . . ." entertains becoming the other as an invitation for the self to understand itself vis-à-vis the glance of the other.

Her language is graphic, forcing those listening to encounter their gendered selves and the manner in which the penis and the phallic have carried a certain assumption of authority allowing for dominance; but, what if that penis, or better yet, the phallus, were "held" by another? What would men learn about themselves and their movement through the world in relationship to others? And what would women learn and gain through performance of maleness? In other words,

> If I had a dick I would give him a funny name;
> Try to shield him from all the pressure and the dictates,
> The expectations and images how a cock ought to be;
> How he's supposed to function and all the places he's supposed to penetrate.

Once one moves beyond the initial shock of Sookee's lyrics, some things become rather clear: attention to the other and what we learn from that attention is an important topic of philosophical inquiry, seeing our face in the face of the other has prompted certain philosophical challenges and ethical opportunities. In the context of the United States, for sure, such reflexive attention to the other has been a way to rethink racial bias and prejudice: sociologist and philosopher W. E. B. DuBois certainly thought along these lines, also giving attention to the nature and movement of spoken and material bodies in the world of human historical developments.[10]

How does it feel to be a problem? he asked at the turn of the twentieth century. And I find common frameworks in those influenced by him. And then there is gender and sexuality—and opportunities to rethink power through the grammar of gender and sexuality. What does it mean to be a man, and what are the dynamics of masculinity when women, not men, control the discourse and model new modes of behavior for men? How does this reconstruction of masculinity and male identity change the dynamics of self-understanding and communal life?

The markers of identity don't seem so reified, so fixed, when gender is mirrored and performed by the other. The issue here is empathy not duplication. Sookee demands more:

> Who are those fools with their performance principle?
> That makes us sick, me and my dick, basically we don't want beef;
> But the blabber about harder, longer, deeper, gagging, gang ba-bangers
> is dumb shit, all of it, masculinists want to change men;
> He [my dick] doesn't like power games, doesn't like love-hate relationships.

I grew up during the age of hip hop when it wasn't uncommon for the gangsta's stance to involve gripping balls, with an aggressive lean—all followed by harsh words that spoke to power through the ability to use the penis as a weapon, a sword, that can degrade, render docile and control those it "confronts." This was the case with the Houston,

10. W. E. B. Du Bois, *The Souls of Black Folk* (Mineola, NY: Dover Publications, 1994).

Texas–based group, the Geto Boys; the penis became a weapon of derision and denouncement in the feud between Dr. Dre and the late Easy E—after their falling out and the end of NWA. But what if the penis and its activity are viewed through how the "other" understands its proper use and placement, so to speak?

What I am suggesting is another dimension to the question shaping this portion of our time together, an underside to the question that I find compelling: What do we learn about ourselves—our creative and destructive tendencies—through our awareness of the other's awareness of us? More to the point, what do we learn about masculinity and being male when a woman performs masculinity?

Sookee's "If I had a . . ." models a response by playing with, so to speak, the penis. Whether intentional or not I do not know, but I hear something of philosopher Judith Butler in Sookee's lyrics.[11] This isn't Freud's phallus; it's Butler's. And, the idea isn't to destroy difference, to wipe out distinction. The penis maybe biological, but the phallus is a shifting and fluid idea of power; it is cultural. Like Butler, Sookee takes the phallus as a symbol of power and renders it transferable. To discuss it otherwise is to essentialize and reify gender, and there is little we can learn from that process.

Reconstructing rather than destroying the phallus wipes out the male as the eternal subject—although we remain trapped within a certain grammar of life. Life is in relationship—the extension of our selves to others in ways that affirm dignity and the value of difference—mutuality. Such a philosophical shift (and its cultural-social implications) might just free us to be to and with others and ourselves in new and affirming ways.

---

11. See for example, Judith Butler, *Gender Trouble: Feminism and the Subversion of Identity* (New York: Routledge, 2006); Butler, *Bodies That Matter: On the Discursive Limits of Sex* (New York: Routledge, 2011).

There is something of the blues in this take on life—sexual pleasure as affirmation of the beauty and value of embodied bodies—as layered complex, marked by paradox. Early-twentieth-century blues legends Ma Rainey or Bessie Smith might sway in agreement as Sookee spits fire. What is authentic about our embodied bodies as discursive constructions and what is important about others, and us as biological realities, is rethought. Perspective is gained.

How does it feel be another, or at the very least to have all one's "received" postures of identity performed by another? This is uncomfortable to be sure, but it is the type of discomfort that is productive because it pushes from the margins of life to the center and re-envisions possibilities for relationship and mutuality along the way. By extension such a self-understanding in relationship to the other also shows embodied bodies stripped down, so to speak. Performance becomes a mode of being and a method for deciphering the meaning of that being (in connection to space, place, and materiality). Sookee, in a different track, sums it up, I think, by referencing an insight made by RuPaul. "We are born naked," and RuPaul says and Sookee raps, "and the rest is drag."[12] This certainly gives a layered meaning to the idea we drag our embodied bodies through the world . . . uhm.

IN THE WORLD AND OF IT: NOW WHAT . . .?

Proclaimed so often it is a given, or perhaps a cliché, to say hip hop is global. Still, the evidence supporting this statement is graphic. From graffiti with a shared grammar and vocabulary craved into the body of cities across the globe, to the aesthetic of dress that marks bodies of hip hop devotees despite differences in the local culture of their

12. See RuPaul's *Lettin' It All Hang Out: An Autobiography* (New York: Hyperion, 1996); Sookee, "D.R.A.G.—Sookee (official music video HD)," Felix Landbeck, October 20, 2012, https://www.youtube.com/watch?v=BZvF1_XyIKU.

particular national geography, to a style of dance showcased on stages from New York to Tokyo, to Hannover, to the sound—the rhythm, the energy, the unspoken "something" of hip hop culture travels with ease across geographies of meaning, feeling, purpose and desire.

Hip hop culture, as expressed and explored by Spax and Sookee, brings into graphic relief who we are and what we do when we engage the world. Mindful of this, hip hop can be understood as the "soundtrack" for movement—for (in)stability and the shifts as well as twists and turns. It is often movement from the margins to the center of public imagination. It, hip hop, involves a type of cultural inversion to the extent by means of transposition it has embraced socioeconomic arrangements of the modern West in part by rejecting these same markers of meaning.

We move through the world, improving it and aiding those in it, while harming it and damaging those depending on it. And, along this paradoxical path, we bring our troubled and troubling bodies with us. Hip hop . . . for real.

13 HIP HOP CULTURE IS LOCAL

I think the first language I learned to speak was music.

—Brad "Scarface" Jordan

Now if you never been to Texas, there's a picture to paint.

—Bun B

The previous chapter explored hip hop within the context of Germany—an international take on the "culture." This final chapter zooms in, and looks at religious dynamics within the particularities of hip hop culture in Houston (TX).

Not long after hip hop became recognized in the Northeast during the late 1970s and as West Coast gangsta rap announced and mocked the socioeconomic and political dimensions of racial disregard exposed by the California sun in the late 1980s, the South—the "third coast"—flipped the hip hop script.[1] For example, in Houston

1. For information on southern hip hop, see for example: Ben Westhoff, *Dirty South: OutKast, Lil Wayne, Soulja Boy, and the Southern Rappers Who Reinvented Hip-Hop* (Chicago: Chicago Review Press, 2011); Brad Scarface Jordan, *Diary of a Madman: The Geto Boys, Life, Death, and the Roots of Southern Rap* (New York: Dey Street Books, 2016); James Prince, *The Art and Science of Respect: A Memoir by James Prince* (Houston: N-the-Water, 2018); Maco L. Faniel, *Hip-Hop in Houston: The Origin and the Legacy* (Cheltenham, UK: History Press, 2013); Lance Scott Walker, *Houston Rap Tapes: An Oral History of Bayou City Hip-Hop* (Austin: University of Texas Press, 2018).

in the 1980s and 1990s, the Underground Kings (UGK), Geto Boys, DJ Screw and the Screwed Up Click, Slim Thug, Paul Wall, Camillionaire, and others presented a poetics of life dependent on the existential arrangements of the "dirty" South. While the narrative trajectory was rich and complex, dimensions of southern hip hop reflected a particularly strong sense of the signifying nature of life below the Mason-Dixon Line. Given that the music arose in the Bible Belt, one of these dimensions of course entailed reflecting on *and* countering the sensibilities and ritual structures that mark a vibrantly religious terrain.

WHAT IT DO?

Drawing on a shared cultural cartography of southern historical and existential circumstances, Black religion (e.g., the Black church) and hip hop capture creative efforts to render life meaningful. But the manner in which this rendering takes place differs. While Black religion advocates vertical relationships as the ultimate direction of experience, hip hop boasts an irreverent embrace of horizontal relationships. In short, it's the difference between longing for heaven, thus embracing the hood-transcendent realms, and developing a feel for a troubled world.

Both southern Black religion and hip hop give wrestling with life and death an affective quality, that is to say, a "flow" that extends beyond reason (i.e., the mind) to capture and move the body. In either case, visual and sonic performance is central to the extent that it shrouds Blackness in a mood and offers a posture toward/in the social world that signifies that world. Performance here includes ritualized presentation of bodies arranged in time and space and situated in ways meant to speak their importance—for example, church services, chillin', tent revivals, and parties in parks. Yet Black religion and hip hop know that none of this colorful enactment of resistant life safeguards against death (either physical or social).[2] In fact, the existential circumstances framing the emergence of Black religion and hip hop have resulted in them being oversaturated with demise.[3] The Black church, for instance, does not exist without a storied death—the Christ figure murdered by means of crucifixion. Albeit not a transfiguration of the Christ per se (actually more Bacchus-related in tone and intent), hip hop comes from a long history of figures who enact violent demise—from the blues' Stagger Lee (who kills over social disrespect), to R&B chronicles of the mean streets and even meaner antihero, to the contemporary gangsta.

Black churches—through their theo-poetic language, ritual structures, and communal performance—are meant to "tame" death and normalize it as part of a (vertical) relationship with something greater. In hymns like "Precious Lord," written as a theologized articulation of mourning; in elaborate funeral services marking the transition between realms; and in eulogies with an affective quality through which a righteous economy of transcendent well-being is safeguarded, Black churches institutionalize a relationship to demise highlighting "new life" beyond it. The disregard attached to Blackness, to movement through the world within a targeted body, made of churches a location of redress through a form of creative surrender: a spiritualization of death as a moment of transition to "the more" than the world embraced by hip hop. In this way the church seeks to free flesh from material entanglements and, in this moment of surrender, to set the soul against the body—the latter to decompose and go back to the earth and the former to reunite with a spirit realm far from the

2. For information on the nature and meaning of social death, see, for example Orlando Patterson, *Slavery and Social Death: A Comparative Study*, with a new preface (Cambridge, MA: Harvard University Press, 2018).

3. For the purposes of this chapter, attention is limited to one dimension of hip hop's quadratic structure—rap music.

earth. Hip hop's engagement with demise is not the same in that performance is altered, marked, for example, by the grim instructions for dying offered in Scarface's "I Seen a Man Die":

> Stop trying to fight the reaper just relax and let it go
> Because there's no way you can fight it but you'll still try
> And you can try it 'til you fight it but you'll still die.[4]

Death becomes the signifier of life's negative arrangements, the fragility and uncertainty of existence in an environment marked by absurdity. That is to say, southern hip hop doesn't seek to hide from death but rather understands life and death to be always relational, always blended.

In fact, as Sharon Holland notes, some artists have "embraced the culture of death as a way to move their bodies out of space and into time." This, for Holland, poses the problem: the manner in which US society associates the Black body with death or the manner in which "blackness has a special relationship with the dead—that the distance between speaking subject and (in)tangible place is not so vast at all."[5] Black religion often responds to this realization by seeking to shed Black bodies in favor of a more theologically comforting sense of the "beyond" in which being isn't confined and death is no more—the colorless soul over against the suspect, embodied Black body. Hip hop, while recognizing Blackness as chronicled through death, provides an anthropology of vulnerability as inevitable and productive and not short-circuited by talk of arrangements beyond the "pale" of existential circumstances. This pretends a more materialist response that

4. Scarface, "I Seen a Man Die," on Scarface, *The Diary*, Rap-a-Lot Records, 1994.

5. Sharon P. Holland, "Bill T. Jones, Tupac Shakur and the (Queer) Art of Death," in "Gay, Lesbian, Bisexual, Transgender: Literature and Culture," special issue, *Callaloo* 23, no. 1 (Winter 2000): 384, 385.

highlights particular markers of presence as visual and sonic spectacle. In other words, Black churches have their crowns, gospel music, preacher's cars, and communion, and southern hip hop has its grillz, chopped and screwed music,[6] slabs, and sizzurp.

GRILLZ

The philosopher Mikhail Bakhtin speaks of laughter as degrading of life, and by this he means a positive arrangement through which the socially marginalized point out the materiality of existence in such a way as to highlight (and celebrate) the horizontal nature of our interactions.[7] Or one might turn to Ralph Ellison, whose sense of laughter is marked by a history of indifference and disregard racialized in extreme ways. Ellison announces that laughter—the comic impulse—shifts vision, perhaps producing a moment of explosive lucidity wherein "we pierce the veil of conventions that guard us from the basic absurdity of the human condition," a moment when, and this is key, "the world of appearances is turned upside down."[8] In Black churches the Spirit can cause laughter of joy and surrender (of will) emerging from bodies decorated with fine hats, colorful clothing, and shoes not meant for work, but in hip hop it's a bit different. What could those experiencing the conditions chronicled in so much southern rap music—a genre marked by a graphic sense of

6. Scarface says this: "Motherfuckers all over the world know Houston for Screw Tapes, but it was Darryl [Scott] who really made Houston mixtapes a thing. Darryl chopped them up and then Screw came on the scene and slowed them down, and it was the marriage of those two styles that gave Houston mixtapes their sound." Jordan, *Diary of a Madman*, 87.

7. Mikhail Bakhtin, *Rabelais and His World* (Bloomington: Indiana University Press, 1984).

8. Ralph Ellison, "An Extravagance of Laughter," in *Going to the Territory* (New York: Vintage, 1986), 146.

trauma and horror—have to laugh about and what could conjure up a smile?[9] And what of the wide smile, that particular framing of the mouth, that accompanies laughter? The answer: laughter (the type of rebellious pronouncement of survival celebrated by Zora Neale Hurston[10]) opens the world in a defiant manner as it denies or signifies the "conclusive" nature of the tragic markers of life. One might say that this act is even more rebellious when that laughter is tied to the open mouth defined by grillz composed of diamonds and gold!

Think of hip hop artists like Houston's Paul Wall and the elaborately arranged precious metals and stones exposed during a smile or made to shimmer through a laugh. Displaying teeth covered with something as material but less biologically resonant suggests signification layered onto irreverence.

Hip hop artists and fans didn't create decorative tooth coverings; such enhancements are much older than that. But hip hop, as is the case with much of the cultural material it touches, amplifies a particular pose—an abundance of "swag" that speaks against a standard invisibility demanded in line with the anti-Black racist ideology and social structuring of life in the United States. Such is

9. Ellison raises this question concerning African Americans in general when discussing his awkward laughter during his viewing of the Broadway play *Tobacco Road*. In speaking about the joke concerning barrels into which Blacks laughed so as to keep whites from hearing them, he says: "For in the joke the barrels were considered a civic necessity and had been improvised as a means of protecting the sensibilities of whites from a peculiar form of insanity suffered exclusively by Negroes, who in light of their social status and past condition of servitude were regarded as having absolutely nothing in their daily experience which could possibly inspire rational laughter. And yet Negroes continued—much as one side of me was doing—to laugh." Ellison, "Extravagance of Laughter," 188.

10. See, for example, Hurston, *I Love Myself When I Am Laughing—and Then Again When I Am Looking Mean and Impressive: A Zora Neale Hurston Reader*, ed. Alice Walker (Old Westbury, NY: Feminist Press, 1979).

the attitude of the Bacchus-like artist toward regulations—whether political or theological—executed through a visual and sonic disruption.[11] This laughter, spilling out from the bejeweled mouth, flaunts noncompliance—to find a moment of joy within a social world meant to restrict and restrain the bodies hip hop celebrates.

Grillz perform affluence while signifying socially accepted signs of wealth. And so markers of material value are turned against the social norms that once gave them significance, and now they are used to shift the cultural geography of meaning:

> I got the wrist wear and neck wear that's captivating
> But it's what smile that's got these onlookers spectating.[12]

Social normativity is performed against itself, remodeled and twisted—and consumed to the extent that the precious materials are affixed to teeth and presented in the mouth that devours. This is a transmutation of standards through aesthetic exaggeration.

CHOPPED AND SCREWED

The church organ is evident in the songs of Houston's Underground Kings (UGK), blending an instrument best known for guiding religious ritual with the impulses of gritty life. The vertical relationship inspired and encouraged by the organ is subverted and used to a different purpose: highlighting and enhancing a particular

11. This isn't "skin and grin" exposure of the teeth through a smile, marking presumed subservience and often associated with a Jim Crow-ed response to white supremacy in which smiling marks acquiescence in that, even in its fake joy or counterfeit contentment, that smile assumes a hierarchy of importance that maintains mechanisms of dehumanization: the white person must be appeased.

12. Nelly, "Grillz," featuring Paul Wall and Ali & Gipp, on *Sweatsuit*, Universal, 2005.

street-centered mood. There is a hypnotic quality to the sound, a flow between two worlds arranged inadequately around the sacred and the secular. Through a secular sermon UGK mimics the telling of truth, eliciting a call-and-response: verbal acknowledgment but with thematics geared toward presentness real and troubled/troubling. Yet at other times the sound produces a type of stillness, a stripping away to lay bare through exaggeration that offers opportunity for introspection, for meditation, for inspection. More than just southern slang, as informative as that is, this is a poetics of manipulation producing a narrative that demands careful engagement. It is communication with alternate beats and scratches that alter the sound so as to break it up and shift its flow.[13]

ALTERED SOUND

Scholars such as Tricia Rose have noted the manner in which rap music manipulates technology, "revising" traditional use—scratching, cutting, sampling—so as to respond to particular dynamics of cultural life. But in Houston there's a twist to this process in that to chop and screw is more than to revise, even though, as Rose notes of rap in general, "emotional power and presence in rap are profoundly linked to sonic force and one's receptivity to it."[14] To chop and screw is to distort words—beyond but also heightened by the dynamics of the southern drawl—and thereby to deny language centrality of expression. Instead, there is something about the sound (which is also slowed down) and the embodied response to the sound that matters.

---

13. See, for example, T. Brandon Evans, "A Sympathetic Resonance: Sound, the Listener and Affect Theory," *Leonardo Music Journal* 23 (December 2013): 88–89.

14. Tricia Rose, *Black Noise: Rap Music and Black Culture in Contemporary America* (Middletown, CT: Wesleyan University Press, 1994), 63.

Through this manipulation a series of relationships are amplified: original recording to hip hop, DJ Screw to mixed tape, recordings to fans, and so on.

DJ Screw's manipulation of sound and words is reminiscent of throat singing by Buddhist monks. They share, I would argue, a deconstruction of human communication to the extent that language limits and confines.[15] Throat singing and chopped and screwed music turn words against themselves. There is an exaggeration at work that rips at words by pushing against the typical rhythm of wordplay so as to expose sound. And anyone who's been to a charismatic Black church service knows that manipulation of auditory "signs" (highlighting energy and possibility) is reflected in Pentecostal glossolalia. Yet speaking in tongues is meant to reduce the human dimension of language by fostering a mode of communication understood only by select humans (with special gifts) and by transhuman forces. Chopped and screwed music highlights an affective turn tied to a type of mystical materialism.

Both those filled with the Holy Ghost in Christian churches and Buddhist monks mean to limit the human nature of communication—to reduce flesh as barrier by distorting the performative quality of language, stripping it down to sound. These monks and glossolalists seek vertical union. Here performance is meant to puncture the distinction between modalities of being in ways that decenter horizontal connection and instead shift away from bodies so as to highlight the possibility of communicating the dynamics of a special relationship with a trans/historical reality. Yet chopped and screwed music remains focused on the materiality of life, on the energy and trauma of horizontal engagements sonically orchestrated. Sound—the manipulation of rhythmic language—produces alterations, different states of

15. This relationship is even more pronounced when "mumble rap" is compared to throat singing.

awareness, a blurring of social distinctions, and a heightened sense of shifting material presence.

To chop and screw a song is to unleash certain possibilities of meaning and to degrade ritualistically (in a Bakhtinian sense) words so as to highlight a more fundamental "something." The listener learns about the self because the sonic shift invites opportunity for circumspection-introspection. Rather than the content—lyrics—per se, it is the process of manipulation and alteration that is important here: the way in which chopped and screwed songs "speak" a grammar made robust through sound and counter the dominant social arrangements of music presentation and consumption. Perhaps something about chopped and screwed pieces gives them a secular prayer quality—that is to say, a type of internal focus outwardly projected. Through this practice the tragic quality of life remains present, but the degrading of words points toward their deeper meaning, which mutates the intensity of the tragic. In this process the listener finds something regenerative. While I wouldn't label this experience trancelike in nature, it does seem to undercut the demands of existential circumstances because slowing down drowns out social noise.

There is, as numerous scholars note, a "therapeutic" quality to music, here amplified by DJ Screw's ritualized enhancements—his manipulation of sound as a type of conjuration. In this respect he was something of a shaman—one with the capacity to alter time and space through the manipulation of sound so as to foster transportation to a "place" of heightened awareness. Stories of life within social worlds are mutated into something sonically sublime.

Sound is only one modality of *movement*. In the South, one has to ask, how does the song sound when you're behind the wheel, slowly moving down the street?

SLABS

The South is marked by migration—by a long movement of African Americans in pursuit of more freedom—and the slab highlights a particular style of contemporary movement. Lacking the existential urgency of the Great Migration (1916–70), the slab represents slow, colorful, graphically intentional transportation through time and space.[16] The slab isn't simply the secularized preacher's vehicle, but, like the preacher's car, it is meant to bespeak a certain social presence. A slab represents a cultural code—a statement concerning the fantastic fluidity of place. And more than that, it is a signifying or warping of inherited vehicular sensibilities.

Let's be clear, a slab is more than transportation.

Cars have always served as nonverbal statements regarding socioeconomic status and style, but the slab amplifies distinctiveness and offers an alternative model of meaning delivered with a "fuck you" to those who don't appreciate it. Not just a vehicle, the slab makes a necessity within southern geography (i.e., personal transportation) a marker of ideological commitment aesthetically articulated. Bright colors, protruding spokes framing not your average tire, refined interiors, and powerful sound systems mark these custom cars—as the car, in turn, slowly marks out geographic patterns and in a way reconfigures human flesh through the transformative quality of movement. To be in the car is to be a part of the car—to reconceive the human in a sense rendering the hip hop body somewhat transhuman (i.e., machine and flesh). Their very existence speaks a type of signification in that they entail the transformation of old vehicles into new mobile tropes—*S*low, *L*oud, *A*nd *B*angin'. It's stylization, a creative impulse:

> On the older cars you put a hood ornament on it like a woman in the front or something. But on the newer cars you don't really do that too much. We also put a fifth wheel on the back, which is just a spare tire or rim on the back, but you can't use it, it's not for

16. For more on the Great Migration, see, for example, Isabel Wilkerson, *The Warmth of Other Suns: The Epic Story of America's Great Migration* (New York: Vintage, 2011).

> practical purposes, it's for decoration. We put hydraulic pumps on the fifth wheel and on the trunk, so when you hit the switch, the trunk opens up and you got neon lights showing in there with a word or phrase. You've [also] got [to have] speakers in there, and that's pretty much it. . . . You've got to jam Screw in the slab.[17]

The slab, then, is more like a transportable temple for the expression of the transformative language of hip hop—whether alone in one's car or in the company of other slabs. It is a site of alterity or a signification of transit through deliberate movement against standardization.

> If you're from that Texas, you already understand the story
> Money, cups and swangas (swangas), tops chopped with that
> trunk lit.[18]

Cups. What's in the cups?

SIZZURP

The sonic dimension, the altered sound that shifts time and space, doesn't require chemical aid, but such aid can intensify the effects. And when consumed, the popular beverage known as purple drank, sizzurp, or lean has a sacramental quality.[19]

> Take a molly like communion (pop one)
> My lil' girl like, "What you doin?" (flash one)

---

17. Paul Wall, in guestlistener, "Slow, Loud, and Bangin': Paul Wall Talks 'Slab God' Sonics," *Sounding Out*, February 22, 2016, https://soundstudiesblog.com/2016/02/22/slow-loud-and-bangin-paul-wall-talks-slab-god-sonics/.

18. Bun B, "KnoWhatImSayin," featuring Slim Thug and Lil' Keke, on *Return of the Trill*, 2 Trill Enterprises, 2018.

19. *Purple drank*, *sizzurp*, and *lean* are all names for a combination of soda and cough syrup containing codeine and promethazine hydrochloride.

I'm just tryna even out my odds (ride)
Sip and sip 'til I feel like a God (God).[20]

Lean, that purple drank (maybe in a big Styrofoam cup), is communion in a world marked by the bluesy blending of life and death as it offers a kind of euphoria married to the slow destruction of the body associated with frequent consumption of purple drank's drug components (promethazine and codeine). Christian communion speaks of death—physical and spiritual—but seeks to substitute one for all, denying the need for each believer to die because one has already made the sacrifice. In a word, "Jesus paid it all." But lean or sizzurp offers no such protection, no substitute. Instead, it is alchemy of mystic-material meaning, which remains earthy and en/fleshed and reflects a demand for "payment" from each consumer.

Still, as the body succumbs to the effects of purple drank, it opens the mind of the one with the cup to new insights, a lucidity that slows down time within an otherwise racing world. And unlike the hyper-personal quality of communion, in which drinking the representation of Christ's blood is only for particular devotees in place at the time, the ritual consumption of lean is more communal in that one might pour some for those not present as a libational act.

Over against wine, representing (if not becoming) the blood of Jesus the Christ through communion, lean remains its chemical ingredients while encouraging horizontal relationships expressed through a body "open" to (the) influence. Yet, like the Christian communion story, it opens toward demise. How could it be otherwise, when church in the South and hip hop in the South are subject to anti-Blackness and class dynamics death-dealing in nature? In a sense, the communion element of both wine and sizzurp entails the consumption of

---

20. Calvin Harris, "Prayers Up," featuring Travis Scott and A-Trak, on *Funk Wav Bounces*, vol. 1, Columbia, 2017.

death—with the former pointing out death as a vertical relationship and the latter slurring the reality of death as horizontal in nature. Christian communion pulls those who consume the elements away from the body through materials that point beyond themselves, but lean urges a deeper (and enhanced) interrogation of the materiality of life—its sights, its sounds, and its feel.

REMIX

Taken altogether, DJ Screw slowed down the music, slowed down the vocals, and in doing so, he highlighted something earthy yet mystical, enhanced by purple drank. The slab moves at a pace reflecting this sonic pulse. The lyrics reduced to a sound pumped loud might just bring a smile with diamonds glistening. And all this offers revelation of hip hop life in the Bible Belt.

ACKNOWLEDGMENTS

This book has been a good number of years in the making, and I must thank my editor—Bethany Dickerson—for being open to talking about the possibility of this book and then agreeing to publish it. Bethany and the rest of the Fortress Press team have been a joy! Because these pieces were published over almost a thirty-year period, the original files were not necessarily in good shape or easy to work with. If not for Maya Reine, they would have remained a set of documents without formatting consistencies and a host of other issues. Thank you, Maya, for your hard work to get these files together.

My family and friends—in the USA and in Europe—encouraged conversation related to Hip Hop and made space for really important exchanges. All those gatherings inform this book. Thank you!

Finally, I must thank my various publishers who originally published these pieces for permission to reprint these essays—now chapters in this book:

SECTION ONE

Chapter 1: Rap Music as Social Transformation

"How Ya Livin'? Notes on Rap Music and Social Transformation," *The Western Journal of Black Studies*, Vol. 23, No. 1 (1999): 10–21. Reproduced by permission of the *Western Journal of Black Studies.*

Chapter 2: The Blues and Identity

"What's The Theological Equivalent of a 'Manish Boy'? Learning a Lesson from Womanist Scholarship," in Stacey Floyd-Thomas, ed. *Deeper Shades of Purple* (New York: New York University Press, 2006), 275–281. Reproduced by permission of New York University Press.

Chapter 3: What Humanists Might Learn from Hip Hop

"Thoughts on What Humanists Might Learn from Hip Hop," *Free Inquiry*, Vol. 32, No. 6 (October/November 2012): 31–35. Reproduced by permission of *Free Inquiry*.

Chapter 4: Zombies in the 'Hood

"Zombies in the hood: Rap music, Camusian Absurdity, and the Structuring of Death," in Monica Miller, Anthony Pinn, Bernard "Bun B" Freeman, editors. *Religion in Hip Hop: Mapping the New Terrain in the US* (London: Bloomsbury Publishing, 2015), 183–197. By permission of Bloomsbury Academic, an imprint of Bloomsbury Publishing Company.

Chapter 5: The Realism of Kendrick Lamar

"Real nigga conditions': Kendrick Lamar, grotesque realism, and the open body", Christopher M. Driscoll, Anthony B. Pinn, and Monica R. Miller, editors. *Kendrick Lamar and the Making of Black Meaning* (New York: Routledge, 2020), 231–244. Reproduced by permission of Taylor & Francis Group.

SECTION TWO

Chapter 6: Conversion in Hip Hop

"On a Mission from God: African American Music and the Nature/Meaning of Conversion and Religious Life," in Gordon Lynch, editor, *Between Sacred and Profane: Researching Religion and Popular Culture*

(London: I. B. Tauris, 2007), 143–156. Reproduced by permission of I. B. Tauris, an imprint of Bloomsbury Publishing Company.

Chapter 7: Theology, Popular Culture, and Religion

Anthony Pinn, "Cultural Production and New Terrain: Theology, Popular Culture, and the Cartography of Religion," in *Creating Ourselves: African Americans and Hispanics on Popular Culture and Religious Expressions*, eds. Anthony B. Pinn and Benjamin Valentin, pp. 12–33. Copyright © 2009, Duke University Press. All rights reserved. Republished by permission of the copyright holder and the publisher. www.dukepress.edu.

Chapter 8: The Lyrics of Angels and Demons

"When Demons Come Calling: Dealing with the Devil and Paradigms of Life in African American Music," in Christopher Partridge and Eric Christianson, editors, *The Lure of the Dark Side: Satan and Western Demonology in Popular Culture* (London: Equinox, 2009), 60–73. Reproduced by permission of Taylor & Francis Group.

Chapter 9: Tupac Shakur's Life and Death in Music

Anthony Pinn and Paul Easterling, "Followers of Black Jesus on Alert: Thoughts on the Story of Tupac's Life/Death/Life," *Black Theology: An International Journal*, Vol. 7, No 1 (2009): 31–44. Reproduced by permission of Paul Easterling and Taylor & Francis Group.

Chapter 10: The Divine Status in Hip Hop

"God Wears Tom Ford: Hip Hop's Re-envisioning of Divine Authority," *Media Development*, Volume LX4 (2014): 20–23. Reproduced by permission of World Association for Christian Communications.

Chapter 11: Artists Deified

"The End: Thoughts on Humanism and Death," in Whitney Bauman, editor, "Secular Theologies and Theologies of the Secular," a special issue of *Dialog*, Volume 45, Issues 45 (December 2015): 347–354. Reproduced by permission of John Wiley and Sons and *Dialog*.

Chapter 12: Hip Hop Culture Is Global

Parts of the text were published in: J. Manemann/ E. Brock, *Philosophie des HipHop. Performen, was an der Zeit ist* (Bielefeld: transcript Verlag, 2018). Used by permission.

Chapter 13: Hip Hop Culture Is Local

Essay originally published as "Bible Belt Swag: Houston Hip-Hop and Black Religion," in Valerie Oliver, editor. Exhibit Catalogue for *The Dirty South: Contemporary Art, Material Culture, and the Sonic Impulse*, Virginia Museum of Fine Arts (Virginia Museum of Fine Arts, 2021), 80–87. Reproduced by permission of the Virginia Museum of Fine Arts.

SELECTED DISCOGRAPHY

"All I Do, the Church Keep A-Grumbling," https://www.negrospirituals.com/songs/all_i_do_the_chunrch_keep_a_grumbling.htm.

Arrested Development. *Three Years, 5 Months, and 2 Days in the Life of . . .* Chrysalis Records, 1992.

———. "United Front." *Zingalamaduni*. Chrysalis Records, 1994.

Beastie Boys. "(You Gotta) Fight for Your Right (to Party)." *License to Ill*. Mercury Records, 1986

Bessie Smith. "Devil's Gonna Git You." Columbia, 1928.

Boogie Down Productions. *Ghetto Music: The Blueprint of Hip Hop*. Zomba Recording Corporation, 1989.

Brown, James. "Say It Loud—I'm Black and I'm Proud (Part 1)." King, 1968.

Bun B featuring Slim Thug and Lil' Keke. "KnoWhatImSayin." *Return of the Trill*. 2 Trill Enterprises, 2018.

Cardi B. "Best Life." *Invasion of Privacy*. Atlantic Records, 2018.

Da Lench Mob. "Freedom Got an A-K." *Guerilla's in Tha Mist*. EastWest/Atlantic Records, 1992.

Dr. Dre. *The Chronic*. Interscope Records, 1992.

———. "Li'l Ghetto Boy." *D.O.D. Do or Die*. The Legion Records, 2005

Earth, Wind, and Fire. "Fantasy." *The Best of Earth, Wind & Fire*. Vol. 1. Columbia Records, 1978.

Flo Rida. "In the Ayer." *Mail on Sunday*. Atlantic, 2018.

Geto Boys. *Geto Boys Best: Uncut Dope*. Rap-A-Lot Records, Inc, 1992.

———. *Grip It! On That Other Level*. Priority Records, 1989.

———. "Mind Playing Tricks on Me." *We Can't Be Stopped*. Rap-A-Lot Records, 1991.

Grand Master Flash and the Furious Five. "The Message." *The Message*. Sugar Hill Records, 1982.

Harris, Calvin, featuring Travis Scott and A-Trak. "Prayers Up." *Funk Wav Bounces*. Vol. 1. Columbia, 2017.

Hopkins, Lightin'. "Black Ghost Blues." *Soul Blues*. Prestige, 1965.

Ice Cube. "Li'l Ass Gee." Lethal Injection. Priority Records, 1993.

———. "My Skin Is My Sin." *Bootlegs & B-Sides*. Priority Records, 1994.

———. "Robbin' Hood (Cause It Ain't All Good)." *Bootlegs & B-Sides*. Priority Records, 1994.

Ice-T. *Rhyme Pays*. Sire, 1987

Jay Z. "Crown." *Magna Carta Holy Grail*. Roc-A-Fella/Universal, 2013.

———. "Empire State of Mind." *The Blueprint 3*. Roc Nation, 2009.

———. "F.U.T.W." *Magna Carta*. Roc-A-Fella Records, 2013.

———. "Heaven," *Magna Carta*. Roc-A-Fella Records, 2013.

———. "Moment of Clarity," *The Black Album*. Roc-A-Fella/Def Jam, 2003.

Jay Z and Kanye West. "Niggas in Paris." *Watch the Throne*. Roc-A-Fella Records, 2011.

———. "No Church in the Wild." *Watch the Throne*. Roc-A-Fella Records, 2011.

———. "Who Gon Stop Me." *Watch the Throne*. Roc-A-Fella Records, 2011.

Johnson, Robert "Hell Hound On My Trail." https://genius.com/Robert-johnson-hellhound-on-my-trail-lyrics.

———. "Me and the Devil Blues." http://www.everydaycompanion.com/lyrics/songs/me_and_the_devil_blues.asp.

———."Ramblin' On My Mind." https://genius.com/Robert-johnson-ramblin-on-my-mind-take-2-lyrics.

KRS-One and Scott La Rock. *Criminal Minded*. B-Boy, 1987.

Lamar, Kendrick. "Alright" *To Pimp a Butterfly*. Top Dawg Entertainment, 2015.

———. "ELEMENT." *DAMN*. Interscope Records, 2017.

———. "YAH." *DAMN*. Interscope Records, 2017.

London, October. "Black Man in America." *Color Blind: Love*. Cadillacc Music, 2016.

Megan Thee Stallion. "Savage." *Suga*. 1501 Certified, 2020.

"Members Don't Get Weary." https://www.negrospirituals.com/songs/members_don_t_get_weary.htm.

Nelly featuring Paul Wall and Ali & Gipp. "Grillz." *Sweatsuit*. Universal, 2005.

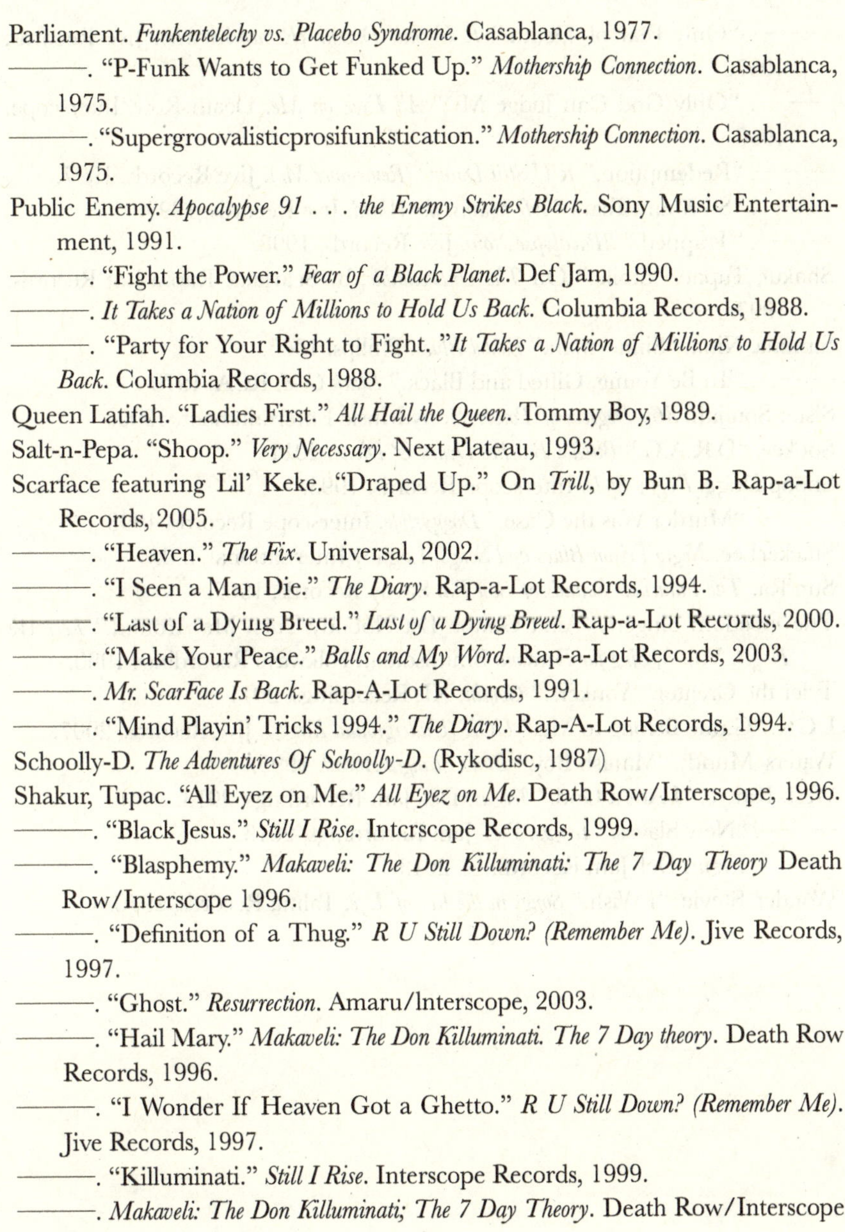

Parliament. *Funkentelechy vs. Placebo Syndrome.* Casablanca, 1977.

———. "P-Funk Wants to Get Funked Up." *Mothership Connection.* Casablanca, 1975.

———. "Supergroovalisticprosifunkstication." *Mothership Connection.* Casablanca, 1975.

Public Enemy. *Apocalypse 91 . . . the Enemy Strikes Black.* Sony Music Entertainment, 1991.

———. "Fight the Power." *Fear of a Black Planet.* Def Jam, 1990.

———. *It Takes a Nation of Millions to Hold Us Back.* Columbia Records, 1988.

———. "Party for Your Right to Fight. "*It Takes a Nation of Millions to Hold Us Back.* Columbia Records, 1988.

Queen Latifah. "Ladies First." *All Hail the Queen.* Tommy Boy, 1989.

Salt-n-Pepa. "Shoop." *Very Necessary.* Next Plateau, 1993.

Scarface featuring Lil' Keke. "Draped Up." On *Trill,* by Bun B. Rap-a-Lot Records, 2005.

———. "Heaven." *The Fix.* Universal, 2002.

———. "I Seen a Man Die." *The Diary.* Rap-a-Lot Records, 1994.

———. "Last of a Dying Breed." *Last of a Dying Breed.* Rap-a-Lot Records, 2000.

———. "Make Your Peace." *Balls and My Word.* Rap-a-Lot Records, 2003.

———. *Mr. ScarFace Is Back.* Rap-A-Lot Records, 1991.

———. "Mind Playin' Tricks 1994." *The Diary.* Rap-A-Lot Records, 1994.

Schoolly-D. *The Adventures Of Schoolly-D.* (Rykodisc, 1987)

Shakur, Tupac. "All Eyez on Me." *All Eyez on Me.* Death Row/Interscope, 1996.

———. "Black Jesus." *Still I Rise.* Intcrscope Records, 1999.

———. "Blasphemy." *Makaveli: The Don Killuminati: The 7 Day Theory* Death Row/Interscope 1996.

———. "Definition of a Thug." *R U Still Down? (Remember Me).* Jive Records, 1997.

———. "Ghost." *Resurrection.* Amaru/Interscope, 2003.

———. "Hail Mary." *Makaveli: The Don Killuminati. The 7 Day theory.* Death Row Records, 1996.

———. "I Wonder If Heaven Got a Ghetto." *R U Still Down? (Remember Me).* Jive Records, 1997.

———. "Killuminati." *Still I Rise.* Interscope Records, 1999.

———. *Makaveli: The Don Killuminati; The 7 Day Theory.* Death Row/Interscope 1996.

———. "Only Fear of Death." *R U Still Down? (Remember Me)*. Jive Records, 1997.

———. "Only God Can Judge Me." *All Eyez on Me*. Death Row/Interscope, 1996

———. "Redemption." *R U Still Down? (Remember Me)*. Jive Records, 1997.

———. "So Many Tears." *Me against the World*. Jive Records, 1995.

———. "Trapped." *2Pacalypse Now*. Jive Records, 1998.

Shakur, Tupac. "Smile." On *The Untouchable*, by Scarface. Rap-a-Lot Records, 1997.

Simone, Nina. "Sinnerman." *Pastel Blues*. Philips, 1965.

———. "To Be Young, Gifted and Black." *Black Gold*. RCA, 1970

Sister Souljah. *360 Degrees of Power*. Sony Music Entertainment, 1992.

Sookee. "D.R.A.G." *Bitches Butches Dykes & Divas*. 2011

Snoop Dogg. *Doggy Style*. Interscope Records, 1993.

———. "Murder Was the Case." *Doggystyle*. Interscope Records, 1993.

StackerLee. *Negro Prison Blues and Songs*. Legacy International, n.d.

Sun Ra. *The Futuristic Sounds of Sun Ra*. Savoy Records, 1962.

The Freedom Singers. "Ain't Gonna Let Nobody Turn Me Around." *Lest We Forget*. Vol. 3, *Sing for Freedom*. Smithsonian Folkways Recordings 1980.

Tyler the Creator. "Yonkers." *Goblin*. XL Recordings, 2011

UGK. "Game Belong to Me." *UGK (Underground Kingz)*. Jive Records, 2007.

Waters, Muddy "Manish Boy." *Blues Straight Ahead*. 1995.

West, Kanye. "I Am a God," *Yeezus*. Def Jam Recordings, 2013.

———. "New Slaves." *Yeezus*. Def Jam Recordings, 2013.

———. *Yeezus*. Def Jam Recordings, 2013.

Wonder, Stevie. "I Wish." *Songs in the Key of Life*. Talma Records, 1976.

SELECTED BIBLIOGRAPHY

Alvarez, Lizette and Cara Buckley. "Zimmerman Is Acquitted in Trayvon Martin Killing." *New York Times*. July 13, 2013.

Anderson, Benedict. *Imagined Communities: Reflections on the Origin and Spread of Nationalism*. Rev. ed. London: Verso, 2006.

Anderson, Victor. *Beyond Ontological Blackness*. New York: Continuum, 1995.

Appiah, Anthony. *Cosmopolitanism: Ethics in a World of Strangers*. New York: W. W. Norton & Company, 2007.

Bakhtin, Mikhail. *Rabelais and His World*. Bloomington: Indiana University Press, 1984.

Baldwin, James. *Go Tell It on the Mountain*. New York: Vintage International, 2013.

Barrett, Lindon. "Dead Men Printed: Tupac Shakur, Biggie Small, and Hip-Hop Eulogy." *Callaloo* 22, no. 2 (1999): 306.

Bataille, Georges. "The 'Old Mole' and the Prefix Sur in the Words Surhomme [Supeprman' and Surrealist." In *Vision of Excess: Selected Writings, 1927–1939*, edited by Allan Stoekl. Minneapolis: University of Minnesota Press, 1985.

Butler, Judith. *Bodies That Matter: On the Discursive Limits of Sex*. New York: Routledge, 2011.

———. *Gender Trouble: Feminism and the Subversion of Identity*. New York: Routledge, 2006.

Bluijs, Siebe. "From Compton to Congress: The Barbarians Inside the Gates—an Exploraiton of 'Black Subjectivity' in Kendrick Lamar's To Pimp a Butterfly." *Thamyris/Intersecting: Place, Sex & Race* 32 (2017): 72–87.

Callahan, Allen. *The Talking Book: African Americans and the Bible*. New Haven, CT: Yale University Press, 2006.

Campbell, Alice P. "Notorious Rapper's Supposed Death Surrounded by Speculation." *lutercol11* College of the Mainland, December 2003.

Camus, Albert. "Fourth Letter." In *Resistance, Rebellion, and Death: Essays*. New York: Vintage International, 1995.

———. *The Myth of Sisyphus and Other Essays*. Translated by Justin O'Brien. New York: Alfred A. Knopf, 1969. Repr., New York: Vintage International, 1991.

———. *Notebooks: 1935–1951*. New York: Marlowe & Company, 1998.

———. *The Plague*. New York: Vintage International, 1991.

———*Rebel: An Essay on Man in Revolt*. New York: Vintage International, 1991.

———. "The Renegade, or a Confused Mind." In *Exile and the Kingdom*. New York: Vintage International, 2007.

———. *Resistance, Rebellion, and Death: Essays*. New York: Vintage International, 1995.

Cannon, Katie Geneva. *Black Womanist Ethics.* Eugene, OR: Wipf and Stock, 2006 [1988].

———. "Resources for a Constructive Ethic: The Life and Work of Zora Neale Hurston." In *Katie's Canon: Womanism and the Soul of the Black Community*. New York: Continuum, 1995.

Castronovo, Russ. *Necro Citizenship: Death, Eroticism, and the Public Sphere in the Nineteenth-Century United States*. Durham, NC: Duke University Press, 2001.

Clark, David. *The Sociology of Death*. Cambridge, MA: Blackwell Publishers, 1993.

Cleaver, Eldridge. *Soul on Ice*. New York: Delta Books, 1968.

Cone, James H. *A Black Theology of Liberation*. Maryknoll, NY: Orbis Books, 1989.

———. *The Spiritual and the Blues*. Maryknoll, NY: Orbis Books, 1991.

———. "Strange Fruit: The Cross and the Lynching Tree." *Harvard Divinity Bulletin* 35, no. 1 (Winter 2007): 47–55.

Cone, James H., and Gayraud Wilmore, *Black Theology: A Documentary History.* Vols. 1–2. Maryknoll, NY: Orbis Books, 1993.

Connelly, Frances S., ed. *Modern Art and the Grotesque*. New York: Cambridge University Press, 2003.

Connor, Marlene Kim. *What Is Cool? Understanding Black Manhood in America*. New York: Crown Publishers, 1995.

Craddock-Willis, Andre. "Rap: Taking It from the Streets." *Keyboard* 14, no. 11 (November 1988).

———. "Rap Music and the Black Musical Tradition: A Critical Assessment." *Radical America* 23 (October 1989): 4.

Christgau, Robert, and Greg Tate. "Chuck D All Over the Map." *The Village Voice*, October 1991, 12–18.

Christian, Margena A. "Rap Star Snoop Dogg Talks about Fame, Fatherhood and Family." *Jet Magazine*, May 2000.

Cumber, Daryl Dance. *Shuckin' and Jivin': Folklore from Contemporary Black Americans*. Bloomington: Indiana University Press, 1978.

Davis, Wade. *The Serpent and the Rainbow: A Harvard Scientist's Astonishing Journey into the Secret Societies of Haitian Voodoo, Zombis, and Magic*. New York: Touchstone, 1997.

De Genova, Nick. "Gangster Rap and Nihilism in Black America: Some Questions of Life and Death." *Social Text* 43 (Autumn 1995): 91.

Dogg, Snoop. *The Doggfather: The Times, Trials, and Hardcore Truths of Snoop Dogg*. New York: William Morrow and Company, Inc., 1999.

Du Bois, W. E. B. "Of the Sorrow Songs." In *The Souls of Black Folk*, edited by Henry Louis Gates Jr. and Terri Hume Oliver. New York: W. W. Norton & Company, 1999.

———. "On the Passing of the First-Born." In *The Souls of Black Folk*, edited by Henry Louis Gates Jr. and Terri Hume Oliver. New York: W. W. Norton & Company, 1999.

———. *The Souls of Black Folk*. Edited by Henry Louis Gates Jr., and Terri Hume Oliver. New York: W. W. Norton & Company, 1999.

Dyson, Michael Eric. *Between God and Gangsta Rap: Bearing Witness to Black Culture*. Oxford University Press, 1996.

Dyson, Michael Eric. *Holler If You Hear Me: Searching for Tupac Shakur*. New York: Basic Civitas Books, 2001.

———. "Rap Culture, the Church, and American Society." In *Sacred Music of the Secular City: From Blues to Rap*, edited by Jon Michael Spencer, 268–73. A special issue of *Black Sacred Music: A Journal of Theo-musicology* 6, no. 1 (1992).

Earl, Riggins. *Dark Symbols, Obscure Signs: God, Self, and Community in the Slave Mind*. Maryknoll, NY: Orbis Books, 1993.

Editors of Vibe, The. "Inside the Mind of Shakur." In *Tupac Shakur*. New York: Crown Publishers, 1997.

Ellison, Ralph. "An Extravagance of Laughter." In *Going to the Territory*. New York: Vintage, 1986.

———. *The Invisible Man*. New York: Random House, 1952.

———. "Living with Music." In *Shadow and Act*, 189–90. New York: Vintage International, 1995.

Evans, James, Jr. *Spiritual Empowerment in African American Literature*. Lewiston, NY: Edwin Mellen Press, 1988.

———. *We Have Been Believers: An African American Systematic Theology*. Minneapolis: Fortress Press, 1992.

Evans, T. Brandon. "A Sympathetic Resonance: Sound, the Listener and Affect Theory." *Leonardo Music Journal* 23 (December 2013): 88–89.

Faniel, Maco L. *Hip-Hop in Houston: The Origin and the Legacy*. Cheltenham, UK: History Press, 2013.

Fletcher, Karen Baker. *A Singing Something: Anna J. Cooper & the Foundations of Womanist Theology*. Pennsylvania: Crossroad, 1994.

Franklin, Clyde W. II. "Men's Studies, the Men's Movement, and the Study of Black Masculinities: Further Demystification of Masculinities in America." In *The American Black Male: His Present Status and His Future*, edited by Richard G. Majors and Jacob U. Gordon, 3–19. Chicago: Nelson-Hall Publishers, 1994.

Foreman, Murray, and Mark Anthony Neal, eds. *That's the Joint! The Hip-Hop Studies Reader*. New York: Routledge, 2004.

Foucault, Michel. *Ethics: Subjectivity and Truth*. Edited by Paul Rabinow. New York: The New Press, 1997.

———. *Technologies of the Self: A Seminar*. Amherst: University of Massachusetts Press, 1988.

Gates, Henry Louis, Jr. *Signifying Monkey: A Theory of African-American Literary Criticism*. New York: Oxford University Press, 1988.

George, Nelson. *Buppies, B-Boys, Baps & Bohos: Notes on Post-soul Black Culture*. New York: Harper Perennial, 1994.

Gibbs, Jewelle Taylor. "Anger in Young Black Males: Victims or Victimizers?" In *The American Black Male: His Present Status and His Future*, edited by Richard G. Majors and Jacob U. Gordon, 127–43. Chicago: Nelson-Hall Publishers, 1994.

Giddings, Paula. *When and Where I Enter: The Impact of Black Women on Race and Sex in America*. New York: Bantam Books, 1984.

Gilkes, Cheryl Townsend. *If It Wasn't for the Women . . . : Black Women's Experience and Womanist Culture in Church and Community*. New York: Orbis Books, 2000.

Gilroy, Paul *Black Atlantic: Modernity and Double Consciousness*. New York: Oxford University Press, 1995.

Girard, Rene. *Violence and the Sacred*. Baltimore: Johns Hopkins University, 1979.

Gonzalez, G. M. "Of Property: On 'Captive' 'Bodies,' Hidden 'Flesh,' and Colonization." In *Existence in Black: An Anthology of Black Existential Philosophy*, edited by Lewis R. Gordon. New York: Routledge, 1997

Gordon, Lewis, ed. *Existence in Black: An Anthology of Black Existential Philosophy*. New York: Routledge, 1996.

Grant, Jacquelyn. *White Women's Christ, Black Women's Jesus*. Altanta: Scholars Press, 1989.

Graham, Natalie. "What Slaves We Are: Narrative, Trauma, and Power in Kendrick Lamar's Roots." *Transition* 122 (2017): 123–32.

Guralnick, Peter. *Searching for Robert Johnson: The Life and Legend of the "King of the Delta Blues Singers."* New York: Plume, 1998.

Hallam, Elizabeth, Jenny Hockey, and Glennys Howarth. *Beyond the Body: Death and Social Identity*. London: Routledge, 1999.

Holland, Sharon Patricia. "Bill T. Jones, Tupac Shakur and the (Queer) Art of Death." In "Gay, Lesbian, Bisexual, Transgender: Literature and Culture." Special issue, *Callaloo* 23, no. 1 (Winter 2000): 384, 385.

Holland, Sharon Patricia. *Raising the Dead: Readings of Death and (Black) Subjectivity*. Durham, NC: Duke University Press, 2000.

hooks, bell. *Outlaw Culture: Resisting Representations*. New York: Routledge, 1994.

Hooten, Christopher. "Why Kendrick Lamar Just Re-released DAMN. in Reverse." *Independent*, December 8, 2017. http://www.independent.co.uk/arts-entertainment/music/news/kendrick-lamar-damn-album-collectors-edition-backwards-reverse-back-to-front-explanation-why-twitter-a8098561.html.

Hopkins, Dwight. *Being Human: Race, Culture, and Religion*. Minneapolis: Fortress Press, 2005.

———. "Black Theology on God: The Divine in Popular Religion." In *The Ties That Bind: African American and Hispanic American/Latino/a Theologies in Dialogue*, edited by Anthony B. Pinn and Benjamin Valentin. New York: Continuum, 2001.

———. *Down, up, and Over: Slave Religion and Black Theology*. Minneapolis: Fortress Press, 1999.

———. *Introducing Black Theology of Liberation*. Maryknoll, NY: Orbis Books, 1999.

———. *Shoes That Fit Our Feet: Sources for a Constructive Black Theology*. Maryknoll, NY: Orbis Books, 1993.

Hopkins, Dwight, and George Cummings, editors. *Cut Loose Your Stammering Tongue: Black Theology in the Slave Narratives*. 2nd edition. Louisville, KY: Westminster/John Knox, 2003.

Horsman, Reginald. *Race and Manifest Destiny: The Origins of American Racial Anglo-Saxonism*. Cambridge, MA: Harvard University Press, 1981.

Howard-Pitney, David. *The Afro-American Jeremiad: Appeals for Justice in America*. Philadelphia: Temple University Press, 1990.

Hughes, Langston, and Arna Bontemps. *The Book of Negro Folklore*. New York: Dodd, Mead & Company, 1959.

Hurston, Zora Neale. *I Love Myself When I Am Laughing—and Then Again When I Am Looking Mean and Impressive: A Zora Neale Hurston Reader*. Edited by Alice Walker. Old Westbury, NY: Feminist Press, 1979.

———. "Spirituals and Neo-Spirituals." In *The New Negro*, edited by Henry Louis Gates Jr. and Gene Andrew Jarrett. Princeton, NJ: Princeton University Press, 2007.

Hurt, Mississippi John. "Stack O'Lee Blues." *The Blues*. Vol. 2. Washington, DC: Smithsonian Collection of Recordings, 1993.

Jones, William R. *Is God a White Racist? A Preamble to Black Theology*. Boston: Beacon Press, 1999.

Jordan, Brad. *Diary of a Madman: The Geto Boys, Life, Death, and the Roots of Southern Rap*. New York: Dey Street, 2015.

Kellehear, Allan. *A Social History of Dying*. London: Cambridge University Press, 2007.

Kelley, Robin. "Kickin' Reality, Kickin' Ballistics: Gangsta Rap and Postindustrial Los Angeles." In *Droppin' Science: Critical Essays on Rap Music and Hip Hop Culture*, edited by William Eric Perkins. Philadelphia: Temple University Press, 1996.

Labov, William et al. "Toasts." In *Mother Wit from the Laughing Barrel: Readings in the Interpretation of Afro-American folklore*, edited by Alan Dudnes, 335–50. Englewood Cliffs, NJ: Prentice-Hall, 1973.

Laderman, Gary. *Rest in Peace: A Cultural History of Death and the Funeral Home in 21st Century America*. New York: Oxford University Press, 2003.

Lamar, Kendrick. "Kendrick Lamar: The Rolling Stone Interview." Interview by Bryan Hiatt. *Rolling Stone*, August 9, 2017. https://www.rollingstone.com/music/features/kendrick-lamar-on-humble-bono-taylor-swift-mandela-w496385.

Langley, Merlin R. "The Cool Pose: An Afrocentric Analysis." In *The American black Male: His Present Status and His Future*, edited by Richard G. Majors and Jacob U. Gordon, 231–44. Chicago: Nelson-Hall Publishers, 1994.

Levine, Lawrence W. *Black Culture and Black Consciousness: Afro-American Folk Thought from Slavery to Freedom*. New York: Oxford University Press, 1997.

Locke, Alain. "The New Negro." In *The New Negro*, edited by Alain Locke. New York: Atheneum, 1986.

Long, Charles. *Significations*. Philadelphia: Fortress Press, 1986.

Lovell, John, Jr. *Black Song: The Forge and the Flame; The Story of How the Afro-American Spiritual Was Hammered Out*. New York: Paragon House Publishers, 1986.

Majors, Richard G., et al. "Cool Pose: A Symbolic Mechanism for Masculine Role Enactment and Coping by Black Males." In *The American Black Male: His Present Status and His Future*, edited by Richard G. Majors and Jacob U. Gordon, 245–59. Chicago: Nelson-Hall Publishers, 1994.

Makarechi, Kia. "Kanye West's 'I Am a God' Inspired By Fashion Week Diss." Huffington Post, Jun 24, 2013. http://www.huffingtonpost.com/2013/06/24/kanye-west-i-am-a-god-fashion-week-diss_n_3490688.html.

Malcolm X. "Ballot or Bullet Speech." In *Malcolm X Speaks: Selected Speeches and Statements*, edited by George Breitman. New York: Pathfinder, 1989.

Margolick, David. *Strange Fruit: The Biography of a Song*. New York: Harper Perennial, 2001.

Marriott, Rob. "Last Testament." *Vibe Magazine*, November 1996, T7.

McLeod, James D., Jr. "If God Got Us: Kendrick Lamar, Paul Tillich, and the Advent of Existentialist Hip Hop." *Toronto Journal of Theology* 33, no. 1 (2017): 123–35.

Mellor, Philip A. "Death in High Modernity: The Contemporary Presence and Absence of Death." In *The Sociology of Death*, edited by David Clark. Cambridge, MA: Blackwell Publishers, 1993.

Miller, Monica, Anthony Pinn, and Bernard "Bun B" Freeman. *Religion in Hip Hop*. London: Bloomsbury, 2015.

Mitchem, Stephanie Y. *Introducing Womanist Theology*. Maryknoll, NY: Orbis Books, 2002.

Monmonier, Mark. *How to Lie with Maps*. Chicago: University of Chicago Press, 1991.

Morrison, Toni. *Beloved*. New York: Vintage, 2004.

———. "The Site of Memory." In *Out There: Marginalization and Contemporary Cultures*, edited by Russell Ferguson et al. Cambridge, MA: MIT Press, 1990.

Moses, Wilson J. "The Black Jeremiad and American Messianic Traditions." In *Moses, Black Messiahs and Uncle Toms: Social and Literary Manipulations of a*

Religious Myth, 30–48. University Park: The Pennsylvania State University Press, 1982.

Murray, Albert. *From the Briar Patch File: On Context, Procedure, and American Identity*. New York: Pantheon Books, 2001.

Neal, Mark Anthony. *Soul Babies: Black Popular Culture and the Post-soul Aesthetic*. New York: Routledge, 2002.

Ogbar, Jeffrey O. G. "Slouching toward Bork: The Culture Wars and Self-Criticism in Hip-Hop Music." *Journal of Black Studies* 33, no. 2 (November 1999): 167.

Palmer, Robert. *Deep Blues: A Musical and Cultural History, from the Mississippi Delta to Chicago's South Side to the World*. New York: Penguin Books, 1982.

Patterson, Orlando. *Slavery and Social Death: A Comparative Study*. Cambridge, MA: Harvard University Press, 2018 [1985].

Paulston, Rolland G. "Preface: Four Principles for a Non-innocent Social Cartography." In *Social Cartography Mapping Ways of Seeing Social and Educational Change*, edited by Rolland G. Paulston. New York: Garland Publishing, Inc., 1996.

Pinn, Anthony B. *African American Humanist Principles: Living and Thinking Like the Children of Nimrod*. New York: Palgrave Macmillan, 2004.

———. "Black Theology in Historical Perspective: Articulating the Quest for Subjectivity." In *The Ties That Bind: African American and Hispanic American/Latino/a Theologies in Dialogue*, edited by Anthony B. Pinn and Benjamin Valentin. New York: Continuum, 2001.

———. *Deathlife: Hip Hop and Thanatological Narrations of Blackness*. Durham, NC: Duke University Press, 2024.

———. "The End: An Essay on Humanist Theology, Rap Music, and Death." *Dialog: A Journal of Theology* 54 (December 2015): 347–54.

———. *End of God-Talk: An African American Humanist Theology*. New York: Oxford University Press, 2012.

———. "'Gettin' Grown': Notes on Gangsta Rap Music and Notions of Manhood." *Journal of African American Men* 1, no. 4 (1996): 23–35.

———. *Humanism: Essays on Race, Religion, and Cultural Production*. London: Bloomsbury Academic, 2015.

———. *Interplay of Things: Technology of Religion, Art, and Presence Together*. Oxford University Press, 2021.

———. *Noise and Spirit*. New York: New York University Press, 2003.

———. *Terror and Triumph: The Nature of Black Religion*. Minneapolis: Fortress Press, 2003.

———. *Varieties of African American Religious Experience*. Minneapolis: Fortress Press, 1998.

———. "Zombies in the 'Hood: Rap Music, Camusian Absurdity, and the Structuring of Death." In *Religion in Hip Hop: The New Terrain*, edited by Monica Miller and Anthony B. Pinn. London: Bloomsbury Academic, 2015.

Pinn, Anthony B., and Allen D. Callahan, eds. *African American Religious Life and the Story of Nimrod*. New York: Palgrave Macmillan, 2008.

———, eds. *Loving the Body: Black Religious Studies and the Erotic*. New York: Palgrave Macmillan, 2004.

Pomorska, Krystyna. "Foreword." In *Rabelais and His World*, by Mikhail Bakhtin. Bloomington: Indiana University Press, 1984.

Powell, Kevin. "2Pac Shakur." *Vibe Magazine*, April 1995, 52.

Prince, James. *The Art and Science of Respect: A Memoir by James Prince*. Houston: N-the-Water, 2018.

Ransom, Stanley Austin, Jr., ed. *America's First Negro Poet: The Complete Works of Jupiter Hammon of Long Island*. Port Washington, NY: Kennikat Press, 1970.

Reed, Annie. "Br'er Rabbit and the Briar Patch." In *Talk That Talk: An Anthology of African-American Storytelling*, edited by Linda Goss and Marian E. Barnes. New York: Touchstone Book, 1989.

Roberts, John W. *From Trickster to Badmen: The Black Folk Hero in Slavery and Freedom*. Philadelphia: University of Pennsylvania Press, 1989.

Rogers, Abraham D. *African Folktales: Selected and Retold by Abraham Rogers*. New York: Pantheon Books, 1983.

Rolsky, Louis. "Black Millennial Music, Critical Studies of Religion, and the Gravitational Pull of Kendrick Lamar." *Sacred Matters*, January 2017.

Rose, Tricia. *Black Noise: Rap Music and Black Culture in Contemporary America*. Middletown, CT: Wesleyan University Press, 1994.

———. "Orality and Technology: Rap Music and Afro-American Cultural Resistance." *Popular Music and Society*, Winter 1989.

RuPaul. *Lettin' It All Hang Out: An Autobiography*. New York: Hyperion, 1996.

Schloss, Joseph. *Foundations: B-boys, B-girls and Hip Hop in New York*. New York: Oxford University Press, 2009.

Schumacher, Thomas. "'This Is a Sampling Sport': Digital Sampling, Rap Music and the Law in Cultural Production." *Media, Culture and Society* 17, no. 2 (April 1995).

Seale, Clive. *Constructing Death: The Sociology of Dying and Bereavement*. Cambridge: Cambridge University Press, 1998.

Sigurdson, Ola. *Heavenly Bodies: Incarnation, the Gaze, and Embodiment in Christian Theology*. Grand Rapids: William B. Eerdmans Publishing Group, 2016.

Smith, Jonathan Z. *Map Is Not Territory: Studies in the History of Religions*. Chicago: University of Chicago Press, 1993.

Smith, Thee. *Conjuring Culture: Biblical Formations of Black America*. New York: Oxford University Press, 1994.

Spady, James G., and Joseph D. Eure, eds. *Nation Conscious Rap*. New York: PC International Press, 1991.

Spencer, Jon Michael *Blues and Evil*. Knoxville: The University of Tennessee Press, 1993.

———, ed. *The Emergency of Black and The Emergence of Rap*. A special issue of *Black Sacred Music: A Journal of Theo-musicology*. 5, no. 1 (Spring 1991).

———. *Protest and Praise: Sacred Music of Black Religion*. Minneapolis: Fortress Press, 1990.

Stephens, Ronald Jemal. "The Three Waves of Contemporary Rap Music." *Black Sacred Music: A Journal of Theo-musicology* 5, no. 1 (Spring 1991): 25–40.

Stewart, Dianne. *Three Eyes for the Journey: African Dimensions of the Jamaican Religious Experience*. New York: Oxford University Press, 2005.

Sullivan, Rachel E. "Rap and Race: It's Got a Nice Beat, but What about the Message?" *Journal of Black Studies* 33, no. 5 (May 2003): 605–22.

Townes, Emilie M. "Ida B Wells-Barnett: An Afro-American Prophet." *Christian Century* 106 (1989): 285–86.

Turchi, Peter. *Maps of the Imagination: The Writer as Cartographer*. San Antonio, TX: Trinity University Press, 2004.

Walker, Alice. "Alice Walker on Writing, Dancing, and Bursting into Song." *Literary Hub*, October 2, 2018. https://lithub.com/alice-walker-on-writing-dancing-and-bursting-into-song/.

———. *Anything We Love Can Be Saved*. New York: Random House, Inc., 1997.

———. *The Color Purple*. New York: Washington Square Press, 1982.

———. *In Search of Our Mother's Gardens: A Womanist Prose*. New York: Harcourt Brace Jovanovich Publishers, 1983.

Walker, Lance Scott. *Houston Rap Tapes: An Oral History of Bayou City Hip-Hop*. Austin: University of Texas Press, 2018.

Wall, Paul. "Slow, Loud, and Bangin': Paul Wall Talks 'Slab God' Sonics." Interview by Guestlistener, *Sounding Out!* February 22, 2016. https://soundstudiesblog.com/2016/02/22/slow-loud-and-bangin-paul-wall-talks-slab-god-sonics/.

Watkins, Mel. *On the Real Side: Laughing, Lying, and Signifying—the Underground Tradition of African-American Humor That Transformed American Culture, from Slavery to Richard Pryor*. New York: Simon & Schuster, 1994.

Wei-Han Ho, Fred, ed. *Sounding Off: Music as Subversion/Resistance/Revolution*. Brooklyn: Autonomedia, 1995.

Welch, Sharon. *A Feminist Ethic of Risk*. Minneapolis: Fortress Press, 2000.

Wert, Adam. "Tension and Ambiguity: Paul Tillich and Kendrick Lamar on Courage and Faith." *Toronto Journal of Theology* 33, no. 1 (2017): 113–21.

West, Cornel. *Prophesy Deliverance: An Afro-American Revolutionary Christianity*. Philadelphia: The Westminster Press, 1982.

Westhoff, Ben. *Dirty South: OutKast, Lil Wayne, Soulja Boy, and the Southern Rappers Who Reinvented Hip-Hop*. Chicago: Chicago Review Press, 2011.

White, Armond. "Fear of Language: American Media and Public Enemy." *The City Sun*, December 12–18, 1990, 25, 33–36.

———. *Rebel for the Hell of It: The Life of Tupac Shakur*. New York: Thunder's Life Press, 1997.

Wilde, Oscar. *The Picture of Dorian Gray*. Franklin Park, IL: World Library Publications, 2009.

Wilkerson, Isabel. *The Warmth of Other Suns: The Epic Story of America's Great Migration*. New York: Vintage, 2011.

Williams, Delores S. *Sisters in the Wilderness: The Challenge of Womanist God-Talk*. Maryknoll, NY: Orbis Books, 1993.

Wilmore, Gayraud. *Black Religion and Black Radicalism*. Maryknoll, NY: Orbis Books, 1973.

Wright, Richard. *Eight Men*. New York: Harper Perennial, 1996.

Wuethrich, Matthew. "Sun Ra: *The Futuristic Sounds of Sun RA*." *All About Jazz*, January 19, 2003. https://www.allaboutjazz.com/the-futuristic-sounds-of-sun-ra-sun-ra-savoy-jazz-review-by-matthew-wuethrich.

INDEX